LOST CAUSES

Lost Causes

Blended Sentencing, Second Chances,

and the Texas Youth Commission

CHAD R. TRULSON, DARIN R. HAERLE,
JONATHAN W. CAUDILL, AND MATT DELISI

FOREWORD BY JAMES W. MARQUART

UNIVERSITY OF TEXAS PRESS ꙮ *Austin*

The research contained in this document was coordinated in part by the
Texas Youth Commission. The contents of this publication reflect the views
of the authors and do not necessarily reflect the views or policies of the Texas
Youth Commission.

All illustrations and photos courtesy of the authors.

Requests for permission to reproduce material from this work should be sent to:
　　Permissions
　　University of Texas Press
　　P.O. Box 7819
　　Austin, TX 78713-7819
　　http://utpress.utexas.edu/index.php/rp-form

♾ The paper used in this book meets the minimum requirements of ANSI/NISO
Z39.48-1992 (R1997) (Permanence of Paper).

LIBRARY OF CONGRESS CATALOGING-IN-PUBLICATION DATA

Trulson, Chad R., author.
　Lost causes : blended sentencing, second chances, and the Texas Youth
Commission / Chad R. Trulson, Darin R. Haerle, Jonathan W. Caudill, and
Matt DeLisi ; foreword by James W. Marquart. — First edition.
　　pages　cm
　Includes bibliographical references and index.
　ISBN 978-1-4773-0786-1 (cloth : alk. paper) — ISBN 978-1-4773-0845-5 (pbk. :
alk. paper) — ISBN 978-1-4773-0787-8 (library e-book) — ISBN 978-1-4773-0793-9
(nonlibrary e-book)
1. Juvenile justice, Administration of—Texas. 　2. Sentences (Criminal
procedure)—Texas. 　3. Juvenile corrections—Texas. 　4. Juvenile
delinquency—Texas. 　5. Juvenile courts—Texas. 　6. Texas Youth
Commission. 　I. Haerle, Darin R., 1979– author. 　II. Caudill, Jonathan W.,
1977– author. 　III. DeLisi, Matt, author. 　IV. Marquart, James W. (James
Walter), 1954– writer of supplementary textual content. 　V. Title.
　KFT1795.T78　2016
　364.3609764—dc23　　　　　　　　　　　　　　　　　2015021600

doi:10.7560/307861

FOR MY FATHER, RICHARD, AND MY FAITHFUL CATHOLIC
MOTHER, PATRICIA, WHO MADE SURE WE WALKED THE
LINE SO AS NOT TO END UP AS LOST CAUSES.
—CHAD R. TRULSON

TO MY MOM, FROM HER BIGGEST FAN.
—DARIN R. HAERLE

TO MY FAMILY.
—JONATHAN W. CAUDILL

TO MY WIFE AND CHILDREN.
—MATT DELISI

CONTENTS

Foreword ix
James W. Marquart

Acknowledgments xiii

Introduction 1

*Determinate Sentencing and the Texas Youth Commission:
A Timeline* 5

CHAPTER 1. Origins and Discoveries 11

CHAPTER 2. The Determinate Sentencing Act in Texas 33

CHAPTER 3. The Sheep That Got Lost 50

CHAPTER 4. Doing Time in the Texas Youth Commission 70

CHAPTER 5. Another Second Chance 87

CHAPTER 6. The Burden of Second Chances 111

CHAPTER 7. Three Decades Later 135

CHAPTER 8. The Last Word 150

Notes 171

Index 195

IN BEAUMONT, TEXAS, around 10:30 a.m. on January 10, 1901, the ground began to shake and shudder. Soon after, a booming explosion rang out that sent pieces of pipe and remnants of an oil derrick hundreds of feet into the air and showered oil onto the earth and the workers nearby. The well was a gusher, and the river of oil it released radically changed the state of Texas, as well as the world's economy, forever. Once trapped in the ground, the oil was now free, and it soon became a major commodity—a thing of value—with all who wished to speculate on the liquid's value buying, selling, and trading it. Yet there were risks and costs: it takes a great deal of time, expertise, and financial resources to turn what comes out of the earth's depths into something useful. The liquid must be handled with great care if one is to avoid disaster.

The same can be said for raising children, who are often characterized as precious commodities, things of intense emotional value, for they represent the future. Parents typically will do anything in their power to make things right for their children. Indeed, they often go to great lengths to support their children, investing in them, refining them, and assisting them in their life journeys. For the most part, moreover, parents want much the same for every child, not just their own, with the cycle of giving and caring extending into the future.

Through the nineteenth-century doctrine of *parens patriae*, the state of Texas functions as a parent. The state sees to the protection of children who suffer abject neglect, cruel mistreatment, or violent abuse and, when and where necessary, gives them second, third, or even fourth chances. However, not every child responds positively to parental wishes or the state's benevolence. Despite the best of efforts, rupture to the good order of things occurs and can result in disasters.

Texas has a long and awkward history when it comes to managing or "parenting" juvenile offenders who have meandered from the straight and narrow. The authors of this book take great care in laying out the history of juvenile justice systems both nationally and within Texas. With respect to Texas, the authors primarily focus on a unique sentencing structure reserved for Texas's most serious and violent juvenile offenders. This structure, called determinate sentencing, was the brainchild of Texas legislators, academicians, and policy makers of the late

1980s who wished for options beyond simply sending juvenile offenders directly to the adult justice system for their crimes. As envisioned, determinate sentencing was to be a scheme of second chances meant to ensure that even the most serious and violent juvenile offenders received a chance at rehabilitation despite their horrific crimes. This unique sentencing structure also provided the possibility of adult punishment in the Texas prison system in the offing if the second-chance rehabilitation effort did not take.

In its experience with determinate sentencing for its wayward children, Texas represents a microcosm of the nation, replete with cycles of reform and neglect—the generation of social and political movements calling at some times for retribution and lengthy incarceration and at other times for benevolence and restoration, for second and third chances. Working across this spectrum determinate sentencing was an attempt to blend the desire for rehabilitation with an equivalent desire for some measure of punishment. Significantly, determinate sentencing was not meant as an intervention into the lives of troubled children to prevent disasters. Rather, it was to intervene once disaster had already occurred, so as to prevent further harm and more disasters.

Political, legal, and social fads in juvenile justice come and go, but this book poses an enduring question underlying them: what should be done with the most serious youthful offenders, those who kill, maim, defile, and destroy the lives of others? The pages of this book challenge the reader to consider this question in the shadow of determinate sentencing and the state of Texas's efforts to fix the most broken of its children. It also raises further questions: Are some children too dangerous to live among us? Do all children, no matter their behavior, deserve a second chance?

In the following pages you will read about roughly 3,500 serious and violent juvenile offenders adjudicated via determinate sentencing and then sent to institutions of the Texas Youth Commission (TYC) since 1987. That total breaks down to some 130 offenders per year, or about two per week, over two and a half decades. Some have committed crimes so horrific that if committed by an adult they would have been given the death penalty. Of the youthful offenders studied here, however, two thirds were released from TYC and have since returned to live among us, often after only two or three years of juvenile incarceration. Among those released from TYC, some took advantage of their second chance at life. Others did not and continued to be involved in criminal behavior. A smaller number failed to demonstrate change during their time in TYC, and were determined to need further intervention by being transferred to the Texas prison system.

In this book you will read about shifting sentencing policies, court cases, giant personalities, moral wrestling, institutional instability and brutality, horrific crimes, chances for redemption, and continuity in delinquent and criminal behavior. Indeed, the state of Texas has faced great difficulty in deciding what to do about these young but extreme offenders. This book represents the first long-term systematic effort to understand the trajectories of these offenders once they have been given a second chance through determinate sentencing.

I am proud to say that these authors in many ways represent my professional offspring. Like any parent, I take great pride in their accomplishments, and this book represents a remarkable achievement. Well written, well researched, and well presented, the story that unfolds here evokes a wide range of emotions and feelings. The authors, who rely on their rich practical experience within the juvenile justice system and their equally rich academic careers, marshal important longitudinal data to show that what to do about our most errant of children, our riskiest commodities, is a never-ending story with few easy answers. Today, as a benevolent parent, Texas still cannot confidently say how many second chances we should extend. I leave it to the reader to study the findings in this book and then to draw their own conclusions to this most complex of questions.

JAMES W. MARQUART
November 2014

THIS BOOK SIMPLY would not have been possible without the kind help of numerous individuals.

First and foremost, we would like to thank Chuck Jeffords, longtime research director of the Texas Youth Commission (TYC). Dr. Jeffords has been a constant source of support, knowledge, and assistance for us on research projects involving juvenile offenders in Texas for more than a decade. It was this same unyielding support that led to the research within the pages of this book. It cannot be emphasized enough that without his support this book would have never even come close to seeing the light of day. We and dozens of other researchers in Texas and elsewhere owe Dr. Jeffords a tremendous debt of gratitude.

A special thanks also goes to James W. Marquart of Lamar University. Dr. Marquart kindly agreed to write the foreword to this book, and his willingness to do so was just another example of the valuable mentorship and guidance he has provided to the authors of this book in our various roles as his students, colleagues, and friends. This book would not be possible without him, and we are fortunate to have benefited from his mentorship.

Thanks also to Jene Anderson, Jerry Holdenried, and the entire group of media production specialists at TDCJ Media Services, in Austin, for helping us to obtain images of Gatesville and Mountain View State Schools. A special thanks goes to Jene, for she has weathered more than her fair share of requests throughout the years on other projects and has always helped with tremendous efficiency and knowledge. She has also been extremely pleasant to work with. Thanks also goes to Laura Saegert and John Anderson, at the Texas State Library and Archives Commission, for helping us locate various TYC photographs and for pointing us toward excellent sources we used to complete this book. Thanks also go to Michelle Hassell, an MSCJ student at the University of North Texas, for helping us with formatting photographs and other associated details.

We would also like to thank William S. Bush, Associate Professor of History at Texas A&M University–San Antonio, and Michael G. Vaughn, Professor in the School of Social Work at Saint Louis University, for their extremely valuable comments and insights, which improved this book in its earlier forms. We also thank the many anonymous reviewers who have scoured over our work the last several years, culminating in the final version of this book.

Thanks also go to those at the University of Texas Press who made sure this book was printed. Allison Faust and Theresa May got this project off the ground and on track, and then Casey Kittrell took over and saw it through. There is nothing better than working with professionals who know how to do their jobs and do them well.

We would also like to recognize the support provided by our colleagues at our respective universities: the University of North Texas, California State University–Chico, and Iowa State University. Special thanks go to Eric J. Fritsch, Professor and Chair of the Department of Criminal Justice at the University of North Texas, for his financial support in the latter stages of this book.

Finally, we owe the highest debt of gratitude to those who matter the most—our families.

LOST CAUSES

Main campus buildings, Gatesville State School for Boys, later known as "Hilltop" once surrounding satellite schools were built. Courtesy of the Texas State Library and Archives Commission.

LOST CAUSES

IN IOWA, IT WAS ELDORA. In Illinois, it was St. Charles. In Florida, it was Marianna. In California, it was Lancaster. In Massachusetts, it was Westborough. In Louisiana, it was Monroe.

In Texas, it was Gatesville.

Every state has that place—the place parents and teachers and priests and old-timers warn the young about. The place where some go, and when they come back, they don't talk about it. These are the places apart that have existed for more than one hundred years, and they are reserved for those youth so far off the straight-and-narrow that they are unfit to be in free society. Although they have been called many other names in the past, these places are today called juvenile correctional institutions.

The Lyman School for Boys in Westborough, Massachusetts (originally known as the State Reform School for Boys at Westborough) is recognized as the first reform school in the nation for delinquent youths. While other places of confinement existed for wayward juveniles before Lyman, such as New York's House of Refuge or Boston's House of Reformation, it was Lyman that ushered in an era in which juvenile institutions were meant to reform the juvenile of his wicked ways and to train him to adopt a life of moral behavior.

In the first several decades it was often the sons of Irish and Italian immigrant Catholics who found their way to the rooms and hallways and work fields of this early American reform school. As the boys were ushered for transport to Lyman, the faithful Catholic mothers would say their final good-byes and sometimes pass on to their sons a medallion of St. Jude Thaddeus—the patron saint of lost causes and hopeless souls. As the wayward youths got farther from home and closer to Lyman, their mothers were already on their way to St. Patrick's or St. Paul's or Our Lady of Sorrows to offer a prayer to St. Jude. At the church a candle would be lit to extend the prayer, as is the tradition among Catholics. At Lyman the lost causes could either mend their ways or confirm their spot on the list of people apart.

More than a century later, the lost causes are still saying their good-byes as they shuffle in their shackles to the transport vans and buses en route to state juvenile correctional facilities in rural backwaters or at the outer edges of cities. What also remains today, just as it did back then, are efforts to deal with the problem of serious juvenile delin-quency, and hopes that intervening in the lives of troubled youths might save them from a life course of crime and failure. And while the lost causes of today have changed considerably from the time of the early Lyman schoolboys—many of the early Lyman schoolboys would not merit a second glance compared to state institutionalized juvenile delinquents of today—what has not changed is that state juvenile insti-tutionalization still functions as a last-ditch place and a last-ditch effort to change the life trajectories of society's delinquent outliers before all hope is lost. This last-ditch effort to change the serious and violent delinquent is especially notable in the state of Texas.

In 1987, roughly a decade after the Gatesville State School for Boys and the high-security, 1960s-era Mountain View State School for Boys had been shut down and then transferred to the Texas prison system, Texas passed a unique sentencing law focused exclusively on serious and violent juvenile offenders. This law, which came exactly one hun-dred years after construction of Gatesville was authorized by the Texas Legislature, was originally called determinate sentencing. Instead of further expanding 1970s-era adult court certification mechanisms by which serious and violent juvenile offenders could face the adult justice system and end up in a Texas prison cell, determinate sentencing af-forded serious and violent juvenile offenders one last chance to change while still remaining under the more protective and rehabilitation-centered umbrella of Texas's juvenile courts and the Texas Youth Com-mission (TYC).

Procedurally, serious and violent offenders prosecuted and adju-dicated in juvenile court under determinate sentencing received an institutional sentence that started first at a TYC state school. If the "sentenced offender" demonstrated change and progress in TYC—as de-termined by TYC staff, psychologists, counselors, judges, prosecutors, and other juvenile justice decision makers—the offender had a chance to reenter free society and get on with his or her life. If change and progress was not demonstrated, the offender was transferred directly to a Texas prison unit by age eighteen to serve the remainder of his or her original determinate sentence—a sentence that could extend to a maximum of forty years. This last-chance opportunity created by determinate sentencing and the juvenile offenders processed through this law are the focus of this book.

In the pages to come, we bring historical records, youthful offender data, personal observations, institutional data, and official rearrest records to bear on the outcomes of every juvenile offender who received a determinate sentence in Texas from 1987 through 2011. This book tells the story of the offenders' institutional behavior while confined in Texas's state juvenile facilities. It tells of the decisions to release the offenders to the streets or to transfer them to the Texas prison system following their time in TYC. It tells of the recidivism outcomes of those offenders who were given another chance at redemption by being released back into the free world after only a few short years in TYC. This book, then, provides a window into what happened to the serious and violent delinquents in Texas who were given another chance to reclaim their freedom and avoid becoming part of the next generation of convicts in the Texas prison system.

Dorm building, Gatesville State School for Boys, ca. 1975. Courtesy of the Texas Department of Criminal Justice.

DETERMINATE SENTENCING AND THE
TEXAS YOUTH COMMISSION: A TIMELINE

1836–1889	When Texas achieves independence in 1836, the age of adult criminal responsibility is 8 years old. It changes to 9 years old in 1856.
	In 1887 the Texas Legislature appropriates funds to build a House of Correction and Reformatory for youthful offenders. It is administered as a branch of the Texas penitentiary system. In January 1889 the House of Correction and Reformatory opens in Gatesville with sixty-eight boys who had been incarcerated with adult felons of the Texas prison system.
1887–1889	In Austin the Deaf, Dumb, and Blind Asylum for Colored Youth begins operations in 1887. It is later renamed the Texas Blind, Deaf, and Orphan School.
	The Texas State Orphan Asylum, later renamed the Corsicana State Home, becomes operational in 1889.
1909	The House of Correction and Reformatory at Gatesville is renamed the State Institution for the Training of Delinquents. Control is transferred from the Texas prison system to a board of trustees.
1916	Gainesville State School for Girls, originally the Texas State Training School for Girls, begins operations as a home for delinquent and dependent girls.
1918	The age of adult criminal responsibility in Texas is raised from 9 to 17.
1919	Texas establishes the State Home for Dependent and Neglected Children in Waco.
1927	The Texas Legislature authorizes the State Board of Control to establish a correctional facility for delinquent black females.

1930	The State Board of Control assumes jurisdiction over the State Home for Dependent and Neglected Children and renames it the Waco State Home.
1939–1940	In 1939 the Texas Legislature renames the State Institution for the Training of Delinquents, designating it the Gatesville State School for Boys. By 1940 Gatesville houses nearly 800 delinquent males under the age of 17 at the time of their commitment. Youths are housed in several campus areas: Hilltop, Riverside, Valley, Hackberry, and Terrace.
1943	The Texas Legislature transforms all matters involving juveniles from criminal matters to civil matters.
1945–1947	In 1945 the Texas Legislature approves the establishment of the State Training School for Delinquent and Dependent Colored Girls in Brady. The fiftieth Texas Legislature creates the State Training School Code Commission in 1947.
1948	Gainesville State School for Girls takes on its present name and houses roughly 200 juveniles.
1949	The State Youth Development Council is created. The council controls the three major training schools in Texas: Gatesville, Gainesville, and Brady.
1950	The Brady State School for Delinquent and Dependent Colored Girls moves to Crockett and is renamed the Colored Girls Training School at Crockett.
1957	The State Youth Development Council becomes the Texas Youth Council (TYC).
1961	Gatesville correctional officer Billy Malone is attacked by nine Gatesville boys and dies after being beaten with a baseball bat. The Gatesville boys flee the facility. Not long after the murder, the Texas Legislature approves funds to construct a "youth prison" for the most violent and serious offenders in Texas Youth Council facilities. James Turman, director of TYC,

becomes a staunch advocate for getting tough on Texas's juvenile offenders.

1962   Mountain View State School for Boys opens on September 5, 1962. Fifty-six boys from Gatesville are transferred to populate this facility reserved for serious and violent offenders.

1971   Alicia Morales is committed to the Texas Youth Council for disobedience without counsel, notice of charges, or court appearance. She becomes the lead plaintiff in a lawsuit against James Turman, executive director of TYC.

William Wayne Justice, federal judge for the Eastern District of Texas, orders further inquiries regarding TYC. The lawsuit expands from a due process case to one also probing physical abuse of TYC wards, racial segregation, solitary confinement procedures, and other concerns.

1972   Giddings State School opens.

1973   Riots commence at the Mountain View and Gatesville State School facilities. TYC officials blame Judge Justice's order prohibiting corporal punishment, racial segregation, and solitary confinement, among other issues.

Texas passes adult court certification law.

1974   Judge Justice provides for sweeping changes to TYC in his 1974 opinion. The provisions include closing Gatesville and Mountain View, hiring more and better-qualified staff, and imposing severe restrictions on solitary confinement and the use of tranquilizers on youths.

Texas's most serious and violent juvenile offenders are mostly sent to Giddings.

TYC appeals Judge Justice's opinion and argues the case should have been heard by a three-judge district panel.

1975   Mountain View State School for Boys closes and youthful offenders are reassigned to other facilities as well as community-based alternatives to confinement. The land and buildings are acquired by the Texas Department of Corrections (TDC).

The Crockett State School reopens as a correctional institution for boys.

1979–1981 The Gatesville State School for Boys closes in 1979 and juvenile offenders are transferred to Crockett, Gainesville, Giddings, or West Texas State School in Pyote.

The Riverside, Valley, and Terrace schools at Gatesville become the Gatesville Unit for Women under control of the Texas Department of Corrections in 1980. (It was later renamed the Christina Melton Crain Unit.) The Hilltop and Hackberry schools at Gatesville become the Hilltop Unit for men, under TDC control, in 1981.

1980 Giddings State School is designated as the maximum security facility of the Texas Youth Council.

1983 The Texas Legislature renames the Texas Youth Council the Texas Youth Commission (TYC). TYC has sole control of secure confinement and community programs for adjudicated delinquents.

By the early 1990s dependent and neglected children, formerly under TYC supervision, are served by the Texas Department of Protective and Regulatory Services, now called the Texas Department of Family and Protective Services (TDFPS).

1984 Judge Justice approves a final settlement agreement in the *Morales v. Turman* litigation.

1985–1994 Texas experiences a massive increase in juvenile crime, including substantial increases in violent behavior by juvenile offenders. The Texas homicide rate among juveniles is nearly double the national rate.

1987 The seventieth Texas Legislature passes the Determinate Sentencing Act (DSA, also later known as the Violent or Habitual Offenders Act). Texas becomes one of the first states to adopt what is broadly known as "blended sentencing."

Determinate sentencing becomes an alternative to lowering the age for adult court certification for juveniles (which stands at age 14 or 15, depending on offense) and also provides serious and violent juvenile offenders with one last chance at redemption.

The initial Determinate Sentencing Act covers six felony offenses: murder; capital murder; aggravated kidnapping; aggravated sexual assault; deadly assault on a law enforcement officer, correctional officer, or court participant; and criminal attempt (only in the case of attempted capital murder). The maximum term of confinement is set at 30 years.

1988   Federal court oversight in the *Morales v. Turman* settled agreement ends.

1990s   The TYC population increases dramatically following Texas's get-tough approach to juvenile offenders. In 1991 TYC incarcerates roughly 2,000 juvenile offenders. By 1999 it houses more than 5,000 youths in secure TYC institutions. The agency struggles to attract and retain qualified correctional officers, and staff and youth injuries skyrocket at the end of the decade.

Complaints of youth abuse and mistreatment percolate, and private groups set their focus on youth treatment in TYC.

1991   The maximum determinate sentence term is increased to 40 years.

1995   The seventy-fourth Texas Legislature expands DSA to dozens of new offenses, from 6 to 30 different offenses (22 offenses with additional offense categories related to attempted and conspiracy acts).

2005   Allegations surface of youth sexual abuse by staff in TYC, in particular at the West Texas State School in Pyote. Accused staff members are not prosecuted.

2007–2008   In March 2007, Texas Rangers and investigators from the Attorney General's Office and the Office of the Inspector General arrive on site at all state juvenile correctional facilities. The TYC abuse hotline becomes operational and receives thousands of calls about alleged abuse.

The TYC board is disbanded and the agency is placed in a conservatorship under Senate Bill 103. Massive changes occur statewide, including the release of thousands of youthful offenders from TYC facilities. Confining misdemeanor offenders in secure TYC institutions is prohibited.

The maximum age of juvenile correctional confinement is also reduced from age 21 to 19.

2011–2015   On December 1, 2011, TYC and the Texas Juvenile Probation Commission (TJPC) merge to create one agency governing both institutional and community justice for juveniles in Texas. This new agency is called the Texas Juvenile Justice Department (TJJD).

SOURCES FOR TIMELINE

"A Brief History of the Texas Youth Commission." Accessed October 7, 2013. http://www.tyc.state.tx.us/about/history.html.

Bush, W. 2008a. *Protecting Texas' Most Precious Resource: A History of Juvenile Justice Policy in Texas (Part I)*. Austin: Texas Criminal Justice Coalition.

Bush, W. 2008b. *Protecting Texas' Most Precious Resource: A History of Juvenile Justice Policy in Texas (Part II)*. Austin: Texas Criminal Justice Coalition.

Bush, W. 2010. *Who Gets a Childhood? Race and Juvenile Justice in Twentieth-Century Texas*. Athens: University of Georgia Press.

Jasinski, L. E. *Texas Youth Commission*. Accessed October 7, 2013. http://www.tshaonline.org/handbook/online/articles/mdt35.

"Juvenile Incarceration: *Morales v. Turman*." Accessed October 7, 2013. http://tarlton.law.utexas.edu/exhibits/ww_justice/morales_v_turman_page3.html.

Markham, J. W., and W. T. Field. *Gatesville State School for Boys*. Accessed October 7, 2013. http://www.tshaonline.org/handbook/online/articles/jjg02.

State Auditor's Office. 2009. *A Follow-Up Audit Report on the Texas Youth Commission*, Report No. 09-036. Austin: State Auditor's Office.

"Texas Youth Commission: An Inventory of Records at the Texas State Archives." Accessed October 7, 2013. http://www.lib.utexas.edu/taro/tslac/20124/tsl-20124.html.

CHAPTER 1

ORIGINS AND DISCOVERIES

DISCOVERING DELINQUENCY

ON JULY 3, 1899, in the old County Building in downtown Chicago, Illinois, Judge Richard Tuthill presided over a court hearing involving Henry Campbell, an eleven-year-old boy who had been arrested for larceny. But this was no regular day and no regular court hearing. On this day, Henry Campbell became the first defendant to be tried in the nation's first juvenile court. Upon pleas from Campbell's parents in the "juvenile court room," Judge Tuthill decided against sending Henry to the state reformatory—one of the few options available to judges at the time. Tuthill sent him instead to his grandmother's home in New York under the belief that there he could "escape the surroundings which have caused his mischief."[1]

So began the nation's first juvenile court—a separate legal arena for children with a mandate "not so much to punish as to reform, not to degrade but to uplift, not to crush but to develop, to make him [the wayward juvenile] not a criminal but a worthy citizen."[2] In the first decade of the court's existence, juvenile court judges handled roughly twelve thousand cases involving children who needed uplifting and development. Most of these cases involved youths detained for theft of items including grain, coal, and various other articles from containers in the old Chicago rail yards and shops. Others facing the juvenile court were tried for loitering on railroad tracks, setting fires, breaking fences, throwing stones at trains, and loafing.[3]

To the progressive reformers who advocated for juvenile courts, known historically as "child-savers," the fact that youthful offenders such as Henry Campbell were far from serious and violent was of no

Aerial photo of Reception Center, with main Gatesville buildings (Hilltop) in the background. Live Oak School is to the left. Courtesy of the Texas Department of Criminal Justice.

matter.[4] To them, behaviors such as idleness, theft, and loitering, left unchecked, would blossom into more serious criminality in adulthood. With juvenile courts focused on these types of behaviors, youths brought to court originated almost solely from the lower or "dangerous" classes, more often than not composed of immigrant children.[5] The disproportionate enforcement was justified in the minds of the child-savers because to them, court intervention was in the best interests of the child in that "removal from the family of origin [and in their view the origin of the problem] was the pathway to moral regeneration."[6]

Fueled by the flame of child-saving, most states by 1910 had established a court to deal with those now considered juvenile delinquents and/or those children who were not delinquent but whose immediate and future welfare depended upon the court's benevolent intervention—the dependent and neglected.[7] By 1925, all but two states had established a juvenile court with wide jurisdiction over all child-related matters.[8] Among other considerations in the development, expansion, and operation of juvenile courts, one pressing need was to find methods for managing the throngs of youths now falling under the courts' wide paternal grasp. The advent of a separate court process specifically for children, regardless of whether they were delinquent or merely dependent or neglected, underscored the need for a host of interventions, treatments, facilities, and sanctions.[9]

To address this need, probation, or a period of proving or trial, became favored as the first-resort disposition for most delinquents who faced juvenile courts.[10] The practice of allowing wayward youths a period of time in the community to prove their worthiness before receiving a more restrictive sanction had been around since the 1840s when a shoemaker named John Augustus asked a Boston police court to let him supervise a local drunk in lieu of imprisonment.[11] Augustus's supervised release program was a natural fit with the juvenile courts' operational philosophy of reformation rather than retribution and judges as wise parents rather than wardens.[12] In short, probation was a second chance.

While probation was the first-resort disposition for most children who came under juvenile courts' jurisdiction, juvenile court judges had other methods at their disposal. For those youths considered more extreme and incorrigible—persistent thieves, those keeping the company of deviants or other lascivious persons, and so on—institutionalization gained sway among the early juvenile court judges.[13] According to juvenile justice scholar Barry C. Feld, the juvenile court's benevolent mission and its judges' "feelings of tenderness did not cause them to shrink from toughness when required."[14] And when toughness was required, institutionalization fit the bill.

DISCOVERING ASYLUMS

In 1825, one hundred years before most states had established a separate juvenile court, 160 young wards were summoned each morning by a loud bell. Fifteen minutes later, a second bell rang out, alerting guards to unlock the youth cells. Directed into the washroom and then quickly into parade formation, the young inmates were inspected for cleanliness and dress. At 7 a.m. the bells chimed again, signaling breakfast, and thirty minutes later the work day started, with wards engaged in making shoes, chair seats, and rat traps. Another bell rang at noon for lunch, another at 5 p.m. terminating the work day, and another at 5:30 p.m. signaling three hours of evening classes and prayers. Following prayers, the young wards were marched to the sleeping halls, doors were locked, and silence was strictly enforced.[15]

The routine of the New York House of Refuge demonstrates that well before the first court for juveniles was established in Cook County, Illinois, places and processes already existed for handling wayward and needy youths.[16] Driven by the familiar philosophy that delinquency and other problem behaviors could be traced back to disorder in the larger society and smaller family unit (e.g., pauperism, parental intemperance, societal temptations of gambling and other vices), houses of refuge emerged across the US landscape to restore proper social order and to train the untrained youngster. Following New York's lead, houses of refuge were established in many major cities in the United States by the 1850s, especially in the East and Midwest. While much fanfare has been placed on the Cook County juvenile court as the starting point for the modern juvenile justice system, in reality, houses of refuge first marked significant changes in the treatment of wayward and needy youths, based on a view that they should be treated differently from their adult counterparts.[17]

Like their precursor institutions the orphanages and almshouses, and to a degree adult penal institutions such as Eastern State Penitentiary in Pennsylvania, houses of refuge were meant to shield susceptible children from the temptations and ills of an increasingly disordered society.[18] Houses of refuge also functioned as vehicles through which to train already wayward children to resist treacherous societal temptations and adopt a life of morality upon their release back into mainstream society. The goal of training youths to resist the temptations of a morally depraved society is no more evident than in the strict regimentation of daily life for wards of the houses of refuge.[19] As scholar David J. Rothman noted:

> The founders of the orphan asylums and houses of refuge shared fully with the proponents of other caretaker institutions a fear that anyone not carefully and diligently trained to cope with the open, free-wheeling, and disordered life of the community would fall victim to vice and crime. The orphan, robbed of his natural guardians, desperately needed protection against these dangers. . . . The vagrant, by definition lacking in supervision, would certainly come under the sway of taverns, gambling halls, and theaters, the crowd of drunks, gamblers, thieves, and prostitutes. The nightmare come true, of course, was the juvenile delinquent, his behavior ample testimony to the speed and predictability of moral decline.[20]

Fueled by the belief that social problems originated largely from the environment, proponents of houses of refuge believed that only by removing them from poor environments and giving them proper discipline and training could such a motley group of rogues, vagrants, beggars, thieves, waifs, and generally weak-natured youths be saved.

SHORTCOMINGS AND CHANGE

By the 1850s, houses of refuge had lost their luster.[21] Despite good intentions, they eventually deteriorated into overcrowded, filthy, and disorganized institutions. Instead of simulating the perfect society with characteristics of hard work, discipline, self-denial, and religious reflection, houses of refuge degenerated into the very condition that they were formulated to check. Among other issues, they were eventually criticized as schools of crime that provided little more than a penitentiary-like experience for their young wards.

Because of their failings, houses of refuge were replaced by a new brand of youth institution, the juvenile reform school. Reform schools were meant to be different from the "old fashioned" houses of refuge, and for a time they functioned in different ways from juvenile institutions of old. For example, reform schools operated under the ideal that education and training, not discipline and rigidity, would transform wayward youths into productive citizens. Moreover, reform schools were often placed in the countryside instead of the city so that reformation could take place under the more calming and wholesome influences of rural areas.[22]

As with houses of refuge, it became evident in time that reform schools did not wholly live up to their promise. Work to support the institution (e.g., farming) often superseded educational efforts, and old claims resurfaced such as that reform schools were little more than places where juveniles became schooled in crime. In short, the change from houses of refuge to reform schools was more symbolic than real.

As institutionalization for juveniles came closer to crossing paths with the 1899 creation of the Cook County juvenile court, approaches to incarcerating wayward and needy youths continued to evolve. By the early 1900s, for example, newly labeled training and industrial schools provided an entirely new institutional experience. Such changes were signified not only by symbolic name changes but also wholesale efforts to change the institutional regime.[23] Instead of being a stark contrast to the "free society," training school administrators sought to normalize the institutional experience so that youths would be better prepared to adapt to regular society upon their release. For example, the complete and rigid routine of houses of refuge, and to a large extent the reform school experience, was replaced by an approach that discarded regimentation for routines such as free time on the common grounds or "yard," recreation time, sports, and other "normal" freedoms such as access to a commissary.[24]

Training schools also featured expanded educational and vocational programming, in addition to more developed classification and grading systems to track youth progress. Moreover, instead of housing juveniles in cage-like prison cells, training schools of the early 1900s were administered on a cottage plan, which called for more sensitive procedures to deal with wayward children, including placement of youths in dormitories or small cottages with a cottage mother and/or father where they might also be able to wear free world clothing.[25] Regular clothing, and not uniforms, signified that the child was an individual, not simply an anonymous part of a larger congregation of "bad kids."

In this same line, training school administrators also instituted treatment programming focused on the individual needs of a particular child. This was a far cry from the congregate and standardized regimentation faced by youths in houses of refuge and reform schools that existed before the development of the juvenile court in 1899.[26] According to Rothman, "the new asylum" [the training school] would ensure that the boy who became adjusted to institutional life would be able to adjust to community life with similar success.[27]

To be sure, the development, routines, and changes among institutions for juveniles varied across the United States. Moreover, evidence suggests that by the early to mid-1900s, many training schools had degenerated much like the houses of refuge and reform schools that came before them—their size was unmanageable and good intentions of caregiving, education, and training gave way to staff abuse, violence, and idleness. These institutions nevertheless survived, but they would continue to face identity crises as the twentieth century progressed.

THE ABSENCE OF SERIOUS AND VIOLENT DELINQUENTS

The creation of the nation's first juvenile court in 1899 was a watershed moment on the way to a modern juvenile justice system. No less important was the development of houses of refuge, a significant precursor to a separate court system for juveniles and whose foundational and operational philosophy was very similar to that of the child-savers who pushed through a juvenile court some seven decades later. The houses of refuge were founded on the belief that behaviors labeled as juvenile delinquency largely originated from environmental forces—weak and lax parenting, intemperance, a loose and free-wheeling society, among others.

In the larger context, however, the common ground was that the youths who came under the control of these juvenile-centric innovations were almost always from the ranks of the underprivileged classes, particularly recent immigrants. Their "crimes" were most often petty offenses. More serious offenders—youthful murderers, rapists, and other violent youths—were simply few and far between in those days, and were never the driving force in the development of early juvenile institutions such as houses of refuge or, for that matter, the juvenile court.

Serious and violent young offenders received limited attention relative to the much more abundant population of young vagrants, thieves, truants, and wanderers. Indeed, even the Glueck boys of the late 1930s—the five hundred institutionalized delinquent youths selected by Sheldon and Eleanor Glueck in 1939 from the Lyman School for Boys in Westborough, Massachusetts, and the Industrial School for Boys in Shirley, Massachusetts, as the foundation for their seminal study *Unraveling Juvenile Delinquency*—were not much to shiver about, being small-time burglars and petty thieves for the most part.[28] This is not to suggest that serious and violent juveniles did not exist at the time, but rather to recognize that well into the twentieth century, institutions and courts for juveniles were largely focused on a select population that was not composed of serious or violent juvenile offenders. As time went on, this trend would change.

SOUTHERN DEVELOPMENTS

In contrast to the broader history of penal development in the United States, the South lagged well behind other regions in terms of institutional development for juvenile delinquents.[29] Yet much like the rest of the country, the institutions and juvenile courts in the South focused largely on petty offenders who belonged to the "wayward, incorrigible, or vagrant classes."[30] A major difference between the South and other parts of the country, however, was the significant preoccupation with race found across a variety of social contexts, including dealings with wayward youths.[31]

The South has always been a region apart regarding crime and punishment broadly and institutional development specifically. This characterization is true for both juvenile and adult justice processes. Prior to the Civil War, however, the South was more or less indistinguishable from other parts of the country in terms of progress toward juvenile institutionalization. Although most southern states were "generally indifferent toward organized treatment of juvenile delinquency prior to the Civil War," some southern states did follow the lead of states such as New York and Pennsylvania.[32] Kentucky, Louisiana, and Maryland, for example, constructed houses of refuge between 1830 and 1855. With the exception that southern houses of refuge were strictly for whites, little else served to distinguish them from their counterpart institutions in the Northeast and Midwest.[33] Before the Civil War, nonwhites, primarily African American youths, simply faced private justice on slave plantations for their transgressions.

In the aftermath of the Civil War, the South began to depart from the rest of the nation in terms of treating juvenile (and adult) offenders. Physically and financially devastated by the North, and no longer backed by profitable slave plantations, southern states entered a period of Reconstruction between 1865 and 1877 to rebuild what had once been a thriving region. To fix the situation, southern lawmakers passed a series of Black Codes or laws designed in part to snare individuals under criminal law so that they could be put to work to rebuild the demolished South.

Generally, Black Codes were designed to keep former slaves "in bondage" and "in their place" so that an orderly society could be maintained.[34] But the Black Codes also supplied much-needed laborers to rebuild the South, replenishing a labor pool that had swiftly evaporated following the end of slavery and the downfall of the old slave plantations. Backed by the force of criminal law, thousands upon thousands of criminals were sent to toil on the newly developed convict leases (or chain gangs or field crews or any other relative of the convict lease) facilitated by the Black Codes and entered into by southern lawmakers. Under the typical agreement, private entities such as railroad, mining, and lumber companies paid the state a price to lease out convicts. Custody and control of the convict population was left to private entities.[35] Not surprisingly, life on the convict lease was characterized by brutal work, abuse, disease, and a staggering frequency of death.[36]

Table 1.1. Juvenile Convicts in Texas Prisons, 1881

Name	Age	County	Color	Crime	Term
Jeff Anderson	16	Galveston	Black	Burglary	2 years
Jesse Brenham	16	Duval	Black	Theft	3 years
Albert Brattow	15	Colorado	Black	Forgery	2 years
Jeff Burleson	16	Tarrant	White	Theft (gelding)	5 years
Virgil Bryant	16	Travis	Black	Theft (cow)	2 years
L. S. Beauregard	12	Harris	Black	Theft	2 years
W. T. Brewster	14	Tarrant	White	Theft (horse)	5 years

After the convict lease system began in the South, more serious juvenile offenders were sometimes sent to work alongside adult criminals on the road crews, chain gangs, and prisoner field squads of the lease.[37] This was particularly true for African American juveniles.[38] White juveniles deemed sufficiently serious offenders were housed in a cellblock in a prison building, if one still existed after the war. In Texas, for example, white juveniles were housed in the East Building of the Huntsville "Walls" unit, or at the Rusk State Penitentiary in Cherokee County in later years. Otherwise, they were sent to the lease as well.

Although juveniles in the South were more or less treated like adults during Reconstruction, such young offenders never really amounted to a major population under the convict lease systems. The number of prisoners in Texas under sixteen years of age hovered around thirty in each year between 1880 and 1912.[39] Despite the relatively low juvenile prison population, Texas governor Richard Coke's message to lawmakers in 1875 noted that building a house of correction for juvenile offenders could ease some of the crowding being experienced in the Texas prison system.[40]

Like the juveniles that might be found in a northeastern reform school in the 1880s, the juvenile "convicts" held in southern prison systems were largely petty offenders that would be considered members of the "dangerous class." A listing of convicts under age sixteen and under the control of the Texas prison system in 1881, for example, describes the offenses perpetrated by the young convicts (see table 1.1).[41]

The evolution of institutionalization and juvenile justice in the South prior to 1899 carries several unique themes compared to juvenile treatment patterns in other parts of the country. Unlike in other regions, there was simply little fanfare in the South attached to the notion of juvenile institutionalization and juvenile delinquency prior to 1865. Indeed, in most southern states the general attitude toward waywardness among youths was indifference at best.[42] Perhaps the "delinquency" problem was not as widespread (or perceived to be as widespread) in the South as in New York or other eastern states with their larger cities and burgeoning ethnic populations. Maybe this attitude of indifference was linked to the more rural undercurrents of the South, where issues such as delinquency and waywardness were viewed and treated as private matters, handled by the family in the home and the community on the streets, or by the slave master and his whip on the plantation.[43] Support for this claim is to some degree evidenced by the absence of houses of refuge and reform schools from the South until the 1850s, well after they had been established in New York and other states. Even by that time, however, these places were found only in a handful of borderline southern states, and certainly not in the Deep South.

After the Civil War, however, the differences between the South and other parts of the nation with respect to containing and controlling juvenile delinquents became much starker. In the South, juvenile institutions were still few in number until the late 1880s. But after the Civil War, wayward youths in the South might easily have found their way to prison cells or, more likely, convict lumber crews in Texas, swamp crews in Louisiana, or chain gangs in Georgia. Regardless of the reasons for this transformation from indifference to adult punishment for wayward juveniles, the South was similar to other parts of the nation in that most juvenile offenders were relatively petty offenders by today's standards.

Although the South lagged behind the rest of the nation in establishing both institutions for juvenile offenders and juvenile courts, by the 1880s the move toward separate legal and institutional arenas for youthful offenders was under way. This was especially true in Texas.

LONE STAR JUVENILE JUSTICE

The confluence of slavery, the Civil War, and postwar Reconstruction slowed the development of institutions for juvenile delinquents in the South. However, by the late 1880s, Texas was more or less in concert with most southern states in developing separate institutions for juvenile offenders.

In 1887 the Texas Legislature passed a bill authorizing construction of a House of Correction and Reformatory for juvenile delinquents. Two

Library, Mountain View State School for Boys, ca. 1975. Courtesy of the Texas Department of Criminal Justice.

years later the Gatesville House of Correction opened to plenty of fanfare and was lauded as a first-class facility for juvenile offenders. Situated on seven hundred acres of land able to support the region's cattle, lumber, and cotton operations, the Gatesville facility was believed to be the perfect place for wayward juveniles in Texas.[44] Indeed, the rural setting was perfect for the Gatesville boys since they could be kept busy growing crops, fixing and tending to "Texas fence" (barbwire), and generally engaging in character-building manual labor on the institution grounds.[45] As with almost all aspects of life in the South and in Texas, Gatesville commitments were strictly segregated by race.[46]

Roughly two decades after Texas opened the Gatesville House of Correction, legislation was passed authorizing juvenile courts across the state. The 1907 Juvenile Delinquency Court Act in Texas led to the establishment of juvenile courts for offenders under sixteen years of age. But one scholar noted that unlike the first juvenile court in Chicago, "the Texas version emphasized punishment over rehabilitation and criminal responsibility over child protection."[47]

The punishment philosophy adopted in the creation of Texas's juvenile courts reflected the general punishment-based culture of the time, a culture that no doubt influenced the operation of the Gatesville House of Correction, which by all accounts was harsh and adult-like. Indeed, by 1909, outside reformers such as the Texas Federation of Women's Clubs and the Texas Congress of Mothers had honed in on Gatesville as a place of torture and abuse that was little different from the adult penitentiaries and developing prison farms in Texas.[48] Examinations into Gatesville at the time uncovered evidence of punishments ranging the gamut from straightforward beatings to a whole host of elaborate methods of corporal punishment. Few educational activities were provided to the young wards, unless one counted hard labor in the cotton fields as an educational activity.[49]

Scrutiny into Gatesville continued, and periodic changes came to both this institution and the larger juvenile court system in Texas in the coming decades. For example, by 1913, after Gatesville had drawn the attention of Texas Governor Oscar B. Colquitt and a variety of reform groups in Texas, the facility was repurposed as an educational institution with recommendations that it include not only educational efforts but also training in industrial and agricultural programs.[50] In another development, a 1913 Texas law authorized the placement of boys at Gatesville for a wide range of behaviors and situations beyond delinquency; it also increased juvenile court jurisdiction to cover youths up to age seventeen while allowing juvenile court judges to issue indeterminate sentences and juvenile institution placement up to age twenty-one.[51] Despite these more rehabilitation-focused efforts, one scholar of 1920s Gatesville noted: "Gatesville's program never really broke away from the assumptions of the reformatory era that viewed residents as 'inmates' rather than 'students.' Hard labor, congregate housing, rigid discipline, and the use of untrained staff as 'guards' rather than 'mentors' all persisted during what proved to be a short-lived period of reform."[52]

ON THE BRINK OF CHANGE

By 1943 Texas juvenile courts had become classified as civil rather than criminal entities, signaling further change toward a more rehabilitative approach for juvenile offenders. Moreover, in the late 1940s state authorities continued to tinker with juvenile institutionalization, with the intention of making the institutions more rehabilitative in practice. For example, in 1947 the Texas Legislature created the State Training

School Code Commission in part to examine the regime at Texas juvenile state schools and offer change recommendations (facilities for delinquent and wayward youths in Texas by this time were referred to as State Juvenile Training Schools). In 1949 the commission's report led to the creation of the Texas State Youth Development Council, which had a mandate to administer state juvenile training schools and oversee a program of rehabilitation and successful reentry back into free society.[53]

The creation of the State Youth Development Council and its mandate was a pivotal event in the care and control of delinquents and other youths needing state intervention. A bill written by the members of the State Training School Code Commission was touted as a blueprint for one of the most innovative and expansive youth development programs in the nation.[54] The bill was embraced by Texas governor Beauford H. Jester. But the highly publicized changes were never fully realized. Motivation problems, funding problems, escapes, and sensational crimes committed by a handful of the state's juvenile offenders were significant barriers that all but crushed the good intentions of fixing Texas's troubled youths and youth institutions through more rehabilitative means.

As time went on, further efforts of change came to Texas juvenile justice, specifically to juvenile institutionalization. In 1957 the Texas State Youth Development Council was renamed and reorganized as the Texas Youth Council (TYC). In a progression of change originating from the early cries of those who examined the Gatesville regime, the new TYC was structured to provide rehabilitation in line with new developments in the fields of psychology, sociology, and social work. Detailed diagnostic procedures, classification systems, treatment plans, trained and professional staff, and other rehabilitation-related functions were the foundations of this brave new plan to again change from old thinking that lauded punishment to a new way of thinking that embraced care, rehabilitation, and nurturing.[55]

TEXAS TOUGH

Like previous efforts, the new mandate was never realized. Although there were numerous reasons for this failure, a leadership transition in the Youth Council was key to a new course of action. By 1957 the Texas Youth Council was headed by James A. Turman. Unlike his predecessors, Turman wielded significant influence over not only his board of

Aerial photo of Mountain View State School for Boys. Courtesy of the Texas Department of Criminal Justice.

directors but also the Texas Legislature. With his political savvy and mounting rhetoric that juvenile offenders were taking advantage of a system that was too soft, Turman ushered in a new era in which the focus was much more on punishment than rehabilitation. In the late 1950s and early 1960s his mounting get-tough arguments—strengthened by a murder committed by several Gatesville parolees in 1957 and the murder of a Gatesville guard by nine youth wards in 1961—meant that the juvenile justice atmosphere was about to change rapidly in Texas.

Under Turman, perhaps no other development was more symbolic of the get-tough approach than the move to build an "interim reformatory" for older and more serious delinquents.[56] Mountain View, opened in 1962, represented a significant shift in the handling of delinquents in Texas and in TYC's general philosophy.[57] It signified the dawn of change for an era in which more extreme delinquents would slowly but surely begin to populate Texas's juvenile facilities.

Despite the new get-tough policies that were fueled in large part by isolated but still troubling instances of extreme juvenile offenses, those sent to Texas's juvenile facilities in the late 1960s and into the 1970s were still not yet fully of the class of severe and violent offenders.

Although this more dangerous element did exist in Texas state schools by that time, in the 1970s nearly 80 percent of boys in TYC were committed for lesser offenses such as stealing, disobedience, and immoral conduct. Only 9 percent were committed for more serious offenses of varying sorts. Further, nearly 70 percent of girls were committed to TYC for disobedience and immoral conduct and only 4 percent for more serious offenses.[58] The "dangerous classes" still remained locked up, but for the most part they were far from dangerous. But this too would change. Ironically, the change to a more serious and violent TYC population was fueled by an unlikely lawsuit meant to reform juvenile justice and juvenile institutionalization in Texas. But as with most good intentions, unintended consequences arose.

TOO TOUGH?

By 1971, TYC was on the brink of massive changes to its operations. In that year, fifteen-year-old Alicia Morales became the unlikely lead plaintiff in a lawsuit that grew from a case involving confidential lawyer access to TYC youths to one that addressed not only juvenile court commitment procedures in Texas but also the treatment that juvenile delinquents received while they were institutionalized. This case was styled as *Morales v. Turman*.

Alicia Morales's path to TYC institutionalization was similar to the experiences of many other youthful commitments to TYC at the time. She had committed no gruesome murder, no violent robbery, no persistent thievery, no real offense at all in fact. Rather, Alicia Morales was committed to TYC for disobedience after she refused to turn over her work wages to her father. In violation of procedures established by the US Supreme Court in the case of *In re Gault*, Morales was committed to TYC without a notice of charges, a court appearance, or even legal representation.[59]

The seeds of *Morales v. Turman* were sown in January 1971, when attorney Steven Bercu of the El Paso Legal Assistance Society was retained to represent Johnny W. Brown, a TYC ward from El Paso.[60] Brown, essentially committed to Gatesville State School for Boys by his mother, was locked up for running away several times to see his girlfriend, who had been deported to Juarez, Mexico. After receiving reports from her son of the abuse he suffered at Gatesville, Martha Brown sought out Bercu to secure Johnny's release.[61] In the course of representing Brown, Bercu filed and was later granted a discovery order from the El Paso court permitting him to interview other TYC inmates in an effort to understand the procedures for which they were adjudicated and institutionalized.[62]

A short time later, on January 27, 1971, Steven Bercu and William Hoffman Jr. arrived at Gainesville State School for Girls to interview six wards regarding their commitment to TYC under the previously granted discovery order. Their effort to conduct confidential interviews with the girls was met with resistance from TYC officials, including James A. Turman, executive director of TYC. Turman, who had already been alerted to Bercu's discovery order, insisted that supervisors be present during the attorney-client interviews. During later attempts to privately interview TYC youths at other Texas state schools, Bercu and Hoffman were again denied the ability to meet with their clients in private. Because of this treatment, in February 1971 Bercu and Hoffman filed a civil action in the federal court for the Eastern District of Texas to prevent TYC officials from interfering with their clients, both in person and by impeding their clients' access to confidential counsel through the mail.[63]

In July 1971, federal judge William Wayne Justice sent a survey to all twenty-five hundred youths under commitment in TYC. The survey inquired about the due process procedures TYC youths received during their adjudication hearings and later institutional commitment to TYC. The results of this survey, which garnered a response rate of 92 percent, revealed that only one-third of the youths committed to TYC had a court hearing prior to commitment, most had not been represented by counsel, and nearly three hundred youthful respondents had neither a hearing nor representation prior to being institutionalized. In addition to due process responses, roughly fifty TYC youths wrote narratives describing constant and brutal abuse by TYC officials.

Following these findings, every youth confined in TYC was interviewed by Bercu and Hoffman in 1972 with the assistance of several students from the law schools of the University of Texas and Southern Methodist University. Based on the responses, Bercu and Hoffman amended their original filing with the court, and the case expanded to focus on the treatment of TYC youths during their period of confinement.[64]

The *Morales v. Turman* trial was held over a six-week period in the summer of 1973. The trial revealed shocking abuse of youths by TYC officials as well as substantial evidence that juveniles committed to TYC were denied due process in their adjudication hearings. TYC commit-

Entrance sign, Mountain View State School for Boys, ca. 1975. Courtesy of the Texas Department of Criminal Justice.

ments at Mountain View and Gatesville, for example, were beaten by both staff and other juveniles for such infractions as speaking Spanish, talking when not authorized, or failing to answer a question. "Office boys," the TYC equivalent to the Building Tenders or inmate enforcers of the Texas prison system,[65] were given special privileges by staff members for falsifying incident reports, provoking incidents with other TYC youths, and participating in the beatings of other TYC wards.

TYC youths who violated arbitrary rules such as talking back or who simply irritated a correctional officer were also subjected to a host of exotic corporal punishments. For example, offending youths faced a variety of "make work" tasks such as "grass pulling," where they were dispersed on the institution grounds to pull grass, with straight knees, for hours on end. Others were "racked" (kicked in the teeth and beaten while on their knees), placed "on shovel" (moving piles of dirt from one place to another), placed "on crumb" (sitting on a chair all day long while facing the wall), or made to watch "Texas TV" (standing with face against a wall for several hours).

Eventually, the *Morales* litigation led to wholesale operational changes in TYC regarding both juvenile court processes and juvenile institutionalization. As one example, Judge Justice's 1974 opinion and ruling eventually led to the transfer of both Gatesville State School and

Mountain View State School to the Texas prison system, the hiring of more qualified staff, and stricter rules for the use of tear gas, tranquilizers, and solitary confinement. The *Morales* litigation eventually ended with oversight by a special committee in 1984. Monitoring of progress in the settlement ended in 1988; by then substantial change had come to Texas's juvenile institutions.[66]

DISCOVERING EXTREME DELINQUENTS

The end of the *Morales* monitoring signified that changes to the processes of adjudication for juveniles and the treatment they received upon commitment to TYC had been fully implemented. The year 1988 also marked another change that would not only alter the correctional landscape in the renamed Texas Youth Commission but also throughout the state of Texas.

By the late 1980s a second wave of juvenile crime blew across the nation, adding to the aftermath of the earlier wave that began building in 1972 and reached a temporary zenith in 1974. This was especially true in Texas, where the number of juvenile arrests nearly doubled between 1988 and 1994 and arrests of juveniles for violent crimes in Texas increased at a fast and furious pace, even surpassing violent crime rate increases among adult criminals. These developments caused tremendous fanfare on a national level, culminating in dire and frequent warnings by criminologists and others of the coming juvenile "super-predator."[67] "Get ready for the bloodbath" was the message. Texas responded.[68]

Texas has never been a state to shy away from dealing with violent crime. This is no less true for juvenile offenders than for adult criminals. For example, Texas's response to the first juvenile crime wave of the 1970s was to enact an adult court certification law in 1973 that allowed juvenile felons age fifteen and older to be tried in adult court and sent to the Texas prison system, with potential sentences including the death penalty.[69] By the thick of the second violent juvenile crime wave in 1987, Texas responded again by passing an innovative law for prosecuting serious and violent juvenile offenders. In an effort to respond to juveniles as young as age ten who had committed serious and violent crimes but were not old enough for adult court certification, and as an alternative to further lowering or even abolishing the minimum age for adult court certification, Texas passed the Determinate Sentencing Act (DSA), later known as the Violent or Habitual Offenders Act. This law, which is fully described in chapter 2, ushered in a new era in re-

Aftermath of youth riot, Mountain View State School for Boys, ca. 1975. Courtesy of the Texas Department of Criminal Justice.

sponding to serious and violent juvenile offenders. In place of previous approaches that sought either the mutually exclusive choice of rehabilitation or getting tough, this new Texas law embraced both in one fell swoop. In combining both rehabilitation and punishment with a last-chance opportunity for serious and violent juvenile offenders, determinate sentencing, like everything in Texas, was big.

CONCLUSION

In 1993, nearly one hundred years after Henry Campbell faced Judge Tuthill in the nation's first juvenile court, two Houston teens, fourteen-year-old Jennifer Ertman and sixteen-year-old Elizabeth Pena, were walking home after leaving a pool party at a friend's apartment complex. It was a perfect day in late June for a pool party, with the weather a hot and sticky ninety degrees, the kind of unbearable and smothering heat that one can only escape at a pool or lake or river.

Jennifer and Elizabeth left the apartment complex around 11 p.m., long after the hot Texas sun had set. They followed the nearby railroad tracks, taking a shortcut along White Oak Bayou near T. C. Jester Park so that they would be home before their 11:30 p.m. curfew. On their way through the park, Jennifer and Elizabeth passed two boys without incident. A short while later, however, they happened upon the aftermath of a "jumping in" ceremony by a local gang known as the Black and Whites. In short order, the gang members seized Elizabeth and pulled her down the railroad track embankment. Jennifer had initially gotten free, but returned to her friend when she heard her cries for help.[70]

With ferocity, the girls were repeatedly gang raped—orally, anally, and vaginally—for more than an hour. The girls were assaulted by two or more gang members at a time. After the sexual assaults, the girls were strangled with a belt; when the belt snapped from the violent force, the girls' shoelaces were used. To ensure that Jennifer and Elizabeth were dead, the gang members then repeatedly kicked and stomped them until their lifeless bodies lay in the park with broken teeth and snapped ribs. According to one investigator, it was the "most vicious, sadistic, animal-like" crime he had ever seen.[71]

The six gang members who perpetrated the unthinkable assaults and murders ranged from fourteen to eighteen years of age. Peter Cantu, Sean Derrick O'Brien, and Jose Medellin were only a few months past their eighteenth birthdays. Efrain Perez and Raul Villareal were just days shy of their eighteenth birthdays. Venancio Medellin, the younger brother of Jose, was fourteen years old.

With the exception of Venancio Medellin, all were sentenced to death and remanded to the Texas prison system to meet their fates with the needle in a small room located on the northeast side of the Huntsville "Walls" unit—a room just a stone's throw from the old East Building at the Walls, the state of Texas's first cellblock, constructed in 1848. Based on the US Supreme Court ruling in *Roper v. Simmons* (2005), however, Perez and Villareal's death sentences were commuted to life in prison since they were only seventeen at the time of the crimes.[72]

Venancio Medellin, because of his younger age, was processed in juvenile court and adjudicated for aggravated sexual assault. Prosecuted under Texas's DSA passed six years earlier in 1987, the younger Medellin's maximum allowable sentence was forty years. His incarceration would begin in a TYC facility, and it was possible that he could be released and discharged from all sanctions by his twenty-first birthday or roughly six years after his conviction. If he was not released from TYC by his twenty-first birthday, Venancio's remaining term of roughly thirty-four years would be served in the Texas prison system, subject to state parole laws.

By 1993 the vagrants, beggars, thieves, and malcontents were for all intents and purposes long gone from state juvenile institutions in Texas. The offenders that populated juvenile facilities in Texas more and more resembled the super-predators that became the buzzword of the late 1980s and early 1990s. Indeed, by 2010, all 1,056 new commitments to TYC consisted of felony offenders,[73] and 39 percent had previously been adjudicated in juvenile court for at least two felonies prior to their most recent felony commitment.[74] Commitment offenses were as serious as capital murder, with the more frequent offenses being aggravated assault, aggravated sexual assault, aggravated robbery, and burglary. Of the 1,056, only 116 were considered so threatening and violent that they were adjudicated and committed under Texas's DSA.

The changes in juvenile institutionalization and juvenile justice were clearly influenced by the juvenile crime waves that swept Texas and the nation in the early 1970s and then again in the late 1980s. Although not set in motion by juvenile crime increases alone, the pendulum had clearly swung toward more punitive sentencing for juvenile offenders, much as was the case in 1962 when the Mountain View State School for Boys arose from the old cotton fields in Gatesville in response to what seemed a new and frightening form of youth violence.

But at the same time that more punitive measures were being exacted on juvenile offenders, Texas embarked on a bold sentencing and institutionalization experiment which pitted the desire to punish serious and violent juvenile offenders against a wish to give such offenders one more last chance to change their ways before reaching the age of adulthood. Much like the efforts of the child-savers a century earlier, Texas's determinate sentencing process was meant to stop juveniles—even miscreant rapists like Venancio Medellin—from becoming adult criminals. The determinate sentencing law attempted to provide the best of both worlds—a third prong of juvenile justice between the regular juvenile court process first employed in Cook County and the adult-court certification processes that swept the nation in the 1970s. Determinate sentencing, in other words, was a "blended" approach designed to give each young offender between adolescence and adulthood "some rope, enough to yank himself out of a life of crime, or to hang himself and wind up in prison."[75]

This third prong of justice, broadly referred to as nationwide as blended sentencing and signifying the blending of juvenile and adult justice, is the subject of chapter 2. The specific subjects of this book, however, are the serious and violent juvenile offenders, like Venancio Medellin, who were adjudicated and sentenced under Texas's DSA between 1987 and 2011.

With this population as our focus, the question we seek to answer is straightforward: What happened when determinately sentenced offenders—many of whom committed the most serious and violent crimes in Texas—were temporarily spared adult justice and given one more chance at redemption? Driven by this broad question, we seek to explore and understand the institutional behavior of the sentenced offenders during their period of confinement in TYC facilities, the decisions made as to whether such offenders ultimately faced adult prison transfer or TYC release, and the recidivism outcomes of those who avoided the adult prison portion of their sentence and were released directly from TYC to the streets in young adulthood. In sum, we seek to understand whether juvenile offenders sentenced between 1987 and 2011 capitalized on their second chance, or continued on the path of lost causes leading to the Texas prison system.

CHAPTER 2

THE DETERMINATE SENTENCING ACT IN TEXAS

MERGING JUVENILE AND ADULT JUSTICE

THE LAST SEVERAL DECADES of juvenile justice have included efforts by juvenile justice administrators, legislators, and other policy makers to impose harsher and longer sanctions on juvenile offenders than had been customary in the past. These efforts have further blurred the line between juvenile and adult justice systems that were originally created to be both philosophically and operationally distinct. This blending of juvenile and adult sanctions was a direct response to the increasing frequency and changing nature of juvenile delinquency. It was focused on offenders who did not fit neatly within traditional juvenile justice courts and systems, and for whom the full effects of the adult justice system were generally inappropriate.

The juvenile court and justice system was founded under the ideology of *parens patriae*—translated as "parent of the country." Under this paternalistic foundation, it was the duty of the state to take responsibility for wayward youths and other young malcontents who were unable to be controlled by their parents or guardians. In those circumstances, the *parens patriae* philosophy of early juvenile courts mandated that the state take over and provide proper guidance and supervision.

Under this philosophy, the juvenile court and juvenile justice system presumed that youthful offenders were not entirely rational offenders. Therefore, this system focused much more on rehabilitation than punishment and was instituted to bring the lives of juveniles back onto acceptable paths. Alternatively, once a person transitioned into adulthood, the criminal justice system operated under the philosophy that adult criminals were rational actors, and thus it focused less on reha-

Louisiana Hall, Gatesville State School for Boys. Courtesy of the Texas State Library and Archives Commission.

bilitation and more on deterrence and punishment. The blending of these two systems—in response to different and more diverse types of juvenile offenders—ultimately led to the advent of a third justice system. Broadly known nationwide as blended sentencing, in Texas it is called determinate sentencing, and the state's adoption of this blended sentencing scheme is the focus of this chapter.

The blending of juvenile and adult sentencing strategies in Texas began in 1987 and came about via the Determinate Sentencing Act (DSA), later known as the Violent or Habitual Offenders Act (hereafter, determinate sentencing).[1] This chapter will discuss the origins of determinate sentencing in Texas before describing the determinate sentencing process to illustrate the way in which Texas responded to juvenile offenders whose behavior required the type of mid-range sanction that falls somewhere between the more rehabilitative orientation of the traditional juvenile court and justice system and the more punitive punishments historically indicative of the adult justice system.

ORIGINS OF DETERMINATE SENTENCING IN TEXAS

Determinate sentencing in Texas was born in the midst of numerous debates within the Texas Legislature in the 1980s over what to do about serious juvenile crime. At the time of these conversations, serious and violent juvenile offenders fourteen years of age or older could be certified to adult court (also referred to as transfer, waiver, remand, bind over, and other terms in different states) and dealt with in ways traditionally reserved for adults, such as imprisonment in adult correctional facilities. However, this age restriction did not work well in cases of serious and violent offenses committed by those too young to be certified to adult court.[2] While traditional juvenile court processes were available for such young and serious offenders, upper-age maximums limited the reach of the juvenile court and juvenile correctional system to offenders under the age of twenty-one. To be sure, such young, serious, and violent offenders are a small percentage of all delinquents—even in the expansive state of Texas.

The two-prong choice of traditional juvenile court processing with its maximum age of jurisdiction at twenty-one or adult court certification were sufficient for most situations involving juvenile offenders. But in some situations (for example, the case of a fourteen-year-old murderer), a potential maximum of seven years in the Texas Youth Commission (TYC) or alternatively sending the youth to the adult justice system at such a young age did not seem to provide adequate choices. Indeed, it was these in-between offenders—for whom the juvenile court might not be tough enough and adult court was not yet available—that provided the incentive to search for other options.

The logical starting point for this search was to lower the age of adult court certification and hence reduce the age under which youths would be protected by juvenile jurisdiction. Most of the initial debates in the Texas Legislature were centered on this goal of lowering the age of certification.[3] In fact, three different house bills and one senate bill were introduced in an attempt to lower this age from fifteen to thirteen for select offenses, but these bills brought with them a number of other challenges. For example, under two of the bills it would have been possible for youths fifteen and sixteen years of age to be incarcerated in the Texas Department of Corrections (TDC). This move would have created the need for a strategy to segregate such youthful offenders from the rest of the adult population to alleviate concerns of victimization and other negative consequences. The bills, however, articulated no clear way to avoid the problem of housing very young juveniles in adult prisons—especially given the growing problem of overcrowding in the TDC at the time.[4]

In other arguments, it was noted that even violent juvenile offenders processed in juvenile court and committed to TYC facilities served an average of only five months of incarceration—even though TYC had authority to house them until the age of twenty-one.[5] Yet youths certified to adult court for a felony offense could receive a sentence of up to ninety-nine years or life for the most serious and violent capital crimes and first-degree felonies.[6] This stark contrast in sanctions raised the issue of fit yet again, with the juvenile court not tough enough and adult imprisonment, if an option, perhaps too tough. Lawmakers appreciated the need to strike a balance between these two disparate systems of punishment.

The Texas Legislature ultimately found a way to ensure that serious and violent juvenile offenders would be committed to TYC facilities for as long as possible, while also protecting them from premature transfer to adult prison and allowing hope for rehabilitation. The legislature's solution was the Determinate Sentencing Act of 1987, which allowed juvenile offenders to face a juvenile punishment first, followed by a potentially consecutive and contiguous term of adult incarceration in the Texas prison system if adequate rehabilitation and progress did not occur during the initial juvenile term of incarceration. The goal behind this legislation was simple: to apply the rehabilitative foundation of the juvenile justice system, and if that failed, to exercise the more punitive and long-term option of adult incarceration.[7] Determinate sentencing in Texas, for all intents and purposes, featured the best of both worlds— a true blending of juvenile and adult justice.

THE DETAILS

When determinate sentencing was originally enacted by the Texas Legislature,[8] it focused on the following six serious and violent offenses: murder, capital murder, attempted capital murder, aggravated kidnapping, aggravated sexual assault, and deadly assault on a law enforcement officer.[9]

Aside from minor legislative modifications, the DSA remained unchanged until it was renamed the Violent or Habitual Offenders Act in 1995. The new name reflected an expanded list of offenses addressed

Table 2.1. Offenses Eligible for Determinate Sentencing in Texas

Murder*	Felony Deadly Conduct
Attempted Murder	Aggravated First-Degree Controlled Substance Felony
Capital Murder*	Criminal Solicitation Capital/First-Degree Felony
Attempted Capital Murder*	Second-Degree Felony Indecency with a Child
Manslaughter	Attempted Indecency with a Child by Contact
Intoxication Manslaughter	Criminal Solicitation of a Minor
Aggravated Kidnapping*	–to commit Indecency with a Child
Attempted Aggravated Kidnapping	–to commit Sexual Assault
Aggravated Sexual Assault*	–to commit Aggravated Sexual Assault
Sexual Assault	–to commit Sexual Performance by a Child
Attempted Sexual Assault	First-Degree Arson
Aggravated Assault	Habitual Felony Conduct (3 Consecutive Felonies)
Aggravated Robbery	First-Degree Arson
Attempted Aggravated Robbery	Felony Deadly Assault Discharge of a Firearm
Felony Injury (Child, Elderly, or Disabled)	Aggravated Controlled Substance Felony

Note: * denotes original offenses under Determinate Sentencing Act of 1987

under this act. Indeed, in 1995 and again in 2001, the Texas Legislature expanded the scope of the DSA, ultimately increasing the number of eligible offenses to thirty (see table 2.1).[10] Currently, any of the thirty offenses can qualify a juvenile offender between ten and sixteen years of age for determinate sentencing in Texas. After being charged and adjudicated in juvenile court for one of these offenses, a juvenile offender could receive a *maximum* sentence first set at thirty years.

After modifications to the legislation in 1991,[11] a juvenile could receive a maximum sentence of forty years for a capital or first-degree felony, a maximum sentence of twenty years for a second-degree felony, and a maximum sentence of ten years for a third-degree felony. Other modifications to the DSA will be discussed later in the chapter, but table 2.2 provides a general timeline of noteworthy historical events related to Texas juvenile justice and the DSA.

Although certain changes listed in table 2.2 have slightly modified the DSA over the years, there are numerous steps between a juvenile being charged with one of these DSA offenses and receiving a determinate sentence. Chart 2.1 illustrates these steps and potential pathways, which will be explained in detail throughout the following section.

The case of Venancio ("Vinny") Medellin, whose story was introduced at the end of chapter 1, provides a good example of how the DSA func-

Table 2.2. Determinate Sentencing Act Milestones

1987	Determinate Sentencing Act (DSA) enacted by Texas State Legislature with 6 eligible offenses and a maximum determinate sentence of 30 years.
1987	Capital Offender Program implemented at Giddings State School to provide intensive therapeutic treatment to violent and capital determinately sentenced offenders.
1991	Maximum determinate sentence extended to 40 years for capital and first-degree felonies.
1995	The seventy-fourth Texas Legislature expands DSA from 6 to 30 different offenses (22 offenses with additional offense categories for attempts and conspiracies). Determination court hearings eliminated for sentenced offenders unless TYC requested the transfer of a youth to TDCJ or if they requested release to parole before a sentenced offender served his or her minimum length of incarceration.
2001	Texas Legislature added 2 offenses to the list of those eligible for DSA.
2007	Maximum age of TYC jurisdiction reduced from age 21 to age 19. Youth who have not completed sentence by age 19 and who have not been transferred to the Texas prison system are transferred to adult parole supervision.

tions in the Texas juvenile justice system.[12] Drawing from numerous newspaper articles compiled by the victims' families that chronicled the prosecution and sentencing of Venancio and his codefendants, the following narrative uses details from his story to parallel the process of determinate sentencing for juvenile offenders in Texas.[13]

TRANSITION FROM "JUVENILE" TO "SENTENCED OFFENDER"

The determinate sentencing process begins when a juvenile as young as the age of ten commits one of the thirty serious and violent offenses noted in table 2.1. Recall from chapter 1 that Venancio helped his brother Jose and other older gang members brutally rape and murder two teenage girls in 1993 in Houston. Reports indicate that Venancio urged his brother and one of the other gang members to leave, but then sexually assaulted one of the girls when pressured by the others. According to testimony, Venancio was not present for—and did not participate in—the murder of each victim following the sexual assaults.

Venancio not only met the age requirement for determinate sentencing at fourteen but also was charged with aggravated sexual assault,

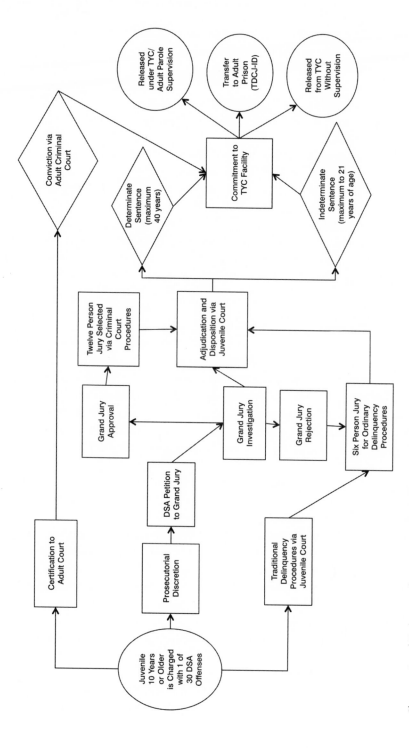

Chart 2.1. Legal Pathways of Determinate Sentencing in Texas

one of the six original eligible offenses for a determinate sentencing prosecution. Since Venancio's crime was committed in 1993, the list of offenses had not yet increased beyond the first six.

THE DECISION TO PURSUE A DETERMINATE SENTENCING PROSECUTION

After Venancio's aggravated sexual assault case was filed in juvenile court, the Harris County prosecutor assigned to the case made a decision that changed the trajectory of this fourteen-year-old's life—and criminal career—from that point forward. It is important to emphasize here that processing an offender under determinate sentencing is triggered by prosecutorial discretion. In Texas, the prosecutor has sole discretion to make one of the following three decisions: allow the case to follow the normal course of action for an ordinary delinquency case via traditional juvenile court, file a certification petition to adult court for a full adult court trial, or pursue a determinate sentencing case in juvenile court.[14] Proceedings for determinate sentencing cases are initiated when the prosecutor decides to use this third option that blends jurisdictions and subjects juvenile offenders such as Venancio Medellin to two systems of accountability simultaneously.

THE GRAND JURY INDICTMENT

To begin the formal DSA process, the determinate sentencing petition for the offense was filed in juvenile court alleging that Venancio committed one of the six covered offenses. The prosecutor then presented the petition to a twelve-member grand jury, whose indictment is required for determinate sentencing proceedings to officially begin.

The grand jury conducts an investigation into the case prior to approving or rejecting the petition.[15] This investigation includes the opportunity for witnesses to the crime, victims, and the accused to testify. It also provides the chance for other evidence and character witnesses to be presented on behalf of the accused. However, during these grand jury proceedings, Venancio would have had no right to be present during the presentation of testimony to the grand jury. The grand jury has discretionary power in these situations to allow (or restrict) Venancio or any other witnesses to testify.

In Venancio's case, his defense attorney, family members, and others may have been allowed to testify on his behalf at the grand jury hearing. Prior to the alleged crime, Venancio was reportedly regarded as a decent boy who possessed potential not usually found among youths on the streets of his north-side Houston neighborhood. Given his reputation, his family and possibly his teachers could have testified that he received good grades in school, stayed out of trouble, and avoided gangs. His defense attorney could also have emphasized that Venancio had been admitted to a magnet school that would help him develop his already demonstrated artistic ability. Venancio may have also testified on his own behalf, to tell his side of the story and to explain the extent to which he was involved in the crimes committed. These proceedings would have been conducted in secret, and an affirmative vote of nine or more of the twelve grand jury members was required to approve the prosecutor's petition to try the case under determinate sentencing.

THE ADJUDICATION PROCEEDING

Once a DSA petition is approved and entered into the record of the case, adjudication proceedings begin. The requirements of determinate sentencing proceedings are very similar to those of ordinary delinquency cases. One difference worth noting is that while a county court may employ a six-person jury for ordinary delinquency cases, determinate sentencing cases require a twelve-person jury. Additionally, the jury must be selected in accordance with the conditions required in adult criminal cases.[16]

Provided the juvenile prosecuted under the DSA is adjudicated in juvenile court, the youth is initially committed to the custody of TYC facing a maximum ten- to forty-year determinate sentence, depending on the severity of the crime and the sentencing by the judge or jury. If the judge or jury delivers a sentence of ten years or less, a probation term rather than a term of incarceration may be granted.[17] Because of the violent nature of his crime, however, Venancio received a forty-year incarceration term for felony aggravated sexual assault on September 30, 1993, just three months after the rape and murder of Elizabeth Pena and Jennifer Ertman. Venancio was then committed to TYC at age fourteen to begin this forty-year sentence.

THE FIRST OPPORTUNITY FOR RELEASE:
THE DETERMINATION HEARING

Roughly three years later in September 1996, Venancio was back in court. In determinate sentencing proceedings, Texas law requires a hearing in front of a judge to decide the next step. For offenses committed prior to 1996, the DSA required TYC to secure juvenile court approval prior to releasing a juvenile who had not served his or her full sentence.[18] Approval or rejection of a juvenile's early release is decided during this hearing (referred to in chapter 5 as a determination hearing), which is scheduled in juvenile court a minimum of thirty days prior to the offender's eighteenth birthday.

The determination hearing is arguably the most pivotal decision-making point in the DSA process. A decision is made during this fail-safe hearing about whether the offender will remain a "juvenile" in the eyes of the justice system or be transferred to the Texas prison system as an "adult" offender who must face the second or adult half of his or her determinate sentence. This hearing is also meant to provide an incentive for youths to participate in juvenile treatment programs that are offered by TYC during juvenile incarceration. The more progress toward rehabilitation a youth has made prior to this hearing, the more likely it is that he or she will receive a positive review. But even then, there is no guarantee of release instead of TDC transfer.

The decision made at this hearing usually triggers one of four general options concerning the juvenile's future: release to the community with supervision requirements; release to the community without supervision requirements; continued incarceration in TYC until the maximum age of jurisdiction (age twenty-one prior to 2007, age nineteen after 2007);[19] or transfer to the Texas prison system to face the remaining balance of the original determinate sentence.[20]

RELEASE TO THE COMMUNITY WITH SUPERVISION

The first option is a decision made by a Juvenile Review Board within TYC prior to the youth's eighteenth birthday to determine if he or she should be released to the community with supervision requirements. If this board decides to pursue such a release, then the TYC has authority to parole a juvenile without juvenile court approval provided that the juvenile has served his or her minimum length of stay.[21] However, if this release occurs prior to completing this minimum sentence length of stay, the TYC is required to seek juvenile court approval.

If released to the community with supervision requirements, the offender could be released under TYC parole supervision and jurisdiction until age twenty-one (changed to nineteen in 2007). Once a youth reached the maximum age of juvenile jurisdiction, he or she could be discharged from agency supervision and either released from supervision entirely, or administratively transferred to adult parole supervision. Although juvenile parole is an option, the released sentenced offender would more typically face transfer to the Texas Department of Criminal Justice Parole Division and then ultimately be placed on adult parole in the community to serve the remainder of his or her sentence once released.

RELEASE TO THE COMMUNITY WITHOUT SUPERVISION

In certain cases, sentenced offenders may be released directly to the community without facing further supervision requirements. Sometimes this outcome is decided by TYC authorities, but only after an offender has served his or her minimum length of stay in TYC as required by the court. In other cases, depending on the length of the determinate sentence, a sentenced offender may have completed his or her entire sentence before the determination hearing and is then mandated by law to be released and discharged from TYC (an example would be a fourteen-year-old who received a two-year determinate sentence). In a final situation, a sentenced offender who was ordered to continue his or her incarceration in TYC at the determination hearing could be released without supervision requirements at age twenty-one, after having served the minimum length of stay but not the entire sentence.

CONTINUED COMMITMENT TO TYC

The third option is that the youth could continue to serve his or her time in TYC. For example, at the determination hearing prior to an offender's eighteenth birthday, decision-makers could "recommit" the offender to remain incarcerated at the juvenile level until the maximum age of TYC jurisdiction. At that time, the sentence is effectively served, and the juvenile ages out of juvenile jurisdictional control and is released to the community without parole supervision.

TRANSFER TO THE TEXAS PRISON SYSTEM

The fourth option available for sentenced offenders following a determination hearing is transfer to the Texas prison system to continue the original determinate sentence with the potential for parole release after serving a period of confinement. It is important to note here that in some cases, this transfer to adult incarceration occurs prior to a juvenile's eighteenth birthday, but it must occur after the juvenile has turned sixteen. After a juvenile is transferred to adult prison, any retroactive good-conduct time is added to the period of time committed to TYC, and that combined accrued time counts toward adult parole eligibility. Note, however, that parole eligibility does not mean the offender will be paroled while serving his or her adult portion of the determinate sentence.

VENANCIO'S DETERMINATION HEARING OUTCOME

Venancio Medellin was regarded as a model ward during his commitment to TYC, and a recommendation was made by TYC authorities to release him to serve the remainder of his sentence under adult parole supervision. Since 1998, the committing judge in DSA cases has followed this recommendation from TYC 80 percent of the time.[22] Venancio's case, however, fell into the other 20 percent. Although TYC provided a glowing review of his behavior during his commitment to their juvenile correctional facilities and recommended that his commitment to TYC continue until he reached the age of twenty-one, the committing judge decided to transfer him to the adult side at that time. Dismissing TYC's recommendation report as "psychobabble," Judge Pat Shelton also said that he hoped Venancio's future parole officer was yet to be born—emphasizing his desire for Venancio to serve the entirety of his forty-year sentence in adult prison: "Venancio's offense in and of itself is sufficient to justify that sentence. What we are saying [to him] is that we can't trust you based on what you did that one day, no matter how perfect you were before and after. I think the system has got to put the interests of the victim and the public first."[23]

Shelton's language during this hearing provides a poignant example of how the DSA relies on multiple players to ultimately determine the path that each youth's life will take. "Can we rehabilitate the fifteen-year-old, and is it worth the time and expense (considering) the crime committed?" Shelton asked. "The answer is no. At the time of the transfer hearing, I have to consider what that *offense* [emphasis added] was worth, not what the *offender* [emphasis added] is worth. That's the difference between the court and TYC."[24]

After this hearing, Venancio was transferred to the Texas prison system at age eighteen with credit for the three years he served in TYC, making him eligible for parole in seven years. As mentioned, Judge Shelton could have continued Venancio's commitment to TYC until the age of twenty-one. He decided, however, to immediately transfer him to the Texas adult prison system because in a balancing act of worthiness, Venancio fell short.

SEVEN YEARS LATER: VENANCIO'S ADULT PAROLE HEARINGS

Venancio had his first adult parole hearing in May 2006. Five of the seven members of the Texas Board of Pardons and Paroles had to vote in his favor before he would be released. Even though he was now thirteen years into his sentence, he was denied parole. He was again denied in 2009, at which point he had served sixteen years—two years longer than the number of years he had been alive at the time he committed his crime. On September 4, 2012—nineteen years into his forty-year determinate sentence—he appeared for another parole hearing. The victims' families, as well as advocates of the death penalty and lengthy sentencing, spoke out prior to each parole hearing to mobilize support for keeping Venancio incarcerated. He was again denied parole in 2012. Thirty-three years old at his hearing in 2012, he will continue to go up for parole every three years; if every request is denied, he will not be released from prison until he is fifty-four years old. While Venancio has a chance every three years to be released to the streets, the potential also exists to keep him incarcerated until the year 2033 for an offense he committed at the age of fourteen.

EFFICACY OF THE DETERMINATE SENTENCING ACT (DSA) IN TEXAS

Years after different states implemented blended sentencing schemes, scholars have begun to examine various aspects that are similar to the determinate sentencing method used in Texas. David J. Rothman argues that policies are often motivated by what will be most convenient for correctional practice, rather than by what is most beneficial for offender rehabilitation.[25] In other words, the desire for an effective correctional system trumps society's desire to reform criminal offenders. With the Determinate Sentencing Act, Texas managed to strike a genuine compromise between the two. Since the DSA was enacted in 1987, it has produced a number of consequences—some intended and some not.

While providing a chance for redemption for serious and violent

Old shop building, Gatesville State School for Boys, ca. 1975. Courtesy of the Texas Department of Criminal Justice.

youthful offenders and an opportunity to avoid Texas prison time, the DSA also exerted a significant level of personal accountability on each serious and violent youthful offender subjected to this process. Additionally, the DSA also significantly increased the power of juvenile courts by allowing them to give youths less than sixteen years of age lengthier sentences than were available via normal delinquency procedures in Texas's traditional juvenile courts.[26] Finally, determinate sentencing ensured that offenders served longer terms of confinement than youths convicted as ordinary delinquents.[27]

As another consequence, determinate sentencing has caused the number of juveniles waived to adult court in Texas to decrease over the last several years. For example, there were 596 juveniles certified as adults in the state of Texas in 1994, compared to only 167 ten years later in 2004—a 72 percent decrease in the number of juveniles certified and waived directly to adult court.[28] While this decline is partially attributed to the nationwide drop in juvenile crime that occurred during the mid- to late 1990s and generally continues to this day, some of the 72 percent decrease has arguably been absorbed by an increase in the number of youths who received a determinate sentence.[29] Indeed, while determinate sentencing has led to a decrease in the number of certified juveniles in Texas, it is also likely that its expansion drew in cases that might otherwise have been handled under the traditional juvenile court process. This is particularly relevant after the 1995 expansion of determinate sentencing.[30]

The increase in number of offenses eligible for determinate sentencing also triggered an increase in the overall number of sentenced offenders committed to TYC. Indeed, juveniles committed to TYC with determinate sentences more than quadrupled from 1990 to 1996, increasing from 48 to 207.[31] Since 1996, sentenced offenders have constituted about 7 to 8 percent of those committed to TYC each year.[32] This further defines the scope of the extreme delinquents examined in this book.

The ongoing use of determinate sentencing has also encouraged TYC to develop and maintain numerous specialized treatment programs to target youths committed to its facilities, with one program specifically targeting the most violent and problematic sentenced offenders. Originally called the Capital Offender Program/Group and today known as the Capital and Serious Violent Offender Treatment Program, its creation in 1987 paralleled the implementation of the DSA, and was intended to accelerate the rehabilitation of TYC's most serious and violent offenders via intensive therapeutic treatment. Unfortunately, the demand for such intensive treatment greatly outweighs TYC's ability to supply it to all sentenced offenders who may need it, as only eighteen to twenty offenders can receive such treatment at one time.

The advent of blended sentencing likely also slowed the development of other certification options in Texas. While twenty-nine states possess statutory exclusion laws to automatically certify youths to adult court for certain offenses, Texas does not possess such legislative exclusion for these offenders.[33] While determinate sentencing has perhaps stunted the expansion of certification provisions in Texas, this version of blended justice has arguably yielded other unintended consequences. It has significantly strengthened prosecutorial discretion and created the challenging organizational context that requires collaboration of juvenile justice and adult criminal justice.[34] However, it is also worth noting that the constitutionality of the DSA has been upheld repeatedly in Texas, surviving attacks related to vagueness, double jeopardy, and separation of powers.[35] Given the DSA's established constitutionality as well as its longevity, the time has come to examine its efficacy more carefully and extensively.

Bill Connolly, an attorney with over thirty years of experience litigating juvenile cases in Texas, has been a frequent speaker at the annual Nuts and Bolts of Juvenile Law meeting that is sponsored by the Juvenile Law Section of the State Bar of Texas and Texas Juvenile Probation Commission. In 2005 he used one presentation to tackle some issues and consequences of the DSA head-on:

> Anyone can read a statute and discern what the words mean with some reasonable degree of certainty. It seems that the principal question is one of application. How can a prosecutor, defense attorney, probation officer or Judge take a specific set of facts and apply them in the framework of the sometimes divergent worlds of the Juvenile Justice Code; Texas Code of Criminal Procedure; Texas Rules of Evidence; Texas Rules of Civil Procedure; Texas Constitution; United States Constitution and case law decisions related to all of these areas of law? The prosecutor's duty to see that "justice is done"; the defense attorney's duty "to zealously defend the Respondent within the bounds of the law"; and the Court's duty to serve the dual purposes of "punishment" and "treatment, training and rehabilitation," puts into play a multitude of possibilities in the area of "Determinate Sentencing."[36]

Connolly highlights the challenges associated with not only the interpretation of such legislation, but more importantly with the application of the DSA. Both the interpretation and application rely on many players with divergent perspectives. How, then, do we best tackle an evaluation of such a law?

A logical approach to investigating the impact of blended sentencing is to conduct a case study of a type of sentencing reform in one state that is rarely found elsewhere in the United States.[37] Scholars have set the stage for an in-depth evaluation of the DSA's efficacy,[38] but this book is the first effort to examine this sentencing scheme's impact from numerous angles, and over three decades of Texas juvenile justice. As previously discussed, DSA proceedings are triggered by a single factor: prosecutorial discretion. Here we are unable to examine the motivations of such discretion in the cases of each sentenced offender in our population. Prosecutorial discretion is difficult, if not impossible, to measure, which has made it increasingly challenging to produce any reliable nationwide data on the overall rates of blended sentencing and certification to adult court.[39] While it is impossible to control for factors such as prosecutorial discretion and historical shifts in ideology within the TYC, this book takes a step forward by providing a more extensive case study on a blended sentencing scheme than has been produced with previous empirical research in this area.

The chapters to follow take careful analytical steps to examine the impact of the DSA on Texas juvenile justice outcomes such as institutional misconduct, recidivism, and the persistence of criminal careers as offenders who were juveniles at the time of the commission of their crimes transitioned into young adulthood. In sum, this book represents the first long-term examination of a blended sentencing scheme in one state with a focus on the institutional behavior of sentenced offenders and their recidivism outcomes if and when released from TYC facilities. Chapter 3 will provide a look into the cohort of sentenced offenders to be examined.

CHAPTER 3

THE SHEEP THAT GOT LOST

[Guard talking]: "Ain't nobody talking when I'm talking fellas . . . so shut the fuck up. The following items are placed in the envelope as I call them off . . . empty wallet, legal paperwork. First three out of the tank. Line up single file on the bench, let's go. Open your mouth, stick out your tongue. All right, do your ears, one at a time. Okay, bend your heads over and shake them out with your fingers. Hands above your head, hands out in front of you, over, move those fingers. Reach down and lift up your nut sack. Drop your nut sack. Pull back your dick. Turn around. One foot at a time, pick it up and wiggle the toes. Other foot. Okay, bend over and grab your ass, spread your cheeks, and give me two good coughs." AMERICAN ME (1992, DIR. EDWARD JAMES OLMOS)

A LIFE FOR A LIFE

THE EPIGRAPH TO THIS CHAPTER comes from a movie scene depicting what happens when an offender enters intake at a state correctional facility. Beyond the Hollywood theatrics, the quotation and scene also aptly demonstrate the institutional ceremony that marks the transition of an adolescent from a free child to a state delinquent.[1] Although the initiation is not as harsh and anonymous and indifferent as the adult institutional experience, those who enter state juvenile incarceration have entered a new world of routines, orders, commands, and timetables unlike anything they have yet experienced.

State juvenile incarceration also marks another important life transition. This transition is both symbolic and real, for it is the point signifying the end of one life and the beginning of another—the leaving of an old, familiar, unsuccessful life for the chance at a new and different and better life. But state juvenile incarceration can also be a marker sig-

Outside picket at Reception Center after TDC modifications, Gatesville State School for Boys, ca. 1980. Courtesy of the Texas Department of Criminal Justice.

naling continuity in problem behavior that leads to life failure. Indeed, for the sentenced offenders in Texas, state juvenile incarceration can be a turning point toward change and redemption, or it can be just one more stop on the way to becoming members of the next generation of prisoners in Texas. These are the only options for the sentenced offenders.

TRANSITION POINT

After the gavel falls, and the tears of anger and sorrow and regret have been shed by both the youths and their families, the sentenced offenders, as they are now known, are whisked back to the county detention center where they have resided for the last several weeks or months prior to their court hearing.[2] Back at county detention, the formally adjudicated youthful offenders will likely be placed on suicide watch during the typical few short days until transport to the Texas Youth Commission (TYC) Orientation and Assessment intake facility (Brownwood State School until the 1990s; then Marlin, Texas; and since August 2007 the McLennan County State Juvenile Correctional Facility in Mart for boys or the Ron Jackson State Juvenile Correctional Complex in Brownwood for girls).[3]

Once at state orientation and assessment, the youthful offenders will stay for roughly thirty to sixty days and be processed and evaluated across a number of classification and treatment programming domains—medical, emotional, educational, familial, and psychological. A detailed review of juvenile system involvement for both delinquency- and nondelinquency-related matters will also ensue, and institutional staff will continually evaluate youths on their adjustment to the institutional regime.

At the same time that staff members are evaluating youths at orientation and assessment, the juvenile offenders will also be sizing each other up and assessing their situation: making contacts, acting tough, embellishing their delinquent careers, claiming gang membership, and generally trying to find their "fit" in what is a foreign place to most of them. Despite their serious and violent crimes and tough exteriors, at orientation and assessment most are secretly scared to death. The scene is all too familiar to those who have spent any time in a juvenile correctional facility—the new commitments gaze out the window wishing they had gone to school more, drunk less, huffed less paint, and stayed home on that fateful day they committed the crime. They are wondering about their brothers and sisters and friends and parents, and, oddly enough, the prom that they will not attend. Yet even after their previous stay in juvenile detention, the young delinquents are still not desensitized to the constant buzz created by the batch institutional environment, nor have their senses yet dulled to the uniquely institutional blend of smells from urine, body odor, bleach, and industrial-strength cleaners such as Pine Sol and Simple Green. Despite all of this newness and change, however, the one thing that the new commitments do know is that their incarceration—this time—is for real.

Following evaluation at orientation and assessment, TYC commitments are ushered to a more permanent facility based on their specific treatment needs, proximity to their home, and other institutionally relevant considerations. While some "regular" TYC commitments might be placed in a halfway house or another lower-security facility, most are placed in high-security facilities. All of the sentenced offenders are placed in TYC's high-security facilities such as the state schools at Giddings or Gainesville. Once there, the sentenced offenders face one of two general outcomes related to their determinate sentence. The first is to demonstrate substantial and sustained progress toward rehabilitation and hope for TYC system release to a community context such as adult or juvenile parole or, in rarer cases, outright release and discharge. The second option is to face the balance of the adult portion of their determinate sentence in the Texas prison system, or TDC (Texas Department of Corrections), as the old-time convicts still call it.

This chapter examines the population of juvenile offenders in Texas ages ten to sixteen who committed a determinate sentence–eligible crime and were subsequently prosecuted, adjudicated, and incarcerated in TYC as sentenced offenders between 1987 and 2011.[4] Our goal is to paint a comprehensive picture of the sentenced offenders as they transitioned from the lawful to the delinquent world and from the community or "free world" to the juvenile correctional institution. In short, we seek to describe the general social history and backgrounds of the sentenced offenders, their crimes, and the sentencing for their crimes. We also seek to provide a snapshot of what happened to these youths as they navigated through state juvenile incarceration toward either release to the community and a second chance at redemption, or transfer to the Texas prison system.[5]

DETERMINATE SENTENCES AND THE SENTENCED OFFENDERS, 1987–2011

Between 1987 and 2011, there were a total of 3,382 youths who were prosecuted, adjudicated, and incarcerated in TYC as sentenced offenders.[6] Of those sentenced in the 1980s, 1990s, and early 2000s, all have either been released from TYC into the community or have moved on to the Texas prison system. A few have died following their determinate sentence.[7] Others, such as those sentenced to TYC more recently, are just starting their journey to community release and a second chance or transfer to the Texas prison system.

Table 3.1 provides the yearly breakdown of determinate sentences in Texas from 1987–2011.[8] The table is divided into time intervals corresponding to changes that came to the original 1987 determinate sentencing law (see chapter 2 for specific details of the changes that came in 1991, 1995, 2001, and 2007). For example, one of the early changes to the original law came in 1995.[9] In that year the Texas Legislature added eleven additional offenses or categories of existing offenses (e.g., conspiracy, solicitation) eligible for prosecution under determinate sentencing. The legislature also increased the range of sentence lengths specific to the aforementioned offense additions (e.g., a maximum of ten years for a third-degree felony) and also eliminated the need for juvenile court hearings unless TYC requested to transfer a youth to the Texas prison system or wanted to release a youth before the completion of his or her minimum length of confinement.

Table 3.1. Determinate
Sentences in Texas, 1987–2011

Years	Determinate Sentences
1987–1994	419
1995–2000	1,271
2001–2006	1,095
2007–2011	597
Total	3,382

The mean number of determinate sentences in Texas between 1987 and 2011 was approximately 135 per year. The most active years for determinate sentences were between 1996 and 1999, with more than 200 determinate sentences resulting in TYC incarceration in each of those years. The increased activity in the first several years following 1995 is not altogether surprising since that time period was marked by an expanded list of offenses eligible for determinate sentencing. Despite the increase in the mid- to late 1990s, the number of determinate sentences over the last several years has been on a slight downturn. Since the last change to the determinate sentencing law in 2007, the average number of determinate sentences has been approximately 120 per year.[10]

AGE, RACE, AND SEX

Table 3.2 examines the basic demographics of the sentenced offenders. The sentenced offenders were committed to TYC at an average age of nearly sixteen (15.88), with the youngest being committed at close to age eleven. Roughly equal numbers were African American (38.9 percent) or Hispanic (39.1 percent), and just over 20 percent of the population was composed of whites. Sentenced offenders were disproportionately male (94.5 percent).

OFFENSES LEADING TO COMMITMENT

In chapter 1 we briefly examined the 1993 gang rape and murders of fourteen-year-old Jennifer Ertman and sixteen-year-old Elizabeth Pena. The only juvenile among the perpetrators, fourteen-year-old Venancio Medellin, received a forty-year determinate sentence and was eventu-

Table 3.2. Demographics of Sentenced
Offenders

	Mean/N	Percent
Age at TYC Commitment	15.88	—
Race		
White	686	20.3
African American	1,316	38.9
Hispanic	1,322	39.1
Other	58	1.7
Sex		
Male	3,195	94.5
Female	187	5.5

ally transferred to the Texas prison system to face the adult portion of his determinate sentence.[11] As shocking as this crime was, the reality is that in Texas and the nation as a whole it is rare for these types of crimes to involve juvenile offenders. Despite their rarity, however, such crimes still shock the conscience when perpetrated by such young offenders. Below is a sampling of other juvenile crimes committed in Texas, prosecuted and adjudicated under determinate sentencing, and resulting in sentences served initially in TYC:

- In January 2000, thirteen-year-old Edward "Pete" McCoy was present during the killing of eighty-four-year-old former school-teacher Geraldine Davidson. Davidson, who was first bound and then kidnapped after happening upon McCoy and his friends burglarizing her home, was driven around town in the trunk of a car and shown to other friends. At the Neches River near Palestine, Texas, Davidson had her hands tied behind her back and a cinder block tied to her ankles. She was then thrown into the river, where she drowned. McCoy, who testified against the others, received a twenty-year determinate sentence.[12]
- In June 2003, sixteen-year-old Marcus McTear was given a forty-year determinate sentence for the stabbing death of his fifteen-year-old girlfriend, Ortralla Mosley. McTear stabbed Mosley to death in the hallway of Reagan High School in Austin because they had recently broken up.[13]
- In February 2009, fourteen-year-old Rudy Zuniga participated in

Table 3.3. Sentenced Offender Commitment Offenses

	Frequency	Percent
Aggravated Robbery	1,184	35
Aggravated Sexual Assault	698	21
Aggravated Assault	520	15
Murder	344	10
Capital Murder	195	6
Indecency with a Child	107	3
Aggravated Kidnapping	63	2
Deadly Conduct	57	2
Sexual Assault	55	2
Injury to Child or Elderly	47	1
Manufacture/Delivery Controlled Substance	40	1
Manslaughter	25	1
Unlawful Possession Controlled Substance	14	< 1
Arson	14	< 1
Burglary	6	< 1
Assault	3	< 1
Robbery	3	< 1
Other	5	< 1
Intoxication Manslaughter	2	< 1
Total	3,382	100

Note: All percentages rounded to the nearest whole number except those under 0.5, which are indicated as < 1.

the brutal beating, torture, gang rape, and killing of thirty-five-year-old Rose Marie Gonzalez of Harlingen. Gonzalez's body was stuffed in her refrigerator following the rape-murder. Rose's mother found her in the refrigerator a few days after the killing. Zuniga testified against the three other accomplices, all young adults. Zuniga received a forty-year determinate sentence.[14]

• In April 2010, sixteen-year-old Khianna Laqua Williams and fourteen-year-old Gilbert Ramirez of Clifton, Texas, each received a twenty-year determinate sentence for shooting a Clifton man in the face. The man, Arturo Chavez, died. The motive of the crime was to rob Chavez.[15]

These vignettes are just a sampling of the crimes committed by Texas's sentenced offenders between 1987 and 2011. Table 3.3 examines the offenses of commitment for the entire population of sentenced offenders. The table is arranged in order from the most to least frequent offenses of commitment. Roughly 80 percent of all sentenced offenders were committed for the first four offenses listed (aggravated robbery, aggravated sexual assault, aggravated assault, and murder).[16]

Outside of aggravated robbery commitments (1,184, or 35 percent of all commitments), sexual assault–based offenses (aggravated sexual assault, sexual assault, and indecency with a child) accounted for 860 commitments, or approximately 25 percent of all sentenced offender commitments between 1987 and 2011. Homicide-based offenses (capital murder, murder, manslaughter, and intoxication manslaughter) accounted for 566 commitments, or roughly 17 percent.

Table 3.3 shows that the great majority of all sentenced offender commitments were for violent, person-related crimes. In fact, with the exception of fifty-nine commitments for drug-related offenses (manufacture/delivery of a controlled substance and unlawful possession of a controlled substance) or "other" crimes, roughly 98 percent of all sentenced offenders were committed to TYC for violent acts that boil down to robberies, homicides, sexual assaults, and extremely assaultive and dangerous behaviors. While these findings are unsurprising given the scope and intent of determinate sentencing in Texas, the results do show an extremely serious and violent offender cohort.[17]

SENTENCE LENGTH

Table 3.4 examines the sentence lengths of the cohort of sentenced offenders. As noted in chapter 2, offenders can receive sentences of "not more than forty years" (capital felonies, first-degree felonies, and aggravated controlled substance felonies), "not more than twenty years" (second-degree felonies), and "not more than ten years" (third-degree felonies) corresponding to the list of eligible offenses for determinate sentencing.[18] Thus, while maximum sentence lengths can range from ten to forty years, in practice offenders can receive sentences ranging anywhere from less than one year up to forty years, depending on their crime.

Table 3.4 shows that as a singular category, almost half of the sentenced offenders (48.85 percent) received a sentence in the range of five to ten years. Not shown in the table is that the average determinate sentence was 10.62 years across the entire population of sentenced offenders from 1987 to 2011. Despite the fact that many of the sentenced

Table 3.4. Sentence Lengths of
Sentenced Offenders, 1987–2011

Sentence Length	Frequency	Percent
Less than 5 years	718	21.23
5–10 years	1,652	48.85
11–20 years	670	19.81
21–30 years	221	6.53
31–40 years	121	3.58
Total	3,382	100

offenders committed acts that could potentially justify the forty-year maximum sentence, only 121 (3.58 percent) received a sentence between thirty-one and forty years (not shown is that 86 offenders received a maximum forty-year sentence).

Perhaps one of the most attractive aspects of determinate sentencing in Texas is that it affords latitude in sentencing for the judge or jury. Indeed, there are perhaps no two cases that are alike, despite what may appear on the surface to be equal offenses. Considering variations in the offenses and factoring in all of the circumstances surrounding a youth and his or her delinquent behavior, some youths will not receive the maximum allowable sentence, even when such a sentence could have been assessed. This reality seems to be reflected in table 3.4, where judges or juries in determinate sentencing cases have used their discretion to render sentences below the maximum. Indeed, roughly 70 percent of all sentences were for ten years or less, well below the maximum time range that could have been levied based on the whole range of commitment offenses. Further details regarding sentence length are provided in table 3.5. Again, despite the ability to sentence youthful offenders to longer maximum sentence lengths, judges and/or juries exercised discretion to provide a range of sentences.

BEFORE TYC: EXTREME LIVES

The previous discussion demonstrated that the cohort of sentenced offenders in this study constituted an extremely serious and violent group of state delinquents by the time they arrived at TYC as sentenced offenders. But what is missing, beyond their crimes and sentences, is information about them prior to their TYC commitment. In sum, what were their experiences and situations before they reached state juvenile incarceration as sentenced offenders?

At a basic level, those who hear accounts of juvenile killers, rapists, and muggers usually attribute such behavior to serious deficiencies across several life domains. For someone so young to be so violent and chaotic is viewed as an indication of a life chance ladder that has several broken or missing rungs—violence in the home, absent parenting, rampant substance abuse, criminally involved parents, gang membership, and a long history of involvement with the juvenile justice system, among other red flags.

Table 3.6 presents information on the life situations of the sentenced

Table 3.5. Average Sentence Length (Years) by Commitment Offense

	Frequency	Average Sentence Length	Standard Deviation	Minimum Sentence Length	Maximum Sentence Length
Aggravated Robbery	1,184	8.89	6.17	1	40
Aggravated Sexual Assault	698	9.80	7.74	1	40
Aggravated Assault	520	7.14	4.86	1	40
Murder	344	20.70	10.39	1	40
Capital Murder	195	21.99	11.80	1	40
Indecency with a Child	107	6.51	4.10	1	20
Aggravated Kidnapping	63	12.86	7.19	1	32
Deadly Conduct	57	5.04	2.79	1	10
Sexual Assault	55	6.55	3.37	1	20
Injury to Child or Elderly	47	7.90	6.92	0	40
Manufacture/Delivery Controlled Substance	40	6.33	3.89	1	20
Manslaughter	25	10.04	5.14	4	20
Unlawful Possession Controlled Substance	14	7.57	5.39	1	20
Arson	14	13.21	13.12	3	40
Burglary	6	5.67	2.94	2	10
Assault	3	3.67	0.58	3	4
Robbery	3	4.33	1.15	3	5
Intoxication Manslaughter	2	10.00	0.00	10	10

Note: total does not equal 3,382 because "other" offenders were removed from the table due to lack of any variation among the four separate offenses by the five commitments categorized as "other."

Table 3.6. Sentenced Offender Histories before TYC Commitment

Sentenced Offender Backgrounds	Mean/Percent
Delinquent and Juvenile System History	
Previous Referrals to Juvenile Authorities	4.39 / 99%
Previous Delinquent Adjudications	2.37 / 99%
Prior Out-of-Home Placements	3.69 / 69%
Juvenile Probation Failure	28%
Gang-Related	17
Ever Referred for Running Away	27
Educational History	
Special Educational Needs	26
Highest Grade Completed at Commitment	8[a]
Enrolled in School at Commitment	74
History of Truancy	71
Mentally Ill	14
Mentally Challenged	13
Familial History	
Family in Poverty	59
Chaotic Home Environment	71
Rigid Home Environment	32
Abuse History	
Believed or Confirmed Emotional Abuse	19
Believed or Confirmed Abandoned	12
Believed or Confirmed Medical Neglect	4
Believed or Confirmed Supervision Neglect	23
Believed or Confirmed Sexual Abuse	14
Believed or Confirmed Physical Neglect	9
Believed or Confirmed Physical Abuse	16
History of Substance Abuse	77
Violence History	
Youth Violent toward Family	25
Youth Suicidal Tendencies	11
Youth Danger to Self	18
Youth Danger to Others	70
Youth Sexually Deviant	18
History of Setting Fires	12

Note: percentages refer to those having engaged or experienced the behavior at least one time. Unless otherwise noted, all measures are those collected at the time of state juvenile commitment.

[a]Numeral indicates a grade, not a percentage.

offenders at the time of their commitment to TYC.[19] The table clearly indicates that many of the sentenced offenders were not strangers to the juvenile justice system at the time of their commitment. Indeed, sentenced offenders averaged more than four referrals to juvenile authorities prior to their determinate sentence (99 percent experienced at least one prior referral before being committed for a determinate sentence), and accrued more than two delinquent adjudications on average before their instant commitment offense (99 percent experienced at least one prior adjudication). Moreover, 69 percent of sentenced offenders had previously been placed outside of their home, and the cohort averaged just under four different out-of-home placements prior to their determinate sentence commitments. Twenty-eight percent were on probation at the time of their commitment, 17 percent were confirmed as gang related at their state commitment, and 27 percent had previously been referred to the system for running away.

On average the sentenced offenders had completed the eighth grade at the time of their state commitment (recall the average age at commitment was roughly sixteen years of age). Approximately 74 percent of the sentenced offenders were enrolled in school at the time of their commitment, although 26 percent evinced special educational needs, 71 percent were considered truants, 13 percent were considered mentally challenged, and 14 percent were deemed mentally ill at TYC orientation and assessment. The sentenced offenders often were not at the age-appropriate grade in school and appeared to face several additional educational challenges prior to their commitment.

Roughly 60 percent of the sentenced offenders lived in poverty prior to their state commitment and also faced what was considered by TYC as a chaotic (71 percent) and rigid (32 percent) home environment. Some of the sentenced offenders also faced various forms of abuse and neglect in the home. Indeed, between 4 and 23 percent of the sentenced offenders suffered various forms of believed or confirmed abuse ranging from medical and supervision neglect to sexual and emotional abuse. About 77 percent of all sentenced offenders had a history of substance abuse at the time of their commitment to TYC.

The last category in table 3.6 examines variables indicative of a history of violence and other problematic behaviors beyond those already noted. Not surprisingly, 70 percent of all the youthful offenders were considered dangers to others. Twenty-five percent had been violent toward their family prior to commitment, with under 20 percent con-

Table 3.7. Progression of Sentenced Offenders through TYC, 1987–2011

Status	Total	Percentage
Community Release	2,082	62
Continued Supervision	1,426	68
Served Full Sentence	556	27
Reached Age of Majority	57	3
Unknown Community Release	43	2
Texas Prison System Transfer	1,024	30
Died	4	1
Still in TYC	272	8
Total Cohort	3,382	100

sidered suicidal, sexually deviant, a danger to self, or having a history of setting fires.

Although numbers on a page can give some idea of the histories of the sentenced offenders, they do not provide justice to the extreme and dysfunctional histories of the youths under study. This history applies not only to the behavior of the offenders themselves but also to the conditions they faced in their family, home, and general social environments. There is no doubt that the sentenced offenders were involved in extreme delinquency that led to their state commitment. However, the data indicate that they also faced extreme lives prior to their incarceration in TYC across numerous life domains.

PROGRESSION THROUGH TYC

As noted at the outset of this chapter, the 3,382 sentenced offenders faced two basic options: release from TYC to a community context, or transfer to the Texas prison system for the adult portion of their determinate sentence. Table 3.7 details the outcomes for the cohort of sentenced offenders.

Of the 3,382 sentenced offenders, 272 or roughly 8 percent had still not faced a determination hearing regarding release to a community context or transfer to the Texas prison system at the time of this study.[20] These 272 are those who were more recently adjudicated and incarcerated in TYC as sentenced offenders, and who are just beginning to navigate the juvenile portion of their determinate sentences.

As shown in table 3.7, 2,082 or 62 percent of the cohort of sentenced offenders were released from TYC to a community context, or in other words were "released to the streets." Release from TYC to a community context does not necessarily mean the offender is released free and clear, avoiding the adult portion of the determinate sentence or any sanction at all. It often means instead that the adult portion of the determinate sentence will be served outside of a Texas prison.[21] For example, while some offenders are released directly from TYC for completing their sentence in full, or by reaching the maximum age of TYC supervision authority, others are released to the community on adult parole, adult probation, juvenile parole, or some other nonsecure program based in the community.[22] Approximately 68 percent of those released to a community context (1,426 of the 2,082 community releases) faced further portions of their determinate sentence in the community, with most of them being placed on adult parole under supervision of the Texas Department of Criminal Justice—Parole Division.

Among those released from TYC without further supervision were 556 sentenced offenders (27 percent of all community releases) who had served their full determinate sentence while in TYC, 57 (3 percent) who reached the age of majority while in TYC, and 43 (2 percent) who were released from TYC and did not appear to receive further sanction.[23]

Taking into account those released to the streets (2,082) and those

Main walkway at Hilltop between youth dorms and chow hall, Gatesville State School for Boys, ca. 1975. Courtesy of the Texas Department of Criminal Justice.

who were still in TYC (272) at the time of data retrieval, the remaining 1,028 offenders were either transferred to the Texas prison system to continue their determinate sentence behind bars (1,024), or they died (4).[24] Relative to the entire population of 3,382 sentenced offenders, then, roughly 30 percent of all sentenced offenders were transferred to the Texas prison system to serve the remainder of their determinate sentence. Although chapter 5 will detail the types of offenders who faced the two general outcomes of community release or Texas prison system placement as well as their similarities and differences and the factors related to those outcomes, table 3.7 illustrates the general progression of the sentenced offenders through TYC.

TIME AND ACTIVITIES IN TYC

Chapter 4 focuses on the institutional behavior of the 3,382 sentenced offenders during the time they were incarcerated in TYC institutions. Institutional behavior or misconduct is a main indicator of how sentenced offenders adapted and progressed through TYC, and to some degree of whether they took advantage of their last chance at redemption. However, institutional misconduct is not the only indicator. To provide a look into other aspects of the progression of sentenced offenders during their time in TYC, this section briefly examines factors such as time served and involvement in forms of treatment.

Table 3.8 provides a snapshot of how much time sentenced offenders served and what treatment activities they participated in as they progressed through TYC. Among the entire sample of 3,382 offenders, the average time spent in TYC was just over three years. The average for those who were released to a community context by TYC, transferred to the Texas prison system, or died was 3.17 years in TYC.[25] Of those who were still in TYC on December 31, 2011 (272), table 3.8 shows that they had served an average of 1.85 years of their sentence. Interestingly, although they served an average of only about three years in TYC, most offenders received sentences ranging from five to ten years. Considering the average offender arrived at TYC at almost sixteen years of age, the data suggest that most sentenced offenders were either released to a community context or transferred to the Texas prison system at roughly age nineteen.[26]

In addition to time served in TYC, table 3.8 provides further information relative to forms of generalized and specialized treatment received by the offenders while in TYC. TYC defines certain forms of sex offender,

Table 3.8. Time and Treatment in TYC

Sentenced Offender Backgrounds	Mean/Percent
Time Served in TYC	
Years Served in TYC (3,382)	3.06
Years Served in TYC (3,110)	3.17
Years served in TYC (272)	1.85
Age at TYC Release (3,110)	19.05
Specialized Treatment (3,382)	
Chemical Dependency Treatment	37.67
Sex Offender Treatment	20.67
Mental Health Treatment	16.68
Capital Offender Treatment (all types)	28.86
Residential Capital Offender Treatment	17.21
Received Multiple Forms of Treatment	27.00
Other Treatment Received (3,382)	
Non-Specialized Treatment Programming	94.32

Note: the number 3,110 is a combination of the 2,082 community releases, 1,024 Texas prison transfers, and the 4 sentenced offenders who died. It does not include the 272 sentenced offenders still in TYC.

chemical dependency, mental health, and capital offender programs as specialized treatment, as opposed to numerous forms of general or non-specialized treatment received while incarcerated.

As shown in table 3.8, roughly 38 percent of all sentenced offenders received specialized chemical dependency treatment while confined. This number is lower than the percentage of offenders who were deemed to have a history of substance abuse at intake to state commitment (77). Roughly 21 percent of sentenced offenders received specialized sex offender treatment during their TYC stay (21 percent were committed for aggravated sexual assault, and another 5 percent for sexual assault or indecency with a child). Moreover, approximately 17 percent received specialized mental health treatment (14 percent were deemed mentally ill at state commitment and 13 percent were deemed mentally challenged). In sum, participation in specialized treatment by the sentenced offenders appears to be roughly equivalent to the need for such treatment relative to offenders' specific offenses of commitment and deficiencies and needs identified at orientation and assessment.

Hackberry School entrance sign, Gatesville State School for Boys, ca. 1980. Hackberry was one of several schools at Gatesville dispersed across tracts of land surrounding the main complex (other schools included Hilltop, Live Oak, Riverside, Sycamore, Terrace, and Valley). Schools were fully or partially segregated by race. Courtesy of the Texas Department of Criminal Justice.

Sycamore School entrance sign, Gatesville State School for Boys, ca. 1980. Courtesy of the Texas Department of Criminal Justice.

Terrace School entrance sign, Gatesville State School for Boys, ca. 1980.
Courtesy of the Texas Department of Criminal Justice.

Live Oak School entrance sign, Gatesville State School for Boys, ca. 1975.
Courtesy of the Texas Department of Criminal Justice.

Beyond other forms of specialized treatment, roughly 29 percent of all sentenced offenders received a form of capital offender treatment while at TYC. This type of treatment includes but is not limited to short-term capital offender treatment, longer-term residential capital offender treatment, aftercare, orientation, and aggression replacement training, among other variations. The longer-term residential capital offender treatment, known as the Capital and Serious Violent Offender Treatment Program (CSVOTP) and operated at Giddings State School, was provided to 17.21 percent of sentenced offenders at some point during their time at TYC.[27] Moreover, table 3.8 indicates that 27 percent of all sentenced offenders received multiple types of specialized treatment at TYC.

In addition to treatment types deemed specialized by TYC, sentenced offenders also could have been assigned to more generalized treatment programming, including but not limited to job training (e.g., Project Rio), gang renunciation programs, vocational programs, or any number of other numerous generalized rehabilitative programs offered by TYC. Of the entire population of sentenced offenders, almost 95 percent participated in at least one generalized form of treatment programming provided by TYC.

Although not shown in the table, it should be noted that roughly 72 percent of all sentenced offenders received at least one form of specialized treatment while at TYC. This is in addition to the fact that almost 95 percent of all sentenced offenders also received more generalized treatment. Overall, then, most sentenced offenders received treatment, and nearly three-fourths also received some dose of specialized treatment during their stay at TYC.

CONCLUSION

Our examination thus far has shown that the sentenced offenders were extreme individuals across various life domains, despite their young age. Looking back at their life history, most were squarely situated on the lower rungs of the life chance ladder, with previous delinquent involvement, educational deficits, and problematic and disadvantaged home environments replete with abuse, violence, and general chaos. While this situation does not describe every youth who found his or her way to TYC as a sentenced offender, the overall picture is bleak.[28]

Upon their incarceration, the sentenced offenders were thrust on the path to redemption or continued failure. Texas gave them one last chance to turn away from the path of a wasted life characterized by crime, violence, failure, and adult prison time. After placement into state juvenile confinement, the majority of sentenced offenders received some form of specialized and/or generalized treatment to afford them the best chance for success in the event of community release. Some even received a highly intense form of treatment for violent offenders to improve their chance at redemption.

Following a relatively brief period of time in TYC, on average just three years, 62 percent of all 3,382 sentenced offenders received another second chance by being released from TYC to the community. Most of them faced further sanctioning on juvenile or adult parole, but some were released after serving their full sentences in TYC or for having reached the maximum age of TYC supervision jurisdiction. Regardless of the placement, these are the offenders who escaped (at least for the time being) the Texas prison system and showed enough progress to be considered safe to place back into society. The remaining 1,024 sentenced offenders were transferred to the Texas prison system to face the adult portion of their determinate sentences.

Chapter 5 examines in more detail the choice between community release or Texas prison system transfer. Before that examination, however, chapter 4 explores in more depth the institutional behavior and progress of the sentenced offenders during their time in TYC. An examination of their involvement in institutional misconduct provides more insight as to whether the sentenced offenders took initial advantage of their second chance. Chapter 4 therefore examines continuity or change in the conduct of the sentenced offenders during the time that they were incarcerated in TYC facilities.

CHAPTER 4

DOING TIME IN THE
TEXAS YOUTH COMMISSION

THE INSTITUTIONAL BLEND

GUIDED BY THE DOCTRINE OF *parens patriae*, the past two hundred years of juvenile justice have operated on the tacit assumption that delinquency in the community and, by extension, misconduct within detention and confinement settings was caused by some blend of individual and environmental factors. Delinquency with early life onset or for very serious offenses, for example, was commonly believed to be indicative of high antisocial tendencies. Yet the disproportionate prevalence of delinquency in neighborhoods characterized by poverty, deprivation, and disadvantage suggested that environmental factors "push" some youths into wayward behavior.

This line of thinking is demonstrated in the history of custodial juvenile settings. Historian Steven Schlossman has observed: "The founders of reform school assumed that their clientele would not be exclusively serious offenders but a motley group of lower-class children—some who had already been convicted of criminal acts, others whose incorrigible behavior predicted future confrontations with the law, and still others whose life chances were so circumscribed by poverty and bad example that it would be an act of charity (in the founders' view) to incarcerate them and prevent a lifetime of poverty and crime."[1] This "blend" of delinquents within juvenile justice settings—from houses of refuge, to houses of reformation, to reform schools, to training schools, to contemporary juvenile correctional facilities—and the diverse ways with which delinquents responded to the conditions of their confinement contributed to various problem behaviors within those facilities. Some youths were unfazed by the negative features of juvenile institutions. Others were driven to madness, suicide, and other forms of highly dys-

Youth "lockup" room, Mountain View State School for Boys, ca. 1975. Courtesy of the Texas Department of Criminal Justice.

functional behavior. Some complied dutifully to the guidelines of institutional life. Others were constantly disruptive. Some underwent a reformation and caused no additional problems for staff. Others were predatorily violent.

Against this backdrop, a paradox of sorts characterizes the institutional behavior of the confined. On the one hand, there is reason to expect the "kept" to behave in violent, disorderly, and maladaptive ways given the negative environment in which they live, and, perhaps more importantly, given the many risk factors that institutional wards display. From this perspective, juvenile delinquents on the extreme end of offending should be predicted to behave poorly during confinement precisely because they are extreme delinquents.

Indeed, it is difficult to overstate the severity of the backgrounds of the 3,382 sentenced offenders examined in chapter 3. The average sentenced offender arrived at the Texas Youth Commission (TYC) with an extensive history of delinquency and juvenile justice system involvement, and about 80 percent came with substance abuse problems. Virtually the entire sample was reared in chaotic homes, just the opposite of the supportive, warm, secure, safe, and highly monitored environments that are conducive to healthy, prosocial development. Perhaps because of this, 25 percent of these youths had been physically violent toward members of their family by the time they were committed to TYC.

Approximately two-thirds of the sentenced offenders were raised in moderate to severe poverty, and the prevalence of physical, emotional, and sexual abuse among them was much higher than in the general population. More than 70 percent were deemed at TYC intake to be dangerous to others. Against this backdrop, it is not surprising that this cohort engaged in more than 63,750 incidents of misconduct that encompassed 129,666 violations of facility rules and regulations.[2]

On the other hand, the preponderance of institutional violations committed by this cohort of sentenced offenders involved breaking basic rules of the facility rather than overt criminal acts. More than 55,000 violations pertained to two forms of misconduct: disruption of program, and refusing to follow staff instructions. The most grievous forms of misconduct, homicide and suicide, did not occur in this sample. Other sensationalistic forms of institutional misconduct, such as hostage taking, occurred just once.

A similar type of variation is seen among the delinquent careers of sentenced offenders. Nearly 10 percent of the wards never participated in a single incident of misconduct or accumulated a single citation for violating institution rules. In contrast, one ward was involved in an astounding 483 incidents of misconduct and accumulated 1,254 violations, including several dozen assaults against staff and other wards and 351 counts of disruption of program—a level of misconduct nineteen standard deviation units above the mean! In short, even among extreme delinquents, this youth was an outlier in terms of misconduct.

This chapter explores the delinquent careers of sentenced offenders within TYC by examining the incidence and prevalence of misconduct, the individual-level variation in it, associations between commitment offense and misconduct, and correlates of institutional offending. Although there are a host of risk factors among these wards, a handful were consistently associated with various forms of rule violations and even violent delinquency occurring within TYC facilities. Before delving into the delinquent careers of the 3,382 sentenced offenders, this chapter first places their behavior in context by examining what we know about institutional misconduct among serious delinquents.

INSTITUTIONAL MISCONDUCT AMONG INSTITUTIONALIZED DELINQUENTS

Consistent with the person-environmental understanding of juvenile delinquency across the past two centuries, theoretical models of institutional misconduct pointed first to prison environments as their assorted deprivations (e.g., crowding, squalor, administrative incompetence, staff brutality, lack of treatment options, lack of educational and work training) were thought to "produce" prisoner misconduct and violence. After a few decades of study, a new model of inmate behavior was advanced that pointed to individual-level factors (e.g., criminal history, criminal justice system status, history of violence, gang history, drug history, young age, male gender, minority status) or risk factors that were "imported" into the facility. These risk factors in turn were theorized to manifest in misconduct.[3]

More recently, a compromise of sorts has been reached in the research community whereby elements of importation and deprivation are both seen as important variables in the institutional behavior of confined individuals. On balance, prior investigations of institutional misconduct and violence among youths in juvenile correctional facilities and detention centers reveal how pre-confinement risk factors generally increase the likelihood of emotional and adjustment problems, psychiatric disturbance, noncompliance, misconduct, and victimization within custodial settings. Overall, these works reflect a combination of youth-specific or importation factors, facility-specific or deprivation factors, and interaction between these factors as explanations for misconduct during confinement.

Among these findings, behavioral evidence of violence and recurrent antisocial behavior is of primary importance to understanding continued noncompliance and delinquency behind bars. An early study of misconduct in four juvenile correctional settings spanning four states found that a youth's history of violent delinquency was the strongest predictor of misconduct, and its effects withstood the potentially confounding effects of many other risk factors.[4] In a large-scale study of nearly five thousand youths confined in a southern US correctional system, wards with multiple indicators of serious, violent, and chronic delinquency—including early onset of antisocial behavior, adjudication history, police contacts, and gang involvement—were more likely than other delinquents to commit serious forms of misconduct such as assault against other wards, assault against staff, gang activity, possession of dangerous weapons, and others.[5]

Based on data from more than eight hundred serious delinquents committed to the California Youth Authority (CYA), investigators have found that childhood trauma is an important predictor of subsequent institutional misconduct. Compared to youths who experienced low levels of traumatic experiences, high-trauma youths accumulate more total incidents of misconduct that are reviewed by the parole/aftercare board; display more suicidal activity such as self-injurious behaviors, suicidal ideation, and suicide attempts; engage in more sexual misconduct; and commit more drug violations while in custody.

High-trauma youths also experience dramatically worse mental health during their confinement. They display higher levels of anger and irritability, more anxiety, more depressive symptoms, more somatic complaints, and more severe and frequent thought disturbances. In addition to trauma experiences, a variety of other factors have been found to predict institutional misconduct, including young age, prior incorrigibility, prior violent delinquency, and prior drug problems.[6]

Others have used the CYA data to explore institutional misconduct using different measures and research foci. In a study of violent misconduct among CYA wards, the strongest predictors of institutional misconduct were police contacts, prior history of violence, and prior history of gang involvement. Interestingly, none of these factors were associated with drug use during confinement.[7]

A particularly serious risk factor for misconduct is juvenile sexual offending. Various forms of sexual aggression during adolescence have been shown to predict sexual misconduct in confinement facilities. However, its effects are not limited to sexual misconduct. Juvenile sexual offending has also been linked to diverse forms of misconduct at multiple points in the correctional experience (e.g., the prior twelve months and the previous twenty-four months). Once again, other indicators of criminality were also found to be associated with sexual, other, and/or total misconduct, including prior police contacts and self-reported delinquency.[8]

There is mixed evidence that predictors of misconduct work similarly for male and female delinquents. A recent study of diverse forms of misconduct using CYA data, for example, found that propensity constructs such as low self-control were consistently related to misconduct for boys, but not associated with misconduct and institutional violence among girls. Instead, female misconduct was more strongly associated with psychiatric diagnoses, externalizing or acting-out symptoms, and prior delinquent offenses and adjudications. Other factors such as age and race were similarly associated with misconduct for boys and girls.[9]

Institutionalized delinquents thus carry a staggering array of risk factors that highlight their highly traumatic upbringing, their often woeful socioeconomic circumstances, and, most importantly, their acute and versatile antisocial behavioral history. These risk factors unfold into institutional misconduct in interesting and sometimes surprising ways.

MISCONDUCT CAREERS OF THE SENTENCED OFFENDERS IN TYC

Table 4.1 displays basic descriptive information about the incidence and prevalence of misconduct among the 3,382 wards during their stay in TYC facilities. Incidence is the total number of misconduct events that occurred irrespective of who committed them, and can be understood as the raw number of "incidents" that were perpetrated by all wards combined. Prevalence is the proportion of the sample that committed various acts of misconduct, and is understood as the percentage of sentenced offenders that engaged in a specific misconduct behavior. The

Table 4.1. Incidence and Prevalence of Institutional Misconduct

Form of Misconduct	Incidence	Prevalence (%)
Disruption of Program	40,386	83.83
Refusing to Follow Staff Instructions	14,796	40.45
Danger to Others	6,651	41.28
In Undesignated Area	4,829	28.06
Assault Students	4,538	36.49
Refuse Written Reasonable Request	3,379	19.40
Assault Student with Bodily Injury	2,223	24.04
Assault Student Offender Contact	1,993	21.79
Assault by Threat of Imminent Bodily Injury	1,910	17.56
Injury to Self	1,685	21.61
Violation of Security	935	9.40
Possession of Contraband	865	14.78
Fleeing Apprehension	805	12.42
Dress Code Violation	790	11.56
Assault Staff Offender Contact	745	10.91
Threatening to Harm Self	739	8.60
Gang Activity	728	12.18
Assault Staff	649	10.35
Possession of Unauthorized Substance	566	13.01
Arrest for Misconduct Violation	503	10.50
Destruction of Property	479	9.79
Attempting, Aiding, Abetting Category I Rule Violation	412	9.17
Assault Staff with Bodily Injury	459	7.87
Stealing Under $50	393	7.75
Fight with No Injury	390	5.71
Lying	339	7.13

following example will clarify the differences between incidence and prevalence. Imagine a sample of one hundred offenders where ninety-nine of them never committed murder, but one offender perpetrated ten murders. In this example, the incidence of murder is 10 because it reflects the total amount of a specific form of crime. The prevalence of murder is 1/100 or .01 (1 percent), because just 1 percent of offenders committed the offense. The types of institutional misconduct in table 4.1 are shown in declining order of incidence.

Most forms of institutional misconduct among sentenced offenders pertained to basic violations of the rules and regulations of the facility.

Table 4.1. Continued

Form of Misconduct	Incidence	Prevalence (%)
Attempting, Aiding, Abetting Category II Rule Violation	332	7.69
Vandalism	298	6.42
Participation in a Riot	278	6.21
Fight with Bodily Injury	241	4.35
Tattooing or Body Piercing	228	4.85
Attempted Escape	218	5.00
Possession of a Weapon	203	5.06
Indecent Exposure	191	3.70
Tampering with Security of Technical Equipment	171	3.78
Absconding	143	3.49
Lending	115	2.93
Fail to Do Proper Housekeeping	96	2.42
Improper Use of Phone	92	2.10
Inappropriate Sexual Contact	82	1.71
Violate Any Law	79	2.13
Escape	78	1.92
Misuse of Medication	49	1.09
Extortion	39	1.09
Chunking Bodily Fluids	33	0.77
Stealing Over $50	29	0.80
Gambling	24	0.68
Refusing a Drug Screen	22	0.65
Breach Group Confidentiality	8	0.24
Missed Scheduled Activity	1	0.03
Hostage Taking	1	0.03
Attempted Suicide	0	0

In this way, noncompliance was exceedingly common among the sentenced offender cohort. The most common offense in terms of incidence and prevalence was disruption of program, with more than forty thousand events and nearly 84 percent of the sample involved in at least one disruption of the program. The second most frequent offense was refusing to follow staff instructions, with nearly fifteen thousand events and more than 40 percent of youths involved in this offense. Other offenses, such as being in an undesignated area and refusing a written reasonable request, were also found among the ten most common offenses.

Gatesville State School for Boys, ca. 1980. Courtesy of the Texas Department of Criminal Justice.

Although these forms of misconduct might not appear serious, and may even look petty to some observers, they should not be ignored. The nondelinquent forms of misconduct reveal a pervasive problem in terms of following basic rules and regulations of society. Just as many delinquent youths jeopardize their school careers by refusing to comply with teacher requests and school guidelines, so too the sentenced offenders were generally unable to get along with the most basic behavioral requirements of institutional life. The frequent displays of misconduct also provide context to the severe risk profiles described earlier in this chapter and in chapter 3. The overlapping problems and various negative experiences that these youths have experienced lend themselves to a behavioral style characterized by flaunting the rules of authority and a general unwillingness to adapt to society. Indeed, for the entire sample, each individual accumulated slightly more than three violations for every one hundred days in confinement.

Although noncompliance has the highest incidence and prevalence, it is important to note that four of the ten most common forms of misconduct are assault-related. A fifth offense—danger to others—has an incidence of 6,651 and a prevalence of more than 41 percent. These data indicate that TYC facilities are places where assaults against wards and staff are not uncommon, and to some degree are routine. There were 459 assaults against staff members that resulted in bodily injury, and nearly 8 percent of wards perpetrated an injury-producing assault against staff. Overwhelmingly, the use of violence in TYC pertained to assault, not to more sensationalistic forms of institutional violence such as murder and rape.

Not all violence in TYC facilities was interpersonal; some related to self-harming. The tenth most common form of misconduct was injury to self with an incidence of 1,685 and prevalence of nearly 22 percent. Fortunately, the self-harming did not escalate; there were no reported attempted suicides in the entire cohort.

Other serious forms of misconduct had considerable variation in incidence and prevalence. Nearly 15 percent of youths were cited for possession of contraband (incidence = 865) and more than 12 percent (incidence = 728) were cited for gang activity. This is lower but comparable to the prevalence of gang affiliation at intake, where more than 17 percent of the total sample was gang-involved. Additional forms of serious misconduct were also relatively infrequent, including participation in a riot (incidence = 278, prevalence = 6.2 percent), attempted escape (incidence = 218, prevalence = 5 percent), possession of a weapon (incidence = 203, prevalence = 5.06 percent), inappropriate sexual contact (incidence = 82, prevalence = 1.71 percent), escape (incidence = 78, prevalence = 1.92 percent), chunking bodily fluids (incidence = 33, prevalence = 0.77 percent), and hostage taking (incidence = 1, prevalence = 0.03 percent). Although some of these offenses are portrayed in popular culture as endemic to juvenile confinement facilities, such as in the films *Bad Boys* and *Sleepers* and various *Scared Straight* documentaries, they are actually quite rare.

Just as there is wide variation in individual forms of misconduct (some forms never occurred, whereas others were perpetrated by more than 80 percent of youths), there is also wide variation in misconduct by individual offenders. On average, wards committed more than thirty-eight acts of misconduct during their time in TYC settings. But 260 youths had no misconduct record during their confinement, evidenced by the absence of citations for prison violations. As shown in table 4.2, other wards were significantly more disruptive. Wards in the 75th percentile had at least 46 citations for misconduct and those at the 90th percentile had at least 100 citations. Those at the 95th percentile accumulated between 150 and 314 citations and those at the 99th percentile totaled between 315 and 1,254 citations. These percentiles in-

Table 4.2. Distribution and Percentiles
for Institutional Misconduct

Percentile	Minimum	Maximum
1st	0	0
5th	0	0
10th	0	1
25th	0	5
50th	16	45
75th	46	99
90th	100	149
95th	150	314
99th	315	1,254

Note: for example, a youth who accumulates 100–149 violations would be in the 90th percentile of the distribution of institutional misconduct, meaning that this youth would account for more misconduct than 90 percent of all sentenced offenders. Youths with at least 150 counts of misconduct were in the 95th percentile, and those with at least 315 counts were in the 99th percentile. This table shows the tremendous variation in institutional misconduct among the sentenced offenders in the sample.

dicate where an individual is on the distribution curve. Thus, a youth with at least 315 violations has more misconduct than 99 percent of his or her peers, while a youth with at least 46 citations committed more misconduct than 75 percent of all sentenced offender peers.

Although importation-based explanations of institutional misconduct (e.g., delinquent history) have enjoyed more support in terms of explaining involvement in misconduct, not all indicators of risk are associated with misconduct in equal proportions. This relationship is particularly true when examining the average misconduct by commitment offense as shown in table 4.3. There is not a clear trend whereby greater offense seriousness is associated with more institutional misconduct. Youths who are adjudicated for the two most serious offenses, capital murder and murder, have among the lowest average levels of misconduct (approximately seventeen to twenty incidents). In contrast, youths committed for assault averaged nearly 416 counts of institutional misconduct.

It is important to acknowledge that mean levels of misconduct by commitment offense are significantly affected by low counts of youths in the category and outliers whose extreme misconduct skews the average by category (this explains the exceptionally high average for wards with assault as their commitment offense). Such counts are also affected by institutional-level variables. For example, misconduct counts could be affected by staff differences at different TYC institutions. Moreover, youth levels of misconduct can be dampened by placement in more secure settings within the institution, generally labeled solitary confinement or administrative segregation in adult prisons— placement that can hinder a youth's ability to engage in misconduct for periods of time. With that point noted, the next section examines

Table 4.3. Institutional Misconduct by Commitment Offense

Offense type	Mean	SD
Aggravated Robbery	39.89	55.16
Aggravated Sexual Assault	46.15	77.48
Aggravated Assault	44.66	78.69
Murder	20.98	33.24
Capital Murder	16.92	24.60
Indecency with a Child	46.04	63.41
Aggravated Kidnapping	27.35	49.53
Deadly Conduct	24.89	34.39
Sexual Assault	27.56	35.10
Injury to Child or Elderly	29.79	43.03
Manufacture/Delivery Controlled Substance	28.45	37.72
Manslaughter	33.76	31.78
Unlawful Possession Controlled Substance	20.71	32.61
Arson	67.21	84.25
Burglary	48.17	33.47
Assault	415.67	206.98
Robbery	12.33	15.37
Intoxication Manslaughter	3.50	3.53

factors associated with misconduct participation among the sentenced offenders.

PREDICTORS OF SENTENCED OFFENDER MISCONDUCT

Thus far, the analyses demonstrate that institutional misconduct is not as straightforward as conventional wisdom might suggest. Given the severe social disadvantages, risk factors, and delinquent histories of the sentenced offenders, it is easy to forecast very high levels of misconduct. Fortunately, the majority of this misconduct relates to violations of rules and regulations rather than delinquent acts per se. In addition, there are high levels of interpersonal violence evidenced by a moderate incidence and prevalence of various forms of assaults against wards and staff members. More extreme forms of violence such as murder, rape, and suicide were not found. There is also tremendous individual-level variation in institutional misconduct. Some youths were extremely compliant and served time without incident. Others were recalcitrantly antisocial even in the most restrictive correctional settings. Most were between these two poles.

The factors that would help explain or predict misconduct participation were examined using two statistical techniques. One approach examines twenty-six predictors of the frequency by which sentenced offenders engage in misconduct. In essence, this model (called a negative binomial model) attempts to explain or predict the actual frequency of misconduct, based on knowledge of twenty-six pieces of information about youthful offenders and their commitment crimes. This approach allows readers to understand the effect of a predictor on the full range of misconduct.[10] The second approach examines the twenty-six predictors of misconduct when misconduct is measured as a binary outcome where sentenced offenders either engaged in misconduct or did not (this statistical model is called logistic regression).[11] An overall picture of how demographics, delinquent history, juvenile justice history, and behavioral risk factors are associated with total misconduct and any misconduct is shown in table 4.4.

In the frequency of misconduct model, fourteen significant predictors were found. Compared to African Americans, who were the reference group, Hispanics, whites, and youths from other racial and ethnic backgrounds were all significantly less likely to accumulate infractions. There was also a strong effect—indeed it was the strongest effect in the model—for age. The younger the ward was upon admission to

Table 4.4. Predictors of Institutional Misconduct

Predictor	Total Misconduct	Any Misconduct (yes/no)
Demographics		
Other Race	–	–
Hispanic	–	–
White	–	–
Sex (Male)	ns	+
Age at TYC Commitment	–	–
Delinquent History, Juvenile Justice, and Behavioral Risk Factors		
Previous Adjudications	ns	ns
Previous Court Referrals	–	ns
Prior Out-of-Home Placements	+	+
Deemed a Substance Abuser	ns	+
Previous Violence toward Family	ns	ns
History of Sexual Deviance	+	ns
Youth Danger to Self	+	ns
Youth Danger to Others	ns	ns
History of Fire Setting	ns	ns
Youth Gang–Related	–	ns
History of Suicidal Behavior	ns	ns
Highest Grade Completed	–	–
Enrolled in School at Commitment	ns	ns
History of Truancy	ns	+
Youth Mentally Challenged	ns	ns
Youth Mentally Ill	+	ns
Youth Raised in Poverty	ns	ns
Youth Raised in Chaotic Home	+	ns
Youth Raised in Rigid Home	ns	ns
Sentence Length	–	–
Time in TYC (Exposure)	+	+

Note: under demographics, African American race was the reference category.

"+" indicates a significant positive relationship at p < .05 or less, "–" indicates a significant negative relationship at p < .05 or less, and "ns" indicates a nonsignificant relationship.

TYC facilities, the greater the misconduct. Youths who received shorter commitment terms engaged in more misconduct than youths who received lengthier sentences. The amount of time in TYC settings, or general exposure, was also positively associated with misconduct.

In terms of delinquent history, juvenile justice involvement, and behavioral risk factors, there was mixed evidence that greater risk translated into more institutional misconduct. For instance, having a greater number of court referrals prior to commitment was negatively associated with misconduct, but having a greater number of prior out-of-home placements was positively associated with misconduct. The effect of prior placements was very large—more than nine standard deviation units above the mean. This suggests that youths who are recurrently removed from the home and placed in detention, treatment, foster, and other correctional settings engage in more deviance during confinement. A strong negative relationship was found for grade completed. Youths who completed more years of education were involved in less misconduct. This supports the notion that education is a protective factor that buffers against antisocial conduct.

A variety of person-centered risk factors were associated with greater institutional misconduct. Youths who were mentally ill, sexually deviant, or a danger to themselves totaled significantly more misconduct than wards without these statuses. Youths who were raised in chaotic homes totaled significantly more violations. Curiously, gang-related inmates had significantly fewer violations than their non-gang peers.

The logistic regression model examined the same predictors, but in this model the dependent variable is whether any misconduct occurred. An added advantage of this approach is that logistic regression coefficients can be readily converted to percentages to indicate the likelihood that a predictor was associated with ever committing misconduct.

Using multiple analytical strategies provides a more robust way to examine predictors of institutional misconduct among TYC sentenced offenders. In the any misconduct model, there were eleven significant effects (compared to fourteen significant findings in the prior model). In addition, there were eight predictors that were differentially predictive of misconduct, depending on how it was measured.

All of the demographic predictors were significantly associated with ever having engaged in misconduct. Large effects were seen for all racial and ethnic groups. African American youths were significantly more likely than Hispanics, whites, and youths from other racial and ethnic backgrounds to engage in any misconduct. Hispanics and whites were about 45–50 percent less likely than African Americans, and youths from other racial backgrounds were 84 percent less likely to commit misconduct. Males were 115 percent more likely to ever be cited, and each year of age was associated with a 32 percent reduced likelihood of misconduct.

Prior placements were associated with about a 14 percent increased likelihood of misconduct, and substance abuse problems increased it by 37 percent. As previously stated, completed years of schooling was associated with less misconduct. Each grade of school reduced the likelihood of misconduct by about 20 percent. Conversely, a history of truancy raised the likelihood of misconduct by 45 percent. Like in the prior model, sentence length was negatively associated with misconduct, whereas total time in TYC was positively associated with engaging in any violations.

CONCLUSION

For serious juvenile offenders, deep-end placements such as juvenile correctional facilities represent the most appropriate sanction, one that commensurately matches their risk profile. As Edward P. Mulvey and Carol A. Schubert have acknowledged, "Some juvenile offenders hurt people severely or threaten community safety substantially, and treating them separately and less harshly offends the sensibilities of many community members about the need for just retribution."[12] The 3,382 sentenced offenders in the current sample certainly match this description.

Despite their shared risk factors and delinquent history, sentenced youths nevertheless select different ways to respond to their institutional confinement situation. A small cadre of sentenced offenders was totally compliant and received no citations for violating facility rules and regulations. Others engaged in a smattering of acts of noncompliance—acts where it is important to acknowledge there is wide room for officer discretion—but otherwise remained free of misconduct during their confinement. Still others engaged in a wide variety of institutional misconduct that spanned diverse forms of delinquency, violence toward self and others, and basic refusals to comply with staff. And those in the 99th percentile of misconduct committed hundreds or, in some cases, more than one thousand acts of misconduct.

Highly noncompliant and violent youths demonstrated without question that they have little interest in modifying their behavior to conform to the rules of institutional life, let alone the rules of society. These are youths who prey on younger and smaller delinquents, and assault them without provocation. They attack correctional officers and other staff members, throw their urine and feces at staff members who walk by their cell, and generally behave like lost causes.

Institutional behavior is effectively a signal of whether the youth is leaning toward desisting from a life of antisocial behavior and attempting to rejoin conventional society, or leaning toward persisting in crime. This signal is an important determinant of the decision to release the youth to society, or to transfer him or her to adult correctional facilities of the Texas prison system. That release decision is examined next in chapter 5.

CHAPTER 5

ANOTHER SECOND CHANCE

THE ROAD TO REDEMPTION

FOLLOWING ADJUDICATION AND DISPOSITION, the road to redemption for sentenced offenders begins in earnest with placement in a secure TYC facility. While the sentenced offenders have been given a second chance to prove that they are not lost causes, the road to redemption is not smooth and obstacle free. Notwithstanding their problematic social, educational, familial, and delinquent life histories or their current status as serious and violent state delinquents, the sentenced offenders must also navigate state juvenile incarceration as they attempt to capitalize on what may be their last chance before facing the full effects of the adult justice system in Texas.

As the sentenced offenders settled in on their second chance, the TYC institutional experience for some was not strong enough to break the ties that bound them to a delinquent and problematic lifestyle. As detailed in chapter 4, the institutional experience for many of the sentenced offenders was characterized by continued involvement in behavior such as staff and ward assaults, dangerous conduct, rioting, and possession of contraband. While not all sentenced offenders engaged in these behaviors during their confinement, the fact remains that many sentenced offenders shunned change and engaged in continued delinquent involvement behind bars. Sentenced offenders accumulated nearly 130,000 institutional violations across nearly 64,000 separate incidents. On average, the cohort of sentenced offenders committed roughly 38 acts of misconduct each during their time in TYC. Sixty-four percent of them assaulted other wards on at least one occasion, and 32 percent assaulted staff on at least one occasion.

In the context of second chances and, for many sentenced offenders,

Youth "lockup" wing, Mountain View State School for Boys, ca. 1975. Courtesy of the Texas Department of Criminal Justice.

the potential for adult prison time, the volume and quality of misconduct detailed in chapter 4 is in some ways surprising. Institutional misconduct is regarded as an important barometer of change or continuity in behavior by TYC administrators, TYC staff, psychologists, counselors, prosecutors, and judges. Indeed, these decision makers rely heavily on indicators of behavior change and progress in determining what exactly to do with sentenced offenders as they approach the decision point for the adult or second portion of their determinate sentence.[1]

It is within this context of change and decision making that this chapter examines what happened to the sentenced offenders as they faced a determination on their future. As detailed in chapter 2, most offenders prosecuted and adjudicated under the Determinate Sentencing Act will face a determination hearing after a period of institutionalization in TYC.[2] This hearing functions as a fail-safe stage where decisions are made to suspend or invoke the adult or second portion of the blended determinate sentence—a decision highly dependent upon youth progress in TYC.[3]

While chapter 2 examined the potential outcomes of this determination hearing as set out by Texas law, the bottom line is that sentenced offenders face one of three options: release from TYC without supervision requirements,[4] release from TYC with supervision requirements, or transfer to the Texas prison system to face the remainder of the original determinate sentence in an adult prison facility.[5] This chapter focuses on the outcomes of sentenced offenders relative to these three options. Before delving into the specific outcomes, however, we will review what is known about the factors relevant to processing and sanctioning juveniles as adults to help inform and guide expectations regarding sentenced offender decision making.

DECISIONS TO PROCESS AND SANCTION JUVENILES AS ADULTS

Options have always existed to deal with youthful offenders in ways traditionally reserved for adult criminals. Prior to the discovery of "delinquency" and the application of this term to young criminals in the late 1800s, young and exceptional offenders could easily find themselves in the back of a transport wagon en route to adult prisons. Young offenders south of the Mason-Dixon line could also be found in nineteenth-century field and work camps, where they toiled alongside adult prisoners on the convict lease. At the turn of the twentieth century, they could also be found on prison farms. In fact, if a young offender's crime was serious enough, adult punishment, including the death penalty, was really the only option prior to a fully realized juvenile justice system of processing and sanctioning.

As the formal juvenile justice system began to take shape following the introduction of child-specific institutions such as houses of refuge and then started in earnest with Chicago's development of the first juvenile court in 1899, the practice of sentencing and punishing juveniles like adults remained a relatively rare event. As these child-centered developments took firmer root in American society, adult-type options to handle the most difficult juveniles did not disappear. Yet the options for dealing with juveniles like adult offenders evolved over time. For example, treating juveniles like adults became much more procedural and subject to more legal scrutiny beginning in the late 1960s. Despite these changes, adult options for juveniles still persisted. Indeed, adult justice was exacted on exceptional juveniles at this time through state provisions that allowed extreme delinquents to be waived or transferred or certified to the adult justice system with the usual list of punishments available, including imprisonment in adult facilities and the death penalty.[6] The long-standing availability of adult justice options for juvenile offenders was acknowledgment that some juvenile offenders were too violent and problematic to fit in the juvenile justice system. These options still persist today.

Despite the survival of mechanisms allowing certain juveniles to be sentenced and punished like adult criminals, such schemes did not escape criticism. A more omnibus criticism of adult court transfer/waiver/certification schemes was that such laws threw out the baby with the bathwater—effectively removing all potential for redemption of the young offenders. Perhaps more than any other criticism, this all-or-nothing characteristic of modern adult court transfer schemes was a significant factor that led to the development of blended sentencing statutes, like determinate sentencing in Texas, beginning in the late 1980s.[7] Although variations abound across the United States, all blended sentencing schemes were meant to provide an in-between sanctioning vehicle for juveniles who were a poor fit for the regular juvenile court and its sentencing limits yet were inappropriate, impractical, or undesirable subjects for adult court waiver and associated adult punishments.[8]

THE BASIS FOR BLENDED SENTENCING

The perspectives in favor of blended sentencing schemes were in many ways arguments against forms of adult court waiver. Proponents of this "third prong" of juvenile justice—a middle ground between regular juvenile court processing and adult court waiver—argued in the first instance that adult court waiver mechanisms abandoned juveniles by labeling them as lost causes, all but sealing their fate as lifetime outcasts from mainstream society.[9] Supporters of blended sentencing also argued that the adult system, particularly adult prisons, was woefully inadequate to deal with the special issues presented by such young offenders. Adult prison placement for juveniles increased their likelihood to be victimized. Adult facilities also lacked the special rehabilitative focus of the juvenile justice system, while adult sentencing and punishment was overly stigmatizing compared to juvenile system intervention.[10] Still other arguments centered on the notion that it was somehow unfair to punish children like adults, especially very young juveniles, since they lacked the maturity to fully appreciate their actions.[11] These are just a sampling of the criticisms.[12]

Beyond these generalized criticisms, perhaps the most influential body of research on the deleterious effects of adult court waiver emerged in the late 1980s and proclaimed in broad fashion that juveniles waived to adult court tended to reoffend quicker, at a higher rate, and more seriously than similarly situated juveniles who were not waived to adult court.[13] In short, this research acknowledged the collateral consequences of adult court waiver noted previously—that it was stigmatizing and nonredemptive, and that adult processes and punishments were a poor fit for such young offenders.

Despite this generally accepted consensus, recent research has revealed the waiver-recidivism relationship may not be so clear cut and that the effects of juvenile waiver on recidivism vary significantly based on the specific and individual characteristics and circumstances of offenders.[14] In short, this new round of research does not broadly proclaim that waiver, in and of itself, automatically translates into higher rates of recidivism for all juvenile transfers. Yet even with this new evidence, little research exists suggesting that waiver has a positive impact—especially for the youthful offender subject to waiver.

PROCESSING AND SANCTIONING
JUVENILES IN THE ADULT SYSTEM

Research in the last several years has also focused on the factors that are influential in determining whether a youthful offender will receive adult punishment for acts committed as a juvenile. While most of this research has focused on the determinants of adult court waiver and associated adult punishment, a smaller body of research has focused on the factors related to invoking the adult portion of a blended sentence. Still another emerging line of research has focused on the determinants of whether a juvenile will receive a blended sentence, regular juvenile court processing, or adult court waiver in the first place.

On the one hand, adult court waiver and blended sentencing schemes are different on a number of levels, perhaps most obviously in that adult court waiver is centered in the adult justice system, whereas blended sentencing is often, but not always, centered in the juvenile justice system.[15] Another main difference is that blended sentencing schemes allow for juvenile system–based sentences, unlike adult court waiver.[16] These and other differences aside, it is appropriate to consult the more developed literature on the determinants of adult court waiver to inform and guide expectations regarding blended sentencing decision making in this chapter. This is because both blended sentencing and waiver processes typically involve highly discretionary decisions (especially concerning judicial discretionary waivers, one of the most frequent types of juvenile waivers). Related to this point is that the blended sentencing decision-making process tends to rely on factors similar to those in adult court waiver determinations in both the initial decision to use blended sentencing and the subsequent decision to invoke or suspend the adult portion of a blended sentence.[17]

Specific to the waiver–blended sentencing comparison, judges in discretionary judicial waiver proceedings focus on such factors as the nature and seriousness of the offense, the presence of aggravating circumstances (e.g., use of a weapon, gang-related crime), protection of society, the sophistication and maturity of the juvenile, prior involvement of the juvenile in the justice system, and a determination of whether the offender is amenable to treatment.[18] Similarly, in Texas's determinate sentencing scheme, the decision to invoke or not to invoke the adult portion of a determinate sentence (and thus the potential transfer of a juvenile to the Texas prison system) focuses on factors such as the experiences and character of the juvenile both before and after TYC commitment, the nature and quality of the offense, and the protection of the victim and victim's family.[19] Thus, while waiver and blended sentencing schemes differ in important ways, the factors driving these decisions are strikingly similar.

Specific to the determinants of adult court waiver, the research evidence generally indicates that offense and previous juvenile justice system involvement carry significant weight in this decision.[20] For example, a number of studies examining the determinants of adult court waiver have revealed that legal factors such as the seriousness of the offense, the nature of the offense incident (e.g., use of a weapon), prior involvement in the system, and other legally based measures are the most influential in waiver decisions.[21] Beyond legal factors, research has also revealed that extralegal factors may also hold some sway in discretionary waiver proceedings. Age, for example, has been consistently related to waiver decisions in that older juveniles are more likely to be waived than younger juveniles, all else being equal.[22] The bottom line is that legal measures tend to be the most influential factors in determining whether a youth is waived to adult court or retained in the juvenile justice system.[23]

If adult court waiver research is instructive to blended sentencing decisions, this literature base suggests that legally based indicators should hold the most sway in decisions to invoke the adult portion of a determinate sentence. These factors should also hold relevance in the initial decision to prosecute a youth under blended sentencing. Unfortunately, only one study has specifically examined the factors related to invoking the adult portion of a blended sentence. In that study, Trulson and colleagues examined blended sentencing outcomes of 1,504 serious and violent male delinquents. Of the 1,504 offenders, roughly 40 percent (608) received a determination requiring them to serve the adult portion of their blended sentence.

Utilizing a rich data source, Trulson and colleagues revealed that commitment offense type, age at commitment, and the frequency of institutional misconduct incidents while confined were significant predictors of facing the adult portion of a blended sentence, even after accounting for relevant measures such as previous adjudications, previous out-of-home placements, and gang affiliation. In short, older juveniles who were committed for the most serious offenses and those who engaged in high rates of institutional misconduct while confined were most likely to face the adult portion of their blended sentence, net the effect of other relevant legal and extralegal measures.[24]

In addition, Brown and Sorenson examined the impact of legal and extralegal factors on the imposition of a blended sentence, a regular juvenile court sentence, or an adult court waiver in Harris County, Texas. Thus, while Trulson and colleagues examined determinants related to invoking the adult portion of the blended sentence for a youthful offender who was already adjudicated via blended sentencing, Brown and Sorenson examined an earlier point in the process—the decision of which prosecution avenue to pursue in the first place. Focusing on this earlier stage of the juvenile justice process, Brown and Sorenson revealed that factors such as the severity and type of felony were influential in youthful offenders receiving a blended sentencing prosecution, net the effects of important measures such as age, race, and sex.[25]

Altogether, existing research on adult court waiver and blended sentencing decision making consistently suggests that legal factors—specifically those relevant to type and severity of offense, prior juvenile justice system involvement, and the like—should heavily influence blended sentencing determinations. Although little research exists, a juvenile's experience while confined, such as involvement in institutional misconduct, also may have an impact on blended sentencing decisions.

THE DECISION FOR TEXAS'S SENTENCED OFFENDERS

Beyond the initial decision to prosecute an offender via determinate sentencing, perhaps the most critical decision with determinate sentencing in Texas occurs after sentenced offenders have had a taste of juvenile institutionalization in TYC facilities. After this period of time, sentenced offenders face a determination hearing that can significantly alter the trajectory of their lives.[26]

Table 5.1 presents information on the outcomes for the sentenced offenders following their institutionalization in TYC. Of the full cohort of 3,382 sentenced offenders, 272 (8 percent) had not faced a determination and were still in TYC at the time of this writing. The largest portion of offenders, 1,426 or 42 percent, were released from TYC but were still required to face supervision requirements in the community. Not shown in the table is that nearly all of the 1,426 sentenced offenders facing community supervision following TYC release were placed on adult parole under the supervision of the Texas Department of Criminal Justice Parole Division. Thus, while these sentenced offenders had to face the adult portion of their sentence, they were not placed in the Texas prison system but were released to the community on parole.[27]

Aside from those sentenced offenders released to the community with parole or other supervision requirements, 1,024 or 30 percent of the cohort were deemed in need of further confinement and transferred to the Texas prison system directly from TYC to face the remaining balance of their blended sentence. Taken together, over 70 percent of the sentenced offender cohort in this study either faced further sanc-

Table 5.1. Sentenced Offender Outcomes
(N = 3,382)

Status	Total	Percentage
Released with Supervision	1,426	42
Texas Prison Transfer	1,024	30
Served Full Sentence	556	16
Reached Age of Majority	57	2
Unknown Community Release	43	1
Died	4	1
Still in TYC	272	8
Total Cohort	3,382	100

Table 5.2. Sentenced Offender Analysis Cohort

Status	Total	Percentage
Released without Supervision	613	20
Released with Supervision	1,426	47
Texas Prison System Transfer	1,024	33
Total Analysis Cohort	3,063	100

tioning on adult parole or another community sanction (42 percent), or were transferred to a Texas prison facility (30 percent). Thus, while the average sentenced offender served only three years of his or her sentence in TYC, almost three-fourths were required to face some part of the adult portion of their blended sentence in the community or behind bars.

Beyond those who were determined to need further supervision or Texas prison system placement, 16 percent or 556 sentenced offenders either served or, following a determination hearing, were allowed to serve their full sentence in TYC without prison transfer or further supervision requirements in the community.[28] In addition to those who served their full sentence in TYC, 57 offenders or 2 percent of the entire cohort were allowed to remain in TYC until they reached the age of majority (twenty-one prior to 2007 or nineteen after 2007) and were released without further supervision requirements.[29]

Of the remaining offenders, 43, or approximately 1 percent, were released from TYC to the community, but it was unknown from the data whether they faced further sanctioning. Although these sentenced offenders are noted here, they will not be included in further analysis in this chapter due to their unknown supervision status. In addition, four sentenced offenders died and their final release status from TYC could not be determined, although it appears death occurred following their release.[30] These offenders were also removed from the analysis in remaining parts of this chapter.

ANALYSIS COHORT

The analysis in this chapter focuses only on those sentenced offenders who received a definitive decision regarding their future. Table 5.2 shows the cohort of 3,063 sentenced offenders that will be analyzed in this chapter.

Of those 3,063, 613 (20 percent) were released from TYC without further supervision requirements after having served their full sentence or after reaching the age of majority while in TYC, 1,426 (47 percent) received a determination that led to TYC release but in most cases with supervision requirements of adult parole, and 1,024 (33 percent) were transferred to the Texas prison system to face the remainder of their determinate sentence.

This chapter next examines the similarities and differences between the three sentenced offender groupings based on a number of important demographic, delinquent history, institutional treatment, and institutional behavior variables. It then examines the factors related to the three major decisions studied in this chapter: release with no supervision, release with supervision, and transfer to the Texas prison system.

COMPARING GROUPS

Table 5.3 compares the three sentenced offender groupings on the basis of a number of variables detailing the histories and circumstances of the sentenced offenders. It should be noted that the variables for this comparison and in further analyses in this chapter were chosen based on previous research regarding factors relevant in juvenile sentencing decisions. For example, both the research on adult court waiver and the limited research on blended sentencing decision making clearly show the relevance of variables indicative of juvenile justice offending history. Other variables groups were selected, such as the variables pertaining to TYC commitment, institutional treatment, and institutional behavior, because these factors are known to be broadly considered by decision makers in Texas relative to invoking or suspending the adult portion of a blended sentence. For example, it was previously noted that decision makers use institutional misconduct behavior in assessing youth progress and change in TYC, and thus variables indicative of institutional behavior are clearly relevant in the decision to invoke the adult portion of the blended sentence.

Table 5.3 provides a descriptive picture of the sentenced offenders as grouped across the three TYC release options. Statistical tests of difference (e.g., chi-square, t-tests, ANOVA) were used to determine whether the groups differed across all the individual variables.[31]

All possible group comparisons were employed in this analysis (R vs. RS, R vs. P, and RS vs. P). If significant differences were detected between groups, such differences were denoted with stars (*). One star denotes that statistically significant differences were found in the comparison of R vs. RS groups. Two stars denote significant differences between the R vs. P groups. Three stars (***) denote significant differences between the RS vs. P groups. Whenever a star or set of stars is shown, it indicates significant differences at a statistical level of at least .05 or less.

As an example, the "Previous adjudications" row in the table shows the average number of previous adjudications across all three groups. The mean number of previous adjudications for R was 1.97, 2.18 for RS, and 2.35 for P. In the "Differences" column, two stars (**) are shown, indicating that in a comparison among all groups, the R vs. P comparison was the only significant difference among the groups (1.97 vs. 2.35 previous adjudications). Here, the Texas prison transfer group (P) had a statistically and significantly greater number of previous adjudications than the release without supervision group (R). No statistically significant differences were found in a comparison of R vs. RS or RS vs. P, relative to previous adjudications. For another comparison, in the male category, there were no significant differences between the R, RS, or P group comparisons, as denoted by "ns" or no significant differences. Indeed, there was little difference relative to the proportion of males: the three groups ranged between 94 and 95 percent.

Table 5.3 reveals a number of significant differences among the groups across several of the variables, some that are perhaps more noteworthy than others. For example, the prison transfer group (P) evinced a significantly greater number of previous referrals than the other two groups. Relative to TYC commitment, there was a significantly greater percentage of homicide commitments in the prison transfer group than in the other groups.[32] Length of sentence combined with time served in TYC was also interesting in that prison transfers received the longest average sentence, but served the fewest number of years in TYC. Perhaps the most marked difference between the groups related to institutional misconduct behavior. Indeed, across all categories, Texas prison transfers were significantly more active relative to misconduct than the other groups. On average, the prison transfers engaged in roughly two to three times more overall misconduct, staff assaults, and ward assaults than the sentenced offender groups released with and without supervision. Furthermore, prison transfers required use of controlling force by TYC staff at a pace significantly greater than the other two sentenced offender groups.

The descriptive statistics presented in table 5.3 do not provide a de-

Table 5.3. Comparisons between Sentenced Offenders Released without Supervision, Released with Supervision, and Texas Prison System Transfers

Variables	Differences	Release without Supervision (613)		Release with Supervision (1,426)		Texas Prison Transfer (1,024)	
		M	SD	M	SD	M	SD
Demographics							
African American	**/***	.35	—	.35	—	.46	—
White	ns	.23	—	.21	—	.19	—
Hispanic	***	.41	—	.41	—	.35	—
Other	**	.02	—	.02	—	.01	—
Male	ns	.94	—	.94	—	.95	—
Female	ns	.06	—	.06	—	.05	—
Delinquent History							
Previous Adjudications	**	1.97	1.81	2.18	1.97	2.35	2.26
Previous Referrals	*/**/***	3.44	3.73	3.99	3.84	4.55	4.63
Previous Out-of-Home Placements	*/***	2.62	4.02	3.36	4.14	3.60	5.10
Previous Probation Failure	*	.32	—	.24	—	.28	—
Previous Violence toward Family	ns	.25	—	.24	—	.27	—
Gang Affiliation	ns	.17	—	.17	—	.18	—
Deemed a Substance Abuser	*/**	.70	—	.78	—	.80	—
History of Fire Setting	*	.14	—	.10	—	.12	—
History of Sexual Deviance	***	.19	—	.16	—	.20	—
History of Running Away	**/***	.28	—	.23	—	.35	—
TYC Commitment							
Age at TYC Commitment	*/**/***	15.49	1.22	16.24	1.03	15.67	1.19
Homicide Offense Commitment	*/**/***	.10	—	.15	—	.26	—
Sexual Offense Commitment	*	.30	—	.24	—	.27	—
Robbery Offense Commitment	*/***	.32	—	.39	—	.27	—
Other Violent Offense Commitment	ns	.22	—	.18	—	.18	—
Drug Offense Commitment	**	.02	—	.02	—	.01	—
Other Offense Commitment	*/**	.04	—	.02	—	.02	—
Length of Determinate Sentence	*/**/***	4.33	4.02	11.36	7.686	13.55	10.25

Table 5.3. Continued

Variables	Differences	Release without Supervision (613)		Release with Supervision (1,426)		Texas Prison Transfer (1,024)	
		M	SD	M	SD	M	SD
Time Served in TYC	*/**/***	3.03	1.19	3.57	1.14	2.71	1.22
Post-1995 Commitment	**/***	.89	—	.90	—	.80	—
Institutional Treatment							
Specialized Chemical Dependency Treatment	ns	.32	—	.37	—	.37	—
Specialized Sex Offender Treatment	ns	.23	—	.21	—	.19	—
Specialized Violent Offender Treatment	*/**/***	.16	—	.33	—	.23	—
Specialized Mental Health Treatment	*	.10	—	.14	—	.13	—
Institutional Behavior							
Total Misconduct Violations	*/**/***	32.39	68.27	20.15	34.72	60.84	69.90
Staff Assaults	**/***	.80	2.21	.50	1.65	2.01	3.75
Ward Assaults	*/**/***	2.40	3.76	1.45	2.31	4.24	4.88
Use of Force by Staff Needed to Control	*/**/***	1.57	4.57	.85	1.98	2.98	4.96

Notes: M corresponds to the mean. For categorical variables (e.g., race), it refers to the percentage within each group size. For example, a mean of 0.35 under R for African American means that 35 percent (or 214) of the 613 released without supervision offenders were African American.

R = release without supervision, RS = release with supervision, P = transfer to prison.

Comparisons between groups: * equals significant differences between R and RS groups, ** equals significant differences between R and P groups, and *** equals significant differences between RS and P groups of p < .05 or less. The indicator "ns" means no significant differences between any group comparisons.

Coding: All variables with a standard deviation listed are metric variables (previous adjudications, previous referrals, previous out-of-home placements, age at TYC commitment, length of determinate sentence, time served in TYC, total misconduct violations, staff assaults, ward assaults, and use of force by staff needed to control). All remaining variables are categorical (1 = yes; 0 = no); for example the variable "gang affiliated" is coded as 1 = gang affiliate; 0 = not a gang affiliate. The table denotes that 17 percent of those released without supervision (R) were gang affiliates.

Gatesville State School for Boys, ca. 1980. Courtesy of the Texas Department of Criminal Justice.

finitive answer regarding the factors related to the decisions to release (R), release with supervision (RS), or to transfer (P) sentenced offenders to the Texas prison system. However, the table provides a clear look into differences among the groups and the factors that may ultimately emerge as predictors of the determination hearing outcomes. It indicates that while prison transfers appeared more equal to the release with supervision (RS) and without supervision (R) groups relative to demographics, delinquent history, and to a large degree TYC commitment (except sentence length) and institutional treatment measures, the prison transfer group clearly departed from the other groups in terms of institutional behavior. Overall, the prison transfers appeared to be highly disruptive to the institutional regime at TYC, and this fact may prove to be a significant reason why they were transferred to the Texas prison system. The next section examines whether this holds true.

FACTORS RELATED TO RELEASE
OR PRISON TRANSFER DECISIONS

The descriptive statistics presented in table 5.3 are instructive on a broad level, but they do not reveal the factors that influence the placement of the sentenced offenders among the three groups. Table 5.4 presents the results of analyses regarding the influence of various demo-graphic, delinquent history, TYC commitment, institutional treatment, and institutional behavior measures on the three outcomes of interest in this chapter. This analysis was accomplished through a statistical technique called multinomial logistic regression (MLR).[33]

In simple terms, MLR allows comparison of the odds of one event occurring relative to a number of other potential events, after consid-ering knowledge across offender life domains (e.g., delinquent history, institutional behavior). For example, is a sentenced offender more or less likely to receive a decision of prison transfer compared to straight release or supervised release after we consider his or her prior delin-quent adjudications, or offense seriousness, or participation in miscon-duct while incarcerated? The analyses enable us to answer this type of question and allow us to understand the factors that can help explain various outcomes for sentenced offenders. Indeed, being able to com-pare different outcome options is important because different factors may influence the different outcomes considered in this chapter.

The information in table 5.4 not only provides an indication of whether a certain factor makes an outcome more or less likely, but also presents information on the percentage increase or decrease in the odds of one event occurring over another event. In other words, the analyses tell us how much a particular measure increases or decreases the odds of an event occurring—also known as magnitude or effect size. They enable us to see, for example, that according to table 5.4, a sentenced offender with a history of probation failure was 66 percent more likely to be released without supervision than with supervision, and was 50 percent more likely to be released without supervision than transferred to prison, compared to someone who did not have a history of probation failure, after accounting for the effects of other variables in the model.

In table 5.4 there are several significant comparisons among the three outcomes of interest in this chapter. The table suggests that the racial/ethnic groups of "white" and "other" were significantly more likely to be released without supervision than transferred to prison compared to African American offenders, or, alternatively, African American offenders were more likely to be sent to prison than to be released without supervision relative to whites and "others." Note that the column labeled "African American" is denoted as a "reference" cate-gory. This means that all of the percentages given (interpreted as per-cent change in the odds of the event occurring) are in relation to the reference category, African American. Thus, the fact that all of the per-

Table 5.4. Determinants of Release without Supervision (R), Release with Supervision (RS), and Texas Prison System Transfer (P)

Group Comparisons	R vs. RS	R vs. P	RS vs. P
Variables			
Demographics			
African American (reference)	—	—	—
White	ns	64%	ns
Hispanic	ns	ns	33%
Other	ns	244%	259%
Male	ns	ns	ns
Female (reference)	—	—	—
Delinquent History			
Previous Adjudications	ns	ns	ns
Previous Out-of-Home Placements	−5%	ns	ns
Previous Probation Failure	66%	50%	ns
Previous Violence toward Family	ns	ns	ns
Gang Affiliated	ns	ns	ns
Deemed a Substance Abuser	ns	ns	ns
History of Fire Setting	ns	ns	ns
History of Sexual Deviance	ns	ns	ns
History of Running Away	34%	ns	−35%
TYC Commitment			
Age at TYC Commitment	−65%	−16%	143%
Homicide Offense Commitment	295%	ns	−69%
Sexual Offense Commitment	ns	ns	−53%
Robbery Offense Commitment (reference)	—	—	—
Other Violent Offense Commitment	ns	ns	ns
Drug Offense Commitment	ns	ns	ns
Other Offense Commitment	ns	ns	ns
Length of Determinate Sentence	−38%	−41%	−5%

centages listed for white, Hispanic, and "other" offenders in the R vs. P and RS vs. P comparisons are positive suggests that those racial/ethnic groups have better odds than African American offenders of being released outright or released with supervision requirements than of being transferred to prison (or to put it another way, African American offenders have increased odds of going to prison, compared to the release outcomes, relative to those racial groups). Table 5.4 also tells us that in the R vs. P comparison by race, Hispanics did not have significantly different odds of release compared to prison transfer than did African

Table 5.4. Continued

Group Comparisons	R vs. RS	R vs. P	RS vs. P
Time Served in TYC	−40%	140%	297%
Post-1995 Commitment	ns	−69%	−38%
Institutional Treatment			
Specialized Chemical Dependency Treatment	ns	ns	−30%
Specialized Sex Offender Treatment	ns	ns	ns
Specialized Violent Offender Treatment	ns	ns	49%
Specialized Mental Health Treatment	−45%	88%	242%
Institutional Behavior			
Total Misconduct Violations	1%	−1%	−2%
Staff Assaults	ns	ns	ns
Ward Assaults	ns	−14%	−14%
Use of Force by Staff Needed to Control	ns	ns	ns

Note: "ns" means not significant. Significance of p < .05 or less is represented in the table. Percentages reported refer to an increase or decrease in the odds of an event (R, RS, or P). For example, under the R vs. RS column, 66 percent indicates that those sentenced offenders who were previous failures on probation prior to their determinate sentence commitment were 66 percent more likely to receive release with no supervision requirements (R) *compared* to release with supervision requirements (RS), after controlling for the effects of other variables in the model.

The parenthetical term "(reference)" denotes that the group was a reference category compared to other groups. For example, African American is the reference group, in comparison to other racial categories. The percent change in odds of R vs. P is 64 percent for white sentenced offenders. This means that compared to African American sentenced offenders, white sentenced offenders are 64 percent more likely to receive release versus transfer to prison, controlling for the effects of other variables in the model.

American sentenced offenders. There were also no significant differences between males and females across the various comparisons. This indicates that males are no more or less likely to receive a particular outcome listed compared to females, after accounting for the influence of other variables in the model.

Very few variables specific to delinquent history were predictive of any comparison outcomes in the table. Consistency was greatest with the measures tapping previous probation failure and those youths with a history of running away. For example, previous probation failures were 66 percent more likely to receive release over supervised release and 50 percent more likely to receive release than prison transfer. Moreover, those sentenced offenders with a previous history of running away were 34 percent more likely to be released without supervision than with supervision, but 35 percent less likely to receive supervised release rather than prison transfer. Interestingly, while previous research on adult court waiver and the limited research on blended sentencing decisions suggest that delinquent history indicators should hold much weight in the types of decisions examined in this chapter, the current analysis is not fully consistent with that finding. While some indicators are influential (e.g., previous probation failure), other staple delinquent history indicators such as previous adjudications or gang affiliation were not related to outcome decisions after accounting for the effects of all other variables in the models.

Offenders who were older at the time of TYC commitment were significantly more likely to receive supervised release or prison transfer than straight release. The analysis shows that a one-unit increase in age at TYC commitment (e.g., from age fourteen to fifteen) was associated with a 65 percent reduction in the odds of getting released without supervision rather than with supervision. A one-unit increase in age also reduced the odds of straight release compared to prison transfer. Older TYC commitments were 143 percent more likely to receive supervised release than prison transfer.

Homicide offenders were 295 percent more likely to be released without supervision than to receive supervised release, relative to the reference category of robbery offense commitments. Homicide commitments were, however, less likely to receive supervised release than prison transfer, in reference to robbery commitments. Sexual offense commitments were significantly less likely to receive supervised release (−53 percent) than prison transfers. No other comparisons were significant among sex offenders.

Those with longer sentences were generally more likely to receive supervised release or prison transfer than straight release. For example, a one-year increase in determinate sentence length decreased the odds of straight release by 38 percent compared to release with supervision and by 41 percent compared to prison transfer. In the model comparing release with supervision to prison transfer, those with longer determinate sentences were significantly less likely to receive a supervised release determination—and hence more likely to face time in the Texas prison system when those two options were compared. Time served in TYC was also predictive of the type of determination option. Longer stays in TYC were related to a decrease in the odds of release compared to supervised release, but they were related to increased odds of release when compared to prison transfer. Those with longer stays in TYC were 297 percent more likely to receive supervised release than prison transfer. Thus, a long stay in TYC was generally related to the outcome of receiving either a supervised release or a straight release from TYC.

While in TYC, sentenced offenders had the opportunity to benefit from not only generalized treatment (e.g., job training) but also specialized treatment. TYC provided specialized treatment programs for chemical dependency issues, sex offender issues, violent offender issues (for which the best-known program is the Capital Offender Program, today known as the Capital and Serious Violent Offender Treatment Program),[34] and mental health issues. Table 5.4 shows few significant effects of specialized treatment participation on the outcomes under examination in this chapter. Those who were involved in specialized chemical dependency treatment were 30 percent less likely to receive supervised release than prison transfer, but no significant differences were found for other comparisons. For example, participating in a specialized chemical dependency treatment program did not affect the odds of receiving unsupervised release rather than release with supervision requirements. Sentenced offenders who received violent offender treatment were 49 percent more likely to receive supervised release than prison transfer. Sentenced offenders who received specialized mental health treatment were 45 percent less likely to be released without supervision than with supervision, and 88 percent more likely to receive straight release than prison transfer. Those who participated in mental health treatment were 242 percent more likely to be released with supervision than to receive prison transfer.[35]

Recall in the descriptive analysis presented in table 5.3 that the release without supervision (R), release with supervision (RS), and prison transfer (P) groups differed most starkly on measures of institutional misconduct participation. Indeed, the group of prison transfers far exceeded the release groups on every misconduct measure, and such differences, with one exception, occurred at a frequency well beyond chance. When considering all of the institutional behavior variables in the MLR models along with other measures, the largest significant effects were found relative to ward assaults. A one-unit increase in ward assaults (e.g., going from one to two ward assaults during TYC incarceration) decreased the odds of release without supervision by 14 percent in favor of prison transfer. The odds also decreased 14 percent for supervised release in favor of prison transfer, net the effects of other variables in the model. In short, sentenced offenders who engaged in ward assaults significantly increased the likelihood of Texas prison system transfer compared to the other potential outcomes, after accounting for the effects of other measures in the model.

THE OVERALL PICTURE

To highlight the most important findings, table 5.5 reduces the analysis to only the statistically significant predictors of the three outcome groups examined previously. This permits us to examine the factors that increase or decrease the odds of prison transfer relative to release with or without supervision.

With some exceptions, the factors that had the most consistent effect on prison transfer centered on the length of the determinate sentence, involvement in total misconduct violations, and involvement in assaults on wards while in TYC. In any comparison where prison transfer was the outcome, sentenced offenders with longer determinate sentences (a proxy for seriousness of the offense that might not be captured by the commitment offense category alone) were much less likely to receive a determination that led to release rather than prison transfer. Furthermore, the frequency of total misconduct violations and involvement in ward assaults appeared to influence decisions that led to prison transfer. In fact, with one exception (R vs. RS model), none of these three institutional misconduct variables was significantly related to the odds of receiving a determination other than further imprisonment.

Moving away from the factors most consistently related to a decision of prison transfer, some variables were more consistently associated with community release options. For example, those who served a longer period of time in TYC were more likely to receive community release outcomes than prison transfer, net the effects of other variables in the models. In terms of race, the analysis shows that whites, Hispanics, and others were more likely than African American sentenced offenders to receive a release option. In addition, participation in specialized mental health and violent offender treatment was associated with increased likelihood of community release rather than prison transfer. This finding was especially consistent for those who received specialized mental health treatment.

The factors most determinative of prison transfer included longer

Table 5.5. Significant Predictors of Sentenced Offender
Outcomes

Predictor	Size of Effect
R vs. RS Comparison	
Increased Odds of R Compared to RS	
Previous Probation Failure	66%
Total Misconduct Violations	1%
Decreased Odds of R Compared to RS	
Previous Out-of-Home Placements	−5%
Higher Age at TYC Commitment	−65%
Longer Length of Determinate Sentence	−38%
Longer Time Served in TYC	−40%
Specialized Mental Health Treatment	−45%
R vs. P Comparison	
Increased Odds of R Compared to P	
Race as White (compared to AA)	64%
Race as Other (compared to AA)	244%
Previous Probation Failure	50%
Longer Time Served in TYC	140%
Specialized Mental Health Treatment	88%
Decreased Odds of R Compared to P	
Higher Age at TYC Commitment	−16%
Longer Length of Determinate Sentence	−41%
Post-1995 Commitment	−69%
Total Misconduct Violations	−1%
Ward Assaults	−14%
RS vs. P Comparison	
Increased Odds of RS Compared to P	
Race as Hispanic (compared to AA)	33%
Race as Other (compared to AA)	259%
Higher Age at TYC Commitment	143%
Longer Time Served in TYC	297%
Specialized Violent Offender Treatment	49%
Specialized Mental Health Treatment	242%
Decreased Odds of RS Compared to P	
History of Running Away	−35%
Homicide Offense Commitment (compared to Robbery)	−69%
Sexual Offense Commitment (compared to Robbery)	−53%

Table 5.5. Continued

Predictor	Size of Effect
RS vs. P Comparison (continued)	
Longer Length of Determinate Sentence	−5%
Post-1995 Commitment	−38%
Specialized Chemical Dependency Treatment	−30%
Total Misconduct Violations	−2%
Ward Assaults	−14%

Note: for metric variables (e.g., total misconduct violations; length of determinate sentence in years), percent change in odds is for a "one-unit" increase in the variable (e.g., for a one-year increase in length of determinate sentence).

sentence lengths and involvement in total misconduct and ward assaults, net the impacts of other variables in the models. This finding is not altogether surprising, since sentence length is a good proxy for seriousness of the offense. Indeed, while we controlled for commitment offense grouping, the reality is that not all homicide or sexual offense or robbery commitments are the same. Sentence length is one important proxy to distinguish *within* these commitment offense categories in more detail relative to seriousness. Those with longer sentences are arguably more serious and, combined with frequent and assaultive misconduct while in TYC, are more likely to receive prison transfer. Such outcomes are indicative of an offender who was serious and violent upon being committed to TYC, and who never embraced the level of change desired by those deciding whether to assign prison transfer or release to the community.

Conversely, the factors that were instructive of release (whether R or RS) had less to do with delinquent background and more to do with factors related to the TYC institutional experience: longer time served in TYC and participation in specialized treatment, in particular violent offender and mental health treatment.[36] Although other variables influenced the odds of release, these were the most consistent across all models. Whether a sentenced offender goes to prison or gets released to the community is most closely tied to their progress while confined in TYC—not necessarily their delinquent history. The one exception was sentence length.[37]

CONCLUSION

The goal of this chapter was to uncover the factors related to the decision to release or to further confine sentenced offenders after they had experienced a period of state juvenile incarceration in TYC. And while this chapter moved us closer to an understanding of which factors are influential in the release or continued confinement of the sentenced offenders, it should be noted that juvenile justice decisions like those examined in this chapter are highly individualized. In short, this chapter could only provide broad strokes as we attempted to paint a picture of the factors related to determination outcomes of more than three thousand sentenced offenders (and over three thousand separate crime victimizations with intricate details and nuances) spanning nearly three decades.

While the broad factors that are considered by decision makers such as judges, prosecutors, and TYC officials are known (e.g., youth progress in TYC, nature of commitment offense), there are many other relevant factors that influence the release or prison transfer decision that could not be attended to in this chapter. For example, there is no doubt that factors such as the specific circumstances of the offense hold weight in determination decisions, but we did not have access to these factors in assessing their influence on the outcomes in this chapter. Likewise, information on victim age, depravity of the offense (recall chapter 1 and the circumstances of the heinous rape-murder of Jennifer Ertman and Elizabeth Pena), localized politics, judicial philosophy, judge experience, media influence, victim participation in the judicial process, and many other variables are all factors that could and likely do influence the decision process beyond those factors examined in this chapter. In fact, in the rare instances when these types of factors can be accounted for, previous research on juvenile justice decision making has made it clear that they do matter in the types of decisions considered here.[38]

We are essentially outsiders looking in on the determinate sentencing process, and on a broad level we may never truly know all of the factors that influence very individualized decisions for *each* determinate sentence case—cases in which individualized and contextualized factors are no doubt meaningful and influential as to the decision of what to do with a specific sentenced offender. But this chapter reveals that in general, those youths with shorter sentence lengths (a proxy for less serious offenders), those who avoided high frequencies of misconduct, especially ward assaults (a proxy for those who abided by the institutional rules and took a break from their past), those who participated in certain treatment programs (a proxy for those who showed motivation to change), and those who served a longer period of time in TYC (a proxy for those who progressed well in TYC and were given an opportunity to continue to benefit from juvenile intervention) were the most likely to receive community release of some sort rather than the other option of placement in the cell blocks and runs of the Texas prison system.

For those who received a second chance via community release, chapter 6 examines whether the released sentenced offenders, under supervision or not in the community, capitalized on that chance or instead veered back onto the path of lost causes by committing more offenses. The chapter examines the recidivism outcomes of the community releases—perhaps the bottom-line measure of "success" in determinate sentencing. It tells us what happened to those who were given another chance at change following a serious and violent offense, and after only a few years of TYC institutionalization.

CHAPTER 6

THE BURDEN OF SECOND CHANCES

DANIELLE NATHANIEL SIMPSON (Texas Department of Criminal Justice [TDCJ] #999370) was executed at age thirty on November 18, 2009. The execution came roughly nine years after Danielle, his brother Lionel, his sixteen-year-old wife, Jennifer, and his thirteen-year-old cousin Edward "Pete" McCoy contributed to the drowning death of eighty-four-year-old Geraldine Davidson.

> On 1/26/2000, Simpson, 20 years old at the time, and three
> co-defendants went to the residence of an 84 year old white female.
> They taped her mouth with duct tape, tied her hands and feet, put her
> in the trunk of her vehicle, drove to the Neches River, tied a rope with
> a block to her, and threw her in the river, causing death. Simpson and
> his co-defendants were in possession of the victim's vehicle at the time
> of arrest.[1]

Nine years later, as Simpson lay on the death gurney, his last statement before execution lacked any sign of remorse for his crime: "Yeah, I want to tell my family I love ya'll. Tell Kate I love her too. Tell brother, my kids I live [sic] ya'll. I'm gonna miss ya'll. I'm ready, ready."

Edward McCoy, the thirteen-year-old cousin of Simpson and the only one not eligible for adult court certification under Texas law, testified against Simpson and received a twenty-year sentence as part of a plea agreement. He spent the first seven years of his sentence in TYC, with the possibility of transfer to the Texas prison system for the remaining thirteen years. McCoy was adjudicated under Texas's Determinate Sentencing Act.

McCoy not only testified against Simpson, but much of the evidence suggested he only watched as Mrs. Davidson was drowned in

Reception Center, Gatesville State School for Boys, ca. 1980. Courtesy of the Texas Department of Criminal Justice.

the Neches River.[2] Undoubtedly, some combination of his age, limited participation in the murder, and testimony against Simpson led to McCoy's second chance. Despite leniency given to McCoy, however, he now carried the burden of second chances. This burden meant that he would have to demonstrate his redeemable qualities in TYC or face transfer to the less merciful Texas prison system.

McCoy, like all subjects in this chapter, started his determinate sentence in TYC. Like some of the sentenced offenders, he participated in the Capital Offender Program (and various other treatment programs) and was given an opportunity to demonstrate he was not a lost cause or hopeless soul, and that he no longer posed a threat to public safety.

During his time in TYC, McCoy demonstrated some level of redemption. Indeed, the convicting court released him back into mainstream society at his determination hearing (McCoy was placed on adult parole for the remaining portion of his sentence). At TYC McCoy successfully completed the Capital Offender Program and became "a model citizen . . . earning a high school diploma and welding certification."[3]

If ever there was the opportunity for redemption, McCoy's case was it. He had been taken under the wing of Simpson, a serious and remorseless offender. Indeed, Simpson was no stranger to local law enforcement. At the time of the murder of Mrs. Davidson, he already had committed separate crimes including sexual indecency with a minor, assault against his sister and juvenile wife, and firing an illegal shotgun at a former girlfriend, among other various run-ins with the law.[4] Simpson was the oldest of the group, the most criminally sophisticated, and the primary aggressor guiding the trajectory of events leading to Mrs. Davidson's violent death.

Simpson's path led to his execution at the Huntsville "Walls" unit. McCoy, on the other hand, was presented with an opportunity for change and redemption. Indeed, all of the serious and violent offenders discussed in this chapter were presented with an opportunity for change, as all were released from TYC to the community based on the convicting court's mid-sentence decision.

This opportunity, however, meant some serious and violent offenders would land back in Texas communities during their late teens and early adulthood years. Once released, some of these second-chance offenders maintained their positive behavior. Some, however, lost their way and returned to crime.

In this chapter, we turn to the recidivism outcomes of Texas's determinately sentenced offenders who were released back to the community instead of being ushered directly to a Texas prison cell. We examine the successes and failures among Texas's sentenced offenders who were given another chance to change, focusing on the factors that would help explain why some sentenced offenders avoided further arrests after release and why some did not.

ATTEMPTING REDEMPTION

In assessing the factors involved in recidivism outcomes of sentenced offenders, this chapter taps into a rich source of data examining various aspects of sentenced offenders' lives before, during, and after their TYC incarceration. This data, which includes information typically found in studies examining recidivism among serious and violent juvenile offenders, forms the foundation for analyses in this chapter.[5]

Once at TYC, the sentenced offenders had an opportunity to demonstrate their redeemable qualities through participation in correctional programming. Although treatment amenability may not carry as much weight as offense seriousness and delinquent histories in assessing recidivism,[6] research suggests correctional treatment has improved recidivism outcomes for some of the most serious offenders.[7] We therefore used measures of general treatment participation at TYC (e.g., educational classes) in our analyses examining sentenced offender recidivism.

In addition to general forms of treatment provided by TYC, some sentenced offenders participated in specialized treatment programs including sex offender, mental health, substance abuse, and violent offender treatment. For instance, the US Department of Justice, through the Office of Juvenile Justice and Delinquency Prevention, pointed to TYC's violent offender treatment program, the Capital Offender Program (COP), and its success in treating serious and violent delinquents.[8] According to the report, TYC's COP was promising. Specifically, the report suggested that homicide offenders who completed the program were only about half as likely to recidivate as were offenders in a comparison group who did not complete the program. Given this potential impact on recidivism outcomes, we included measures of specialized treatment participation in assessing sentenced offender recidivism, including participation in the COP.

Attesting to the significance of the potential for change in TYC, Clyde and Paul Davidson, sons of Mrs. Davidson, testified in favor of McCoy's transfer from TYC to community supervision over transfer to the Texas prison system at his determination hearing in large part due to McCoy's apparent rehabilitation. They based their advocacy on McCoy's model behavior and participation in specialized programming, including the COP, while a ward of TYC. In accordance with the Davidsons' wishes, Anderson County district attorney Doug Lowe did not argue for sending McCoy to an adult prison. "I did see today . . . that rehabilitation is possible," Lowe said.[9]

While it may be too early to assess McCoy's threat to public safety given his record of model institutional behavior, previous research on serious and violent offenders provides a framework to help understand recidivism outcomes of Texas's sentenced offenders. In addition to treatment participation, for example, research has identified consistent relationships between various sociodemographic characteristics (gender, age, and race, for example) and recidivism.[10] Our analyses, therefore, included appropriate measures of these concepts. Scholars also have identified factors such as criminal sophistication and experience[11] and institutional misconduct[12] as factors related to recidivism among serious and violent juvenile offenders. Additionally, previous scholarship has pointed to the influence of correctional treatment[13] and other types of reentry services[14] on post-incarceration recidivism. We use measures of these constructs in assessing the recidivism of sentenced offenders following their community release from TYC.

In the broader context, though, we turn to recidivism data collected by state agencies to paint a picture of risk to public safety from Texas's sentenced offenders.

BACK TO TEXAS STREETS

In this section, we examine various characteristics of the sentenced offenders (e.g., sociodemographic characteristics, delinquent histories, and institutional behavior and correctional treatment) to explore their recidivism following TYC release. Following this descriptive analysis, we examine the results of more advanced statistical analyses designed to isolate the influence of these factors on recidivism.

SOCIODEMOGRAPHICS OF RELEASED OFFENDERS

Table 6.1 presents demographic characteristics of sentenced offenders released from TYC to the community. Of the 3,382 offenders examined in this study, 2,082 were eventually released to the community following their determination hearing (see chapter 5). Of these offenders, 62 percent, or 1,283 offenders, were rearrested at least once following release from TYC, with approximately 75 percent of them being rearrested for a felony offense.

On average, recidivists were similar to nonrecidivists in several regards. For instance, for both recidivists and nonrecidivists, the average age at the time of commitment to TYC was just less than sixteen and the average released offender was just over nineteen. Recidivists and non-recidivists differed in other respects, however. While the full sample of released offenders included 730 (35 percent) African American offenders, a significantly larger portion (40 percent compared to 27 percent in the nonrecidivist category, p <.01) of African American offenders were rearrested after release than avoided rearrest. Whites and Hispanics, on the other hand, made up approximately 60 percent of those released to the community, but were significantly less likely to be rearrested following release (19 percent for whites and 39 percent for Hispanics).[15] Other racial/ethnic backgrounds were statistically indistinguishable across the recidivism classifications.[16]

Given the disproportionate number of males (approximately 95 per-

Table 6.1. Demographics and Backgrounds of Released Offenders

	Full Sample n = 2,082		Non-Recidivist n = 799 (38%)		Recidivist n = 1,283 (62%)	
	f	%	f	%	f	%
Age at TYC Commitment	15.99	0.03	16.05	0.04	15.95	0.03
Age at Release	19.39	0.03	19.40	0.04	19.38	0.03
African American[b]	730	35	217	27	513	40
Caucasian[b]	443	21	201	25	242	19
Hispanic[b]	861	41	359	45	502	39
Other Race	48	02	22	03	26	02
Male[b]	1,961	94	726	91	1,235	96
US Citizen[b]	1,917	92	699	87	1,218	95
Gang Affiliated[a]	359	17	118	15	241	19
Special Education	494	24	176	22	318	25
Mentally Ill	278	13	116	15	162	13

[a] $p < .05$
[b] $p < .01$

cent) under study, it was not surprising that they made up the overwhelming majority (94 percent) of those offenders released to the community. Moreover, there was a significantly larger portion of male recidivists compared to nonrecidivists (96 percent compared to 91 percent for nonrecidivists, $p < .01$).

Table 6.1 also reports offenders' nationalities, associations, and cognitive processing (e.g., whether they were determined to be mentally ill). The overwhelming majority (92 percent) of released offenders were US citizens. Gang affiliates made up 17 percent of offenders released from TYC, but were disproportionately more likely to recidivate than were offenders not affiliated with gangs ($p < .05$). Related to cognitive processing, approximately one-fourth of the released offenders were assigned to special education classes and 13 percent were classified as mentally ill. Neither of the cognitive processing indicators served to distinguish recidivists from nonrecidivists, however.

Beyond the sample demographics, offenders sentenced under Texas's determinate sentencing legislation evinced problematic home environments prior to their TYC commitment as a sentenced offender.[17] Criminologists have focused for decades on how these types of home-based factors relate to a person's potential to offend in the future. Sheldon and Eleanor Glueck discovered significant associations between individual-level traits—such as physical stature, temperament, and attitude—and delinquency in matched samples of five hundred delinquent and five hundred nondelinquent youths.[18] The Gluecks also described the relationship between familial characteristics and delinquency (e.g., disorganized families were more closely associated with delinquents). Given that the vast majority of sentenced offenders (M = 19.39 years old) left the home environment just some three and a half years earlier to begin their TYC confinement, we considered the offenders' home environment when assessing recidivism after TYC release.

As presented in table 6.2, many of the released offenders experienced abuse and poor living environments prior to their commitment to TYC. Just less than one in five offenders reported prior emotional abuse and 11 percent reported abandonment issues. Thirteen percent of the released offenders reported prior sexual abuse, with disproportionately fewer of these offenders being rearrested (p < .01). Approximately 21

Table 6.2. Environmental Factors

	Full Sample n = 2,082		Non-Recidivist n = 799 (38%)		Recidivist n = 1,283 (62%)	
	f	%	f	%	f	%
Emotionally Abused	365	18	149	19	216	17
Abandoned	224	11	86	11	138	11
Sexually Abused[b]	273	13	135	17	138	11
Supervision Neglect	437	21	158	20	279	22
Physical Abuse[b]	310	15	141	18	169	13
Poverty[a,c]	0.72	0.02	0.67	0.02	0.74	0.02
Chaos[a,c]	0.92	0.02	0.88	0.03	0.95	0.02
Rigidity[c]	0.36	0.01	0.35	0.02	0.37	0.02

[a] p < .05
[b] p < .01
[c] Of home environment; 0 = none, 1 = some, 2 = very much

percent of the released offenders reported a lack of supervision in the home, and approximately 15 percent of the released offenders reported prior physical, nonsexual abuse. Similar to the association between offenders with sexual abuse histories, those released offenders with physical abuse histories were significantly less likely to recidivate than those not reporting prior physical abuse (p < .01).

Also reported in table 6.2 are indices (0 = none, 1 = some, 2 = very much) of offenders' home environments. Nonrecidivists and recidivists experienced markedly different home environments, with recidivists reporting significantly greater levels of poverty and chaos than non-recidivists. Of note, however, is that nonrecidivists and recidivists reported similarly rigid home lives.

DELINQUENT HISTORIES

Building on the Gluecks' 1950s study of juvenile delinquency, scholars have explored the concept of criminal desistance—switching from a criminal to a law-abiding lifestyle—of onetime juvenile delinquents while considering the impact of past life events on current and future life events.[19] This orientation suggests behavioral trajectories over an individual's life course. In short, people can change, or they can continue their life trajectory. While opportunities to desist from crime exist (scholars have suggested, for example, that various life events such as marriage or employment may serve to initiate law-abiding behaviors),[20] the idea that offenders enter "pathways" suggests consistent habitual behaviors—whether positive or negative. Consequently, offenders' past behaviors may serve to predict future criminality.

Table 6.3 presents the delinquent histories of offenders released from TYC into Texas communities following the juvenile portion of their determinate sentence. By an average age of nineteen, sentenced offenders had accumulated extensive delinquent histories in comparison to other offenders in Texas's juvenile justice system.[21] Of the full sample of released offenders, 13 percent were committed as homicide offenders, 25 percent were committed as sexual offenders, 37 percent were robbery commitments, 19 percent were committed to TYC for another serious violent crime, and approximately 5 percent were committed to TYC as sentenced offenders for a drug-related offense or other offense.[22] Of these offense classifications, only two were significantly associated with recidivism: sexual offenders were significantly less likely to be recidivists (30 percent nonrecidivists compared to 22 percent recidivists,

Table 6.3. Delinquency Histories

	Full Sample n = 2,082		Non-Recidivist n = 799 (38%)		Recidivist n = 1,283 (62%)	
	f	%	f	%	f	%
Committing Offense						
Homicide	277	13	100	13	177	14
Sexual[b]	528	25	241	30	287	22
Robbery	773	37	284	36	489	38
Other Violent	405	19	145	18	260	20
Drug-Related	41	02	15	02	26	02
Other[a]	56	03	13	02	43	03
Previous Adjudications	2.12	0.04	2.18	0.07	2.08	0.05
Probation Failure[b]	545	26	179	22	366	29
Prior Placements[a]	3.17	0.09	3.46	0.15	2.99	0.11
Substance Abuse	1,583	76	575	72	1,008	79
History[b]						
Violent toward Family	507	24	201	25	306	24
Danger to Self	305	15	126	16	179	14
Danger to Others	1,383	66	549	69	834	65

[a] $p < .05$

[b] $p < .01$

$p < .01$) and offenders categorized as "other offenses" were significantly more likely to be rearrested ($p < .05$).

A further look at the released offenders' delinquent histories provides a clearer snapshot of these offenders before incarceration. For example, the average released sentenced offender had just over two (M = 2.12) previous court adjudications (not including the sentenced offender adjudication). Twenty-six percent had previously failed probation, and, on average, they had more than three (M = 3.17) prior out-of-home residential placements (not including the sentenced offender commitment to TYC). Those offenders who had previously failed probation (22 percent nonrecidivist compared to 29 percent recidivist, $p < .01$) were significantly more likely to be rearrested after TYC release. Just over three-fourths of the released offenders reported substance abuse histories, and they were significantly more likely to be rearrested than

Table 6.4. Institutional Behavior

	Full Sample n = 2,082		Non-Recidivist n = 799 (38%)		Recidivist n = 1,283 (62%)	
	f	%	f	%	f	%
Years in TYC	3.40	0.03	3.35	0.04	3.43	0.03
Assaulted Other Inmates[b]	1.55	0.07	1.13	0.11	1.72	0.09
Assaulted Staff[b]	0.26	0.03	0.13	0.03	0.31	0.03
Refused to Follow Instructions	2.76	0.19	3.17	0.26	2.50	0.27
Institutional Gang Activity	0.13	0.01	0.14	0.02	0.13	0.01
Use of Force by Staff	1.07	0.07	1.15	0.09	1.02	0.09
Use of Mechanical Restraints	0.48	0.03	0.55	0.06	0.43	0.04
Sexual Deviant[a]	358	17	159	20	199	16

[a] $p < .05$
[b] $p < .01$

those without such histories (79 percent compared to 72 percent of nonrecidivist, $p < .01$). Approximately 24 percent of released offenders were classified as violent toward their family or others, 15 percent were categorized as a danger to themselves, and 66 percent were classified as a danger to others. None of these final three classifications, however, were statistically distinguishable in the recidivist and nonrecidivist groups.

INSTITUTIONAL BEHAVIOR AND TREATMENT OF RELEASED OFFENDERS

Institutional misconduct is the natural first post-adjudication signal of criminal persistence into adulthood and thus tends to be a consideration in release decisions.[23] Furthermore, scholars have previously linked institutional behavior to post-release recidivism.[24] As table 6.4 presents, the average released sentenced offender spent just less than three and a half years (M = 3.40) incarcerated and during that time accumulated almost two assaults on other wards, among other forms of institutional misconduct.

Those offenders with more assaults on wards or TYC staff were significantly more likely to be rearrested post-release (p <.01). However, none of the other measures of institutional behavior—refusal to follow staff instructions, institutional gang activity, use of force by staff, or use of mechanical restraints—were significantly associated with recidivism. Interestingly, those offenders classified as sexual deviants while in TYC (approximately 17 percent of this group) were significantly less likely to be rearrested (20 percent nonrecidivist compared to 16 percent recidivists, p < .05).

Table 6.5 presents offenders' participation in correctional programming while at TYC. On average, released offenders participated in approximately two therapeutic programs while incarcerated, but those with a record of more programming were significantly less likely to be rearrested post-release (2.04 programs for nonrecidivists compared to 1.86 programs for recidivists, p < .01).[25] Of the 2,082 released offenders, 28 percent participated in the Capital Offender Program and 21 percent participated in a specialized sex offender program. Thirty-six percent participated in a chemical dependency treatment program and 14 percent participated in a specialized mental health treatment program. Representing a more omnibus treatment exposure, 94 percent of released offenders participated in some form of treatment/programming while in TYC—specialized or general. Participation in three specific treatment programs—specialized sex offender treatment (p < .01),

Table 6.5. Correctional Programming

	Full Sample n = 2,082		Non-Recidivist n = 799 (38%)		Recidivist n = 1,283 (62%)	
	f	%	f	%	f	%
Treatment Programming[b]	1.93	0.02	2.04	0.03	1.86	0.02
Capital Offender Program	584	28	242	30	342	27
Sex Offender Program[b]	441	21	208	26	233	18
Chemical Dependency Treatment[a]	744	36	261	33	483	38
Mental Health Treatment[b]	282	14	160	20	122	10
Other Specialized Treatment	1,962	94	757	95	1,205	94

[a] p < .05
[b] p < .01

specialized chemical dependency treatment ($p < .05$), and specialized mental health treatment ($p < .01$)—were significantly associated with lower recidivism at this basic descriptive level.

Because the underlying motivation behind Texas's determinate sentencing strategy was to provide serious offenders with a second chance while preserving the option for continued sanctions, it is likely that various factors beyond the commitment offense affected the post-release community supervision.[26]

SUMMARY OF SENTENCED OFFENDER BACKGROUNDS AND INSTITUTIONAL PROGRESS

The individual factors associated with determination hearing release decisions for sentenced offenders were examined in the previous chapter. This chapter has thus far focused on basic descriptive recidivism outcomes of those released to the community following their determination hearing. Take, for instance, the case of Edward McCoy discussed previously. Having participated in the Capital Offender Program at Giddings State School and exhibiting good behavior while in TYC, McCoy was released to the Texas Department of Criminal Justice (TDCJ) Parole Division just prior to his twenty-first birthday. In effect, the court extended a second chance to him. How released serious and violent offenders like McCoy behaved during their second chance is of particular interest given the public safety threat they posed in their committing offense. At the end of the day, recidivism is the bottom-line measure of success or failure when it comes to the released sentenced offenders.

The average released sentenced offender sent back to the community was male, was incarcerated at age sixteen, and was released at about age nineteen and a half. The average released offender had approximately two previous delinquent adjudications and over three previous out-of-home placements, a history of substance abuse, and was categorized as a danger to others by state authorities. While incarcerated, released sentenced offenders on average were written up for just fewer than two assaults on another ward and between two and three refusals to follow staff instructions, among other forms of institutional misconduct (see chapter 4). The vast majority of released sentenced offenders participated in some form of general treatment (e.g., educational classes) or specialized treatment programming (94 percent), and specialized treatment program participation aligned closely with offenders' committing offenses. Finally, approximately two-thirds of the released serious offenders were placed under some form of community supervision upon their release. That said, most were rearrested, more often than not for felony-level offenses. To help explain why, we turn to an examination of the timing for recidivism and the factors that can help explain it.

WHEN DOES IT ALL FALL APART?

Beyond the descriptive look at the released sentenced offenders, we were interested in how specific characteristics and pieces of information contribute to an explanation of recidivism among this offender group. A host of demographic data, delinquent history, and other youth-related factors were linked with recidivism, as shown in previous analyses. However, these basic comparisons established only that a significant association existed between these factors and recidivism. A more specific estimation of the relationship between these factors and recidivism required estimating the risk of recidivism through what is referred to as event history analysis.[27] Event history analysis allowed us to isolate the influence of each explanatory variable (e.g., number of previous delinquent adjudications) on the risk of recidivism. In short, we were able to estimate each explanatory variable's contribution to the risk of recidivism while taking into account other relevant information about these offenders.

Estimating the timing to an event, such as recidivism, has a rich history in scientific exploration. In these estimates, social scientists consider the role of time in two general contexts. First, time is cyclical (twenty-four hours in a day, seven days in a week, and so forth) and therefore provides cut-off points for comparison (e.g., how many offenders get rearrested during a particular time interval).[28] The second context shares the standardization purpose (that each offender's "at risk" period of experiencing an event such as recidivism is the same or standardized), but also adds the ability to incorporate time as dynamic.

Known most commonly by a particular statistical model—Cox's regression[29]—event history analysis provides an attractive framework for estimating recidivism risk for Texas's sentenced offenders, because it accounts for cycles of time and allows standardization of risk periods for the released sentenced offenders.[30] Event history analysis allowed us to examine the risk of recidivism for sentenced offenders in the community after taking into account such factors as their delinquent history or participation in institutional misconduct while confined and how long they have been "at risk" or able to recidivate.

RECIDIVISM UP TO FIVE YEARS AFTER TYC RELEASE

The analysis here examines recidivism and recidivism timing among 1,400 sentenced offenders. The entire sample of 2,082 releases is reduced to 1,400 because that is the number of offenders who had at least five years of time after release from TYC to be followed in the community for recidivism. Table 6.6 represents the life table of the sample. A life table is simply a presentation of information that shows at different time intervals the total number of sentenced offenders at risk of recidivism by being in the community, the number who have recidivated at any particular time, and the percent of the sample of sentenced offenders who have not recidivated at a particular time.

Each row in table 6.6 represents in two-month intervals after release from TYC the total number of sentenced offenders at risk of recidivism, the number of offenders rearrested within that time period, and the percentage of the sample "surviving" or not arrested within that time interval. For example, of the 1,400 subjects, 38 were rearrested during the first time period. Thus 3 percent of the 1,400 were rearrested and approximately 97 percent avoided rearrest during the first two months after their release from TYC.[31] Other notable periods of interest include intervals 3, 18, 30, and 31. Interval 3 (months four to six) produced the greatest number of recidivists (n = 66), with approximately 5 percent of the overall sample being rearrested. Interval 18 (months 34 to 36) represents the time at which approximately one-half of the sample had experienced rearrest; thus 50 percent of the sample recidivated within three years after release. Interval 30 represents the final at-risk period, and interval 31 represents those avoiding rearrest. Of the 1,400 sentenced offenders with five years of follow-up after TYC release, 548 (39 percent) were not rearrested, resulting in an overall five-year recidivism of approximately 61 percent.[32]

DETERMINANTS OF FIVE-YEAR RECIDIVISM TIMING

Given the nature of the release decision discussed in chapter 5, we next examine the factors related to recidivism while considering influences such as race, gender, previous delinquent adjudications, and so on.[33] Table 6.7 indicates that of the 1,399 subjects in the full event history model (one offender was excluded from the analysis due to missing data),[34] offenders originating from a chaotic home environment and with a recorded history of substance abuse were at significantly greater

Table 6.6. Five-Year Recidivism Life Table
(n = 1,399)

Interval	Months	At-Risk Total	Recidivists	Survival Percent
1	0–2	1,400	38	97
2	2–4	1,362	43	94
3	4–6	1,319	66	90
4	6–8	1,253	59	85
5	8–10	1,194	48	82
6	10–12	1,146	63	77
7	12–14	1,083	50	74
8	14–16	1,033	39	71
9	16–18	994	47	68
10	18–20	947	35	65
11	20–22	912	40	62
12	22–24	872	34	60
13	24–26	838	30	58
14	26–28	808	22	56
15	28–30	786	22	55
16	30–32	764	25	53
17	32–34	739	20	51
18	34–36	719	18	50
19	36–38	701	22	49
20	38–40	679	10	48
21	40–42	669	12	47
22	42–44	657	12	46
23	44–46	645	10	45
24	46–48	635	11	45
25	48–50	624	13	44
26	50–52	611	13	43
27	52–54	598	12	42
28	54–56	586	12	41
29	56–58	574	11	40
30	58–60	563	15	39
31	60	548	0	39

Note: each period includes the lower bound and excludes the upper bound.

Table 6.7. Event History Models by Offense (n = 1,399)

	Full Sample	Robbery	Sexual	Homicide
Demographics and Background				
African American	+	+	+	+
Hispanic	n/s	n/s	n/s	n/s
White (reference category)				
Male	+	+	n/s	n/s
Gang-Related	n/s	n/s	n/s	n/s
Environmental Factors				
Sexually Abused	n/s	n/s	n/s	n/s
Physically Abused	n/s	n/s	n/s	n/s
Chaotic Home Environment	+	n/s	n/s	n/s
Delinquent History				
Homicide	n/s	Not Used	Not Used	Not Used
Sexual Offense	–	Not Used	Not Used	Not Used
Robbery	n/s	Not Used	Not Used	Not Used
Probation Failure	+	n/s	n/s	n/s
Prior Placements	+	n/s	+	+
Substance Abuse	+	n/s	+	+
Institutional Behavior				
Years in TYC	n/s	n/s	n/s	–
Sexually Deviant	n/s	n/s	n/s	n/s
Staff Assaults	+	n/s	n/s	n/s
Inmate Assaults	+	n/s	+	+
Refusal to Follow Instructions	n/s	n/s	n/s	n/s
Correctional Therapy				
General Treatment	n/s	n/s	n/s	n/s
Chemical Dependency Treatment	Not Used	n/s	Not Used	Not Used
Sex Offender Treatment	Not Used	Not Used	n/s	Not Used
Capital Offender Treatment	Not Used	Not Used	Not Used	–
Post-Release Supervision				
Supervision Received	–	–	n/s	n/s
Observations	1,399	453	363	238

Note: "Not Used" indicates variable was not used in the specific model. With the exception of the variables Prior Placements, Years in TYC, Staff Assaults, Inmate Assaults, and Refusal to Follow Instructions, all other variables are categorical (1 = yes; 0 = no). A plus sign (+) indicates the variable increased recidivism risk, and a minus sign (–) indicates the variable measure decreased recidivism risk.

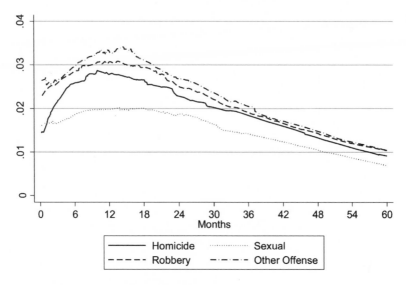

Chart 6.1. Committing Offense Recidivism Hazard

risk of recidivism compared to offenders from stable home environments and without a substance abuse history. Furthermore, delinquent history significantly predicted recidivism, with those sentenced offenders having a previous community supervision revocation and a greater number of previous out-of-home placements also significantly more likely to recidivate post-TYC release. Offenders who engaged in institutional misconduct had significantly greater risks of rearrest, with assaults on both staff and other inmates significantly predicting rearrest. Once back in the community, offenders placed on community supervision services (e.g., adult parole) had a significantly lower risk of recidivism than those offenders released without supervision requirements.

Chart 6.1 represents the full sample's recidivism probability based on committing offense. Overall, offenders of all offense typologies experienced the greatest risk of recidivism between six months and two years post-release. While each offending group had distinguishable trends over time, only those offenders committed for a sexual crime were statistically distinguishable from the other offense groups. In fact, offenders committed to TYC for a sexual offense had significantly lower recidivism hazards than the other offense control group.[35] Given the statistically significant difference presented by offense category and the structure of Texas's DSA,[36] we grouped offenders by offense categories to observe how other individual characteristics influence recidivism within offense categories.

RECIDIVISM RISK BY COMMITTING OFFENSE

For a deeper understanding of factors associated with recidivism, we present the determinants of recidivism risk through separate event history models for different offenses of commitment to TYC: robbery, sexual, and homicide offenders.[37] Table 6.7 also includes these analyses.

ROBBERY COMMITMENTS

This event history analysis included 453 sentenced offenders committed to TYC for robbery. While not shown in tabular form, robbery commitments experienced the highest recidivism risk during months six through eight, with one-half of robbery commitments recidivating within the first thirty months and approximately 66 percent being arrested during the first five years after TYC release.

Table 6.7 presents the event history analysis for robbery commitments. Unlike in the full model, only three individual-level characteristics significantly increased recidivism risk. For robbery commitments, being African American and male significantly increased offenders' risk of rearrest, but experiencing parole supervision after TYC release significantly decreased recidivism risk.

Chart 6.2 presents low-risk and high-risk groupings of robbery commitments based on the event history analysis results.[38] The results show that the low-risk classification group represents non–African American female robbery offenders who experienced post-incarceration supervision in the community following release from TYC. In fact, the low-risk classification group avoided rearrest during the first six months post-release from TYC (as indicated by the low-risk group's hazard ratio starting after six months). Those in the high-risk cohort were at elevated risks of recidivism as soon as they were released. In sum, other than the influences of gender and race, only post-release supervision decreased the risk of recidivism for robbery commitments.

SEXUAL OFFENSE COMMITMENTS

Sexual offense commitments experienced a distinctly different recidivism landscape than robbery commitments. For starters, 48 percent of the 364 sexual offense commitments of focus in this analysis avoided rearrest during the five years after release (52 percent were rearrested

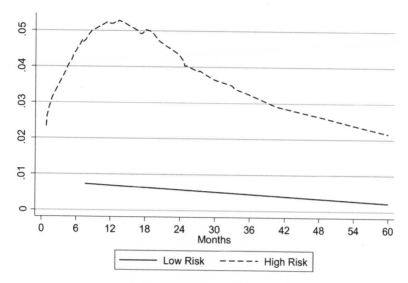

Chart 6.2. Low and High Recidivism Hazard: Robbery Commitments
Note: Recidivism hazard risk is based on significant correlates of the Royston-Parmar model. Low risk category represents non–African American female robbery offenders who experienced post-incarceration supervision. Conversely, the high-risk cohort includes African American male robbery offenders without post-incarceration supervision.

post-release).[39] By comparison, only 34 percent of the robbery commitments avoided rearrest during the first five years after release (66 percent were rearrested post-release).

Sexual offense commitments' recidivism patterns produced a more nuanced and extended recidivism risk peak than that of robbery offenders. For example, sexual offense commitments' recidivism risk peaked during three noncontinuous periods (4–5 months, 10–11 months, and 23–24 months) and one-half of the sample avoided rearrest until the 55–56 month period.

In addition to the lower recidivism risk for sexual offense commitments, those factors associated with predicting recidivism for sexual offense commitments were distinct from those of robbery offenders. Table 6.7 presents the results of the event history analysis for sexual offenders. There were several significant determinants of recidivism within this group. Namely, African American sexual offenders who also had experienced at least one previous out-of-home placement, reported a history of substance abuse, and perpetrated violence against other wards were at elevated recidivism risks. Conversely, non–African

American sexual offenders without a previous out-of-home placement, a history of substance abuse, or a record of assaultive behaviors were least likely to recidivate. These groups are represented in chart 6.3 as the high-risk and low-risk categorizations.

HOMICIDE COMMITMENTS

The final offense group was the homicide offenders. Of the offenders released to the community under Texas's determinate sentencing legislation, 238 were committed for a homicide offense. Of these 238 commitments of focus in this analysis, approximately 42 percent (n = 101) avoided arrest during the five-year period following their release from TYC. Homicide commitments were at the greatest risk of rearrest during months five and six, and one-half of the sample experienced re-arrest within the first thirty-eight months after release.

Table 6.7 presents the results of the event history model for homicide offenders. Much like the previous three models predicting recidivism, African American homicide commitments had significantly greater re-

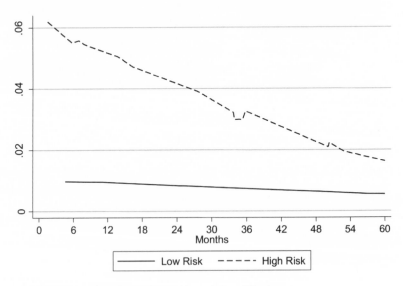

Chart 6.3. Low and High Recidivism Hazard: Sex Offenders
Note: Risk levels categorized by significant correlations produced by the Royston-Parmar model. Low risk represents non–African American sex offenders with no previous out-of-home placements, no recorded substance abuse history, and no reports of assaults on other inmates while incarcerated. High risk includes African American sex offenders with at least one previous out-of-home placement, a record of substance abuse, and at least one assault on another inmate.

Barbershop and clinic, Mountain View State School for Boys, ca. 1975. Courtesy of the Texas Department of Criminal Justice.

cidivism risk than white homicide commitments. Consistent with robbery commitments, male homicide commitments were at significantly greater risk of recidivism than were their female counterparts.

The impact of several institutional factors on recidivism risk highlights the uniqueness of the homicide commitment group. For example, length of incarceration significantly decreased recidivism risk, in that those with longer sentences were at significantly lower recidivism risks (H = 0.83, p < .05). Those homicide commitments with greater participation in ward assaults while in TYC were at significantly higher risks of rearrest compared to other homicide commitments (H = 1.67, p < .05).

After controlling for other treatment participation, homicide commitments participating in the Capital Offender Program had a significantly lower recidivism risk compared to homicide offenders otherwise

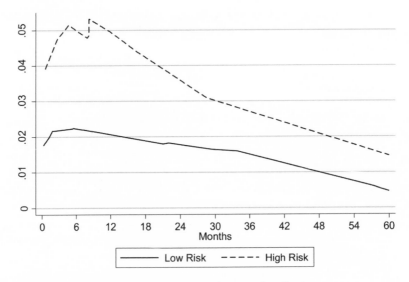

Chart 6.4. Low and High Recidivism Hazard: Homicide Offenders

Note: Risk categorization based on the significant correlations produced by the Royston-Parmar model, excluding race and gender. While the R-P model suggested several significant predictors of recidivism, the exclusionary nature of grouping subjects' recidivism hazards, the small sample size of homicide offenders classified as non–African American or female, the disproportionate distribution of observations across staff assaults, and the omnibus treatment measure's correlation with the capital offender treatment program required risk levels based on a subset of significant correlations. The low-risk category includes homicide offenders with longer than average incarceration stays, no recorded assaults on other inmates, and participation in the Capital Offender Program. The high-risk group included homicide offenders with shorter than average incarceration periods, recorded inmate assaults, and no record of participation in the Capital Offender Program.

situated (H = 0.50, p < .05).[40] This treatment impact departs from the other offending group results, where treatment programming failed to reduce significantly the recidivism risk for robbery and sexual offense commitments. Similar to sexual offenders, however, violence perpetrated on other wards while at TYC significantly increased the recidivism risk for homicide commitments.

As with the presentation of the other three offender groups, chart 6.4 represents low-risk and high-risk homicide classifications based on the event history model.[41] The low-risk group includes homicide offenders without a record of assault of other inmates, with longer stays in TYC, and with a record of participation in the Capital Offender Program.

Conversely, homicide offenders classified as high risk for recidivism had shorter stays in TYC, perpetrated violence against other inmates, and did not participate in the Capital Offender Program.

SUMMARY OF RECIDIVISM OF SENTENCED OFFENDERS

Statistical analyses of available data on Texas's determinately sentenced offenders presented some interesting findings. Of the full sample (N = 2,082), 62 percent (n = 1,283) were rearrested, and of those, roughly three-fourths were arrested for at least one felony offense. Offenders varied in their sociodemographic data, delinquent histories, and institutional behaviors and treatments. In fact, approximately one-third (32 percent) of these serious and violent offenders were released without community supervision. In an effort to refine our estimates, we included a measure of time in the recidivism proxy. Event history analysis allowed us to estimate when recidivism occurred once the sentenced offenders exited TYC facilities and reemerged back into the community. We grouped offenders by their committing offense and discovered sexual offenders had significantly lower recidivism risk compared to other offenders, all else being equal.

In grouping offenders by offense classification and holding other things constant, we discovered several important distinctions. Robbery commitments were most likely to recidivate during months seven and eight, and being an African American male robbery commitment without post-release supervision significantly increased recidivism risk. Sexual offenders, on the other hand, maintained a more nuanced recidivism risk peak, with delinquent history, substance abuse, race, and institutional misconduct measures significantly increasing their recidivism risk. Roughly 60 percent of homicide offenders recidivated within the five-year follow-up period. African American male offenders with institutional histories of ward assaults, and shorter incarceration periods made up the high-risk homicide offender group. In contrast to the correctional treatment programs for the other offense groups, the Capital Offender Program significantly reduced recidivism risk for homicide offenders after controlling for general correctional treatment.

THE EYES OF TEXAS

Upon release from TYC, sentenced offenders given another shot in the community face the difficult burden of second chances. As scholars have suggested, overcoming the social consequences of incarceration for serious crimes, even for juvenile offenders, can be daunting on many levels.[42] Perhaps even some offenders with the best intentions while incarcerated succumbed to committing further offenses once they returned home. For others, something about their experiences or their personal industry provided the necessary motivation to change their criminal trajectory in the transition to adulthood—at least for the time under study.

Collectively, Texas's sentenced offenders traveled the path of either redemption or criminal persistence. Within both trajectories, however, there were more nuanced courses. For example, while correctional programming was associated with reduced recidivism for homicide commitments and post-release supervision was associated with reduced recidivism risk for robbery commitments, sexual offense commitments maintained the lowest recidivism risk regardless of correctional treatment or post-release supervision.

Although our analyses identified factors associated with recidivism timing, our findings are not absolute. Instead of predicting individual pathways, the findings instead estimate the risk of a recidivism event given the failure rate over time. In other words, our analyses speak to the probability of a recidivism event given the statistical likelihood of failure for subjects with similar characteristics. While Edward McCoy was slated for discharge from adult parole during the writing of this book, we are unable to speak to his release from TYC or his progress to this point.

With that noted, our recidivism analyses suggest a few relationships. Statistically, McCoy's demographic characteristics (African American and male) suggest a high risk for recidivism, while his institutional behavior and treatment programming decrease his recidivism hazard. Ultimately, however, we can only estimate the probability of his successful reentry into the community. Whether the court's determination that McCoy's institutional progress made him redeemable comes to reality is yet unanswered on the streets of Texas where he roams. That noted, the eyes of Texas are upon him and the other sentenced offenders who escaped Texas prison time as released sentenced offenders.

CHAPTER 7

THREE DECADES LATER

ALMOST THREE DECADES AGO, on September 1, 1987, Texas's Determinate Sentencing Act (DSA) took effect. Since that time, nearly 3,500 serious and violent delinquents have been prosecuted and adjudicated under determinate sentencing, and then institutionalized as sentenced offenders in the Texas Youth Commission (TYC).[1] Following state institutionalization, some sentenced offenders were released directly from TYC back into Texas's cities and towns and neighborhoods. Although no longer institutionalized, many of the releases faced further supervision in the community on parole, but they were "free" nonetheless. Some sentenced offenders were not released at all, but were instead transferred to the Texas prison system and its population of adult inmates.

Texas was one of the first states in the nation to initiate a juvenile justice process that recognized the shortcomings of both regular juvenile court processing and adult court certification for certain serious and violent juvenile offenders. Known as determinate sentencing in Texas and more broadly as blended sentencing across the nation, this approach included a focus on rehabilitation that recognized the immaturity, malleability, and redemptive potential of youth—even for serious and violent offenders situated on the lowest rungs of the life chance ladder. At the same time, the Texas approach featured a fail-safe measure if rehabilitation was shunned or otherwise failed to take: placement of the serious juvenile offender in the Texas prison system to serve the balance of the original determinate sentence. Looking back, determinate sentencing was structured to provide the best of what the regular juvenile justice system and the adult justice system had to offer—it was an in-between processing and sanctioning scheme with more bite than the regular juvenile court and less determinism

Youth housing building, Mountain View State School for Boys, ca. 1975. Courtesy of the Texas Department of Criminal Justice.

than the adult court and its associated punishments. It was meant to be flexible enough for *both* rehabilitation and punishment.

Roughly thirty years after the first sentenced offenders arrived in Brownwood, Texas, for TYC intake, this book represents the first long-term empirical study of determinate sentencing in Texas and the outcomes of the sentenced offenders. We were afforded a unique opportunity to look back in time and assess sentenced offenders as they began the transition from adolescence to young adulthood by way of their determinate sentence. In doing so, we were able to bring empirical data to bear on the behavioral experiences of the sentenced offenders as they navigated the dorms and hallways and programs of TYC institutions. For those sentenced offenders who were spared Texas prison system transfer, we were able to examine their recidivism outcomes as they exited TYC facilities. In short, this book examined the backgrounds, institutionalization experiences, and recidivism outcomes of sentenced offenders over roughly thirty years as they transitioned from freedom to incarceration and from incarceration to freedom as the most serious and violent juvenile offenders in the state.[2]

SUMMARY OF MAIN FINDINGS

This book has focused on three major analytical areas. After an examination of the Determinate Sentencing Act in Texas and the basic descriptive statistics of the sentenced offender cohort presented in chapter 3, chapters 4–6 provided the analytical foundation. The first major analytical area was an examination of the institutional behavior of the cohort of sentenced offenders as they navigated their time in TYC, before their determination hearing. These analyses were presented in chapter 4, with the major findings as follows. Most forms of institutional misconduct among sentenced offenders pertained to basic violations of the rules and regulations of the facility. However, sentenced offenders were involved in an average of thirty-eight acts of institutional misconduct during their confinement, and some violations, such as assaults on other wards and being considered a danger to others, were among four of the top ten forms of misconduct engaged in by sentenced offenders. These acts, particularly assaultive behaviors, would certainly have been considered continued delinquent violations outside of TYC facilities. Thus, some sentenced offenders continued their violent and generally problematic ways even during their last chance to demonstrate change and redemption, and most still could not follow the most basic of rules.

Beyond the incidence and prevalence of misconduct perpetrated by sentenced offenders, further analyses in chapter 4 examined factors such as youth demographics and delinquent history indicators that would help explain why a sentenced offender became involved in misconduct while confined. Overall, the factors most consistently associated with the frequency of participation in misconduct while in TYC included: being of African American race, being of a younger age at TYC commitment, experiencing a greater number of out-of-home placements, being non-gang related, having a history of sexual deviance, demonstrating self-destructive behaviors (danger to self), having lower educational grade attainment at TYC commitment, being considered mentally ill, being raised in a chaotic home environment, having a shorter TYC sentence, and, intuitively, spending a longer period of time in TYC. Some of the same factors were associated with the analyses that examined whether offenders participated in misconduct during TYC incarceration. The analyses provide general context to the theme that sentenced offender involvement in institutional misconduct depends on a number of different factors, including person-centered risk factors (e.g., mental illness), delinquent history factors (e.g., number of out-of-home placements or age at TYC commitment), and others. The bottom line is that most sentenced offenders were involved in misconduct while confined, but some were involved in much more than others.

Youths committed to TYC as sentenced offenders for assault, arson, aggravated sexual assault, and aggravated assault tended to be the most active in institutional misconduct. Although all youths were considered serious and violent at their commitment, some offender types were clearly more engaged in misconduct than others. At the end of the day, a small group of sentenced offenders avoided any official misconduct sanctions while in TYC. Others engaged in only nominal acts of noncompliance. Still yet, there was a smaller but extremely active group of sentenced offenders who engaged in frequent and generally serious forms of misconduct during their second-chance incarceration. As found in chapter 5, it is likely that these offenders were those for whom Texas prison transfer figured prominently following their determination hearing.

Following an examination of the institutional behavior of sentenced offenders, chapter 5 examined the outcomes of the determination hearing—a hearing that most sentenced offenders will face and that determines their future trajectory. In chapter 5, it was noted that sentenced offenders faced one of three general options following a period of incarceration in TYC: release to the community without supervision, release to the community with supervision, or Texas prison transfer to serve the remainder of the initial determinate sentence.

Of those TYC offenders who faced a determination hearing from 1987 until the end of 2011, 20 percent were released from TYC without supervision requirements, 47 percent were released from TYC with supervision requirements, and 33 percent were transferred to the Texas prison system. The main analyses in chapter 5 sought to determine the factors associated with the three main determination hearing outcomes.

Using advanced statistical analyses, the main findings of chapter 5 can be summarized as follows. First, most sentenced offenders were released from TYC to the streets instead of facing Texas prison transfer. Indeed, 67 percent of all offenders examined in chapter 5 were not transferred to the Texas prison system. Despite their release, however, most faced further supervision in the community, typically on adult parole. Second, the factors most associated with being released (with or without supervision) instead of being transferred to prison included: being of a race other than African American, serving a longer time in

TYC, and participating in specialized mental health treatment or TYC's Capital Offender Program. In contrast, the factors most predictive of prison transfer included having a longer determinate sentence, being older at TYC commitment, and engaging in a higher count of institutional violations, specifically in assaults on other wards during TYC confinement. While other factors were related to the odds of prison transfer depending on the form of community release, the aforementioned factors were the strongest and/or most consistent predictors of prison transfer.

On a last issue regarding the major findings of chapter 5, it was noted that the determinate sentencing process itself, and particularly the outcomes of the determination hearing determining release versus prison transfer, are highly individualized and must filter through numerous actors involved in the juvenile and criminal justice systems. While our analyses demonstrated factors significantly related to the determination hearing decisions, perhaps the bottom line is that these decisions depend on each specific offender and the specific circumstances of each determinate sentencing case. There are nevertheless a number of variables that are clearly relevant in determination hearing decisions that we simply did not have access to in an effort to gauge their influence. These factors, such as victim input at the hearing, judicial philosophy, and others, could not be accounted for in the analysis but are certain to be influential in the determination of whether a sentenced offender is determined to be a lost cause or a hopeful soul.

Finally, chapter 6 presented analyses examining the recidivism outcomes of sentenced offenders who were ultimately released from TYC to the streets, instead of being transferred to the Texas prison system. Results of the analyses in this chapter can be summarized by the following: 62 percent of offenders released to the streets were rearrested and, in general, offenders were at the greatest risk of rearrest between four and twelve months after their release.

More specifically, though, the results of the analyses identified several significant correlates of recidivism timing. For example, African American race was significantly correlated with recidivism across all statistical models, and being male correlated significantly with recidivism only within the robbery offender group. After controlling for these characteristics, it was found that originating from a chaotic home environment, being a habitual offender (previous failed community supervision and placed outside the home), having a history of substance abuse, and engaging in institutional misconduct increased recidivism risks for the full sample of serious and violent offenders. Conversely, those offenders placed on post-release community supervision had significantly lower recidivism risks compared to offenders released without supervision, and offenders sentenced for a sexual offense were at significantly lower recidivism risk than other offenders.

There were several important distinctions across offenders grouped by offense category. Robbery offenders with post-release community supervision, for example, fared significantly better than robbery offenders released without community supervision. However, the protective nature of post-release community supervision disappeared for offenders committed for sexual or homicide offenses. Although offenders committed for a sexual offense were less likely to recidivate than other offenders, those sexual offenders—and, interestingly, homicide offenders—with substance abuse histories, prior residential placement, and a record of institutional violence toward their peers had an elevated recidivism risk level.

While offenders sentenced under Texas's DSA for a homicide offense approximated the same associations as those offenders sentenced for a sexual offense, only homicide offenders demonstrated a clear benefit of correctional treatment. Homicide offenders participating in TYC's Capital Offender Program were less likely to experience recidivism than homicide offenders not participating in the program. The Capital Offender Program was the only correctional treatment program to reduce recidivism risk among these offenders.

Collectively, chapter 6 brings to bear a clearer understanding of DSA offenders released to the community instead of transferred to the Texas prison system. Of particular interest in this context are the failures of second chances. Even those identified through a court's review were more likely to recidivate (roughly 60 percent failed within five years after release) than to succeed. Within this context, however, there are more specific details, such as the public safety benefit of post-release supervision for robbery offenders, on the determinants of recidivism. While offense category influenced recidivism outcomes, extensive delinquent and institutional misconduct histories preceded recidivism for many of Texas's DSA offenders. Chapter 6 offered a glimmer of hope, however, in that the Capital Offender Program decreased recidivism risk for offenders sentenced for a homicide offense. Ultimately, the odds were against these offenders once they were back on the streets, and certain measureable factors increased their risk to public safety in the community.

LIMITATIONS

Before considering the implications of this study, there are limitations that need to be discussed relative to the major findings and themes of this book. While we were able to procure a rich data source from TYC, the official data that constituted the foundation for the analyses in this book were lacking in some respects. While the general benefits and disadvantages to official data have been thoroughly discussed elsewhere and will not be repeated here, it is still the case that the official data limited our ability to answer some questions or provide extended detail in the questions that were assessed. For example, when scrutinizing the institutional behavior of sentenced offenders, we were not able to account for relevant considerations such as official or unofficial changes in documenting youth incidents. Nor were we able to know whether processes for discovering and documenting misconduct incidents occurred differently at different TYC institutions, or across different officers and time frames. For example, it was unknown whether staff at different correctional institutions or at different time periods employed different procedures and criteria to resolve similar youth incidents. Whether these variations happened is unknown, but they could have impacted the analyses by potentially over- or underestimating the true prevalence of incidents within and between youth institutions.

In examining the determination decision as to whether a youth was released from TYC (with or without community supervision) or transferred to the Texas prison system, this study would have again benefited from more detailed data, such as more specific indicators of behavioral and treatment progress in TYC that are known to be broadly influential in the release or transfer decision. While the measures we had access to are close proxies for behavior (e.g., misconduct participation) or treatment participation (e.g., participation in chemical dependency treatment), more finely tuned measures as to actual progress while confined, time in all treatment programs, and other relevant concerns would have provided more specificity to the analyses.

Furthermore, the analyses regarding the release or transfer decision would have benefited from additional variables that are not collected by TYC or organized in another systematic form. For example, data on the characteristics of judges (e.g., experience), prosecutors, specific circumstances of the crime incident, victim characteristics, and other variables would have provided valuable insight. Indeed, the determination hearing in Texas is a highly individualized, discretionary, and largely subjective stage in which a plethora of information is considered *specific* to each individual case.[3] More information on those specific and individualized case-relevant factors would have provided more insight into how release or transfer decisions are made.[4]

Another limitation to our analyses of the determination hearing decision is that we did not have access to information on the Texas prison transfers. In sum, we do not know how long they stayed in the Texas prison system, if they have since gotten out, or what those who did get out have done since release in terms of rearrest, reconviction, or reimprisonment. Indeed, many of the prison transfers may still be in a Texas prison unit, biding their time until their determinate sentence runs out. Some may have been released and reincarcerated, or at the least rearrested. Some may have gone on to lead productive and crime-free lives, avoiding further contact with the justice system. We do not know what happened to them, but information on this group of youths turned adults would have provided substantial perspective on what happened to the lost causes and whether prison transfer may have helped or aggravated their life trajectories.

Relevant to the analysis of recidivism outcomes, this study would have benefited from having access to the specific individual offenses that sentenced offenders were rearrested for upon their release. While we had access to data on some of these offenses, more than half of these recidivism offenses were missing from official data, which prevented any detailed analysis specific to rearrest offenses. While we had knowledge of whether an offender was rearrested, whether the rearrest offense was a felony or misdemeanor, the level of the felony or misdemeanor, and the frequency of rearrest charges, the lack of some other types of information limited our understanding of recidivism. For example, we were not able to provide a systematic sense of offense seriousness escalation or deescalation from each sentenced offender's original commitment offense to TYC—a factor that would have improved the assessment of recidivism from before to after commitment.

The recidivism analyses would have also benefited from information about post-release incarceration. In short, we did not have data on whether released sentenced offenders were reincarcerated following their exit from TYC. Although we know if a youth was arrested postrelease and the general seriousness of the arrest, we do not know if sentenced offenders spent time incarcerated following their rearrest, at either local, state, or federal facilities. This limitation could have resulted in underestimating the true level of recidivism behavior of the released sentenced offenders. This limitation is typical in recidivism studies, but if remedied, it would have improved this study. The study of recidivism would have also been improved by information about the Texas prison transfers and the recidivism outcomes of those released. If nothing else, this information would have provided a more detailed picture of the long-term progress of sentenced offenders upon their exit from the adult side of imprisonment.

More generally, it would have been beneficial to have insight into prosecutorial decision making regarding whether to pursue a determinate sentencing prosecution rather than regular juvenile court processing or adult court waiver proceedings. For example, comparing the sentenced offenders of this study to similarly situated youths who were instead certified to adult court and sanctioned in that arena would have allowed us to address areas such as the similarity or differences between certified and determinately sentenced youths, sentence length differences, time served differences, and the recidivism outcomes among these separate groups. The addition of such comparison groups would have allowed us to examine, even if only broadly, the impact of blended sentencing versus adult court waiver decisions in terms of a variety of indicators such as institutional adjustment and recidivism.

Nevertheless, this book constitutes the first long-term empirical study to examine the institutional behavior, determination decisions, and recidivism outcomes of one of the largest and most serious and violent youthful offender cohorts in the nation. Blended sentencing schemes like determinate sentencing in Texas have become a prominent feature of juvenile justice systems across the country as an alternative to adult court certification. Despite their growing popularity as a processing and sanctioning vehicle for serious and violent juvenile offenders, the research on blended sentencing schemes (and the offenders subject to blended sentencing) is still in its infancy.

We were able to examine the backgrounds, sentencing, processing, institutionalization, and recidivism outcomes across a cohort of more than three thousand serious and violent juvenile offenders over nearly three decades. While we are not able to answer all relevant questions concerning blended sentencing, in Texas or elsewhere, we believe this study presents a significant step toward understanding whether this important change to the structure and function of juvenile justice is beneficial to decision makers who are still debating the age-old question of what to do with youthful offenders who are a poor fit for both the traditional juvenile justice process and the adult justice system.

LOOKING FORWARD: POLICY IMPLICATIONS

On the one hand, policy makers struggle with the serious and violent delinquent because of widespread belief and optimism that juveniles can change and redeem themselves. These hopes are driven in part by evidence that juveniles cannot fully appreciate the wrongfulness of their conduct, have not fully matured, and are not set in their ways like older adult offenders. These perspectives also rest on the fundamental belief that with proper support, treatment, care, and a second or third chance, a youth who has barely experienced life can be rehabilitated rather than staying in prison. Making matters more complex is that many juvenile offenders, especially serious and violent offenders like those considered in this study, arrive at the juvenile justice system with extensive baggage that is not always of their making: poverty-stricken environments, criminalized neighborhoods, histories of extreme abuse and neglect, educational deficits, delinquent siblings, and criminal parents, to name only a few hardships.

On the other hand, it is hard to reconcile the acts committed by the youthful offenders focused on in this study, acts that surely shock the conscience when committed by adults, but are even more shocking when committed by juveniles at the age of thirteen, fourteen, fifteen, or younger. These are the acts, especially the vicious predatory attacks against other people, that make talk about second chances and redemption and change difficult to stomach, even for the most fervent champions of rehabilitation and, ultimately, redemption.

In determining what to do with serious and violent youthful offenders, the growing trend over the last several years in Texas and other states has been to give such offenders one more opportunity to avoid what many believe is the path of lost causes—certification to the adult justice system and its associated adult punishments, including imprisonment in adult institutions. But the emergence of this trend in the form of blended sentencing has not meant that adult court certification and related adult processing options for youthful offenders have disappeared or will in the near future. Certifications still occur in Texas on a regular basis, although they did decline precipitously following the advent of determinate sentencing in 1987. Even so, blended sentencing, however structured, is for many states a last-ditch effort to fix a youthful offender before he or she enters onto a path and a process where life failure is almost a given.

In this story, we found that some youths entered TYC, worked their programs, avoided major institutional infractions, and avoided trouble when given a second chance by being released back into society. Others did not capitalize on their second chance. Some of these failures were identified during their TYC confinement and were transferred to the Texas prison system to contain their risk. Some exited TYC and were re-arrested, and likely found their way to the Texas prison system through the back door. The story told here was one of both successes and failures.

With all of the findings contained within this book, what conclusions can be made? How can the findings contribute to improving juvenile justice and addressing the issue of what to do with serious and violent young offenders? With these broad questions in mind, one of this study's policy implications is that states and local jurisdictions which choose blended sentencing or equivalent options that give serious and violent youthful offenders another chance must continually refine their efforts to identify those who demonstrate the best chance for success and those who are the most likely to be failures. Granted, this is a tall order, since our abilities to predict human behavior are woefully inadequate. There is no crystal ball. In this study, nearly 70 percent of all sentenced offenders were released back to the streets instead of being transferred to the Texas prison system. Many of these releases engaged in tremendous amounts of misconduct while confined, yet were still released. And their release occurred on average just three years after TYC placement. Of those released (and hence determined to be good risks), roughly 60 percent were rearrested at least once, and many of them were rearrested for at least one new felony-level offense. While we did not have specific information as to rearrest offenses and therefore could not assess escalation or deescalation in criminal behavior from TYC commitment to release, the bottom line is that more than half of the best risks recidivated, often for another felony offense. We are not judging whether this rate of failure is good or bad, but we are stating that making a sustained effort to improve the classification and identification of the best risks for release seems a useful practical implication of these findings.

Very little specific information is available in Texas as to how release or transfer decisions are made. While we have no doubt that the decision-makers in Texas, including judges and state juvenile correctional authorities, take this decision seriously, the specific factors that determine whether one homicide offender gets released while another gets transferred into the Texas prison system are still unclear on a day-to-day, case-by-case basis. It is still unclear what factors carry the most weight in release or transfer decisions. Are factors early on in life more important than institutional behavior? Does the seriousness of the commitment offense trump TYC progress? Is there a systematic way to assess risk, or are the release and transfer decisions largely made based on gut feelings and other subjective indicators, supplemented with objective facts? While we were able to examine some of these release-centered issues in chapter 5, we realize release or transfer decisions are highly individualized to a specific youthful offender and his or her own unique individual and case-specific circumstances (e.g., background, delinquent, familial, the specific crime incident, institutional progress, institutional behavior, juvenile court actors, media attention, public outcry) and sometimes defy neat and clear answers even with the rich data source we had.[5] However, more attention to this issue seems a worthy policy implication since the consequences of these decisions are potentially very lofty.

There are those who would put a substantial amount of blame on juvenile justice systems and juvenile correctional authorities for youth recidivism or misconduct or other negative behaviors. We believe this type of criticism is unfair. For years, scholars and others have placed the lion's share of failure on the backs of these entities. To be sure, they tend to receive the credit during times of success. The reality, however, is that juvenile correctional systems are being tasked with changing a lifetime of behavior and thought processes among the most serious and violent and disorganized youths society has to offer. They are asked to make such monumental changes in the course of perhaps two or three years, in an often inconducive environment, and to make sure the changes last a lifetime. This is unrealistic. Simply being sent to a juvenile correctional facility should not lead to the automatic presumption of effective treatment and programming, and hence of rehabilitation.

Some youths will change, and it will be due to the influence and experience they gleaned while confined. Some will change, and their correctional confinement may have little or nothing to do with their transformation. Some will not change, regardless of their circumstances.[6] This is the reality, and the implication is that scholars and researchers and practitioners and policy makers would be best served by recognizing the limits of the correctional sanction. Once it is realized that juvenile justice and juvenile corrections cannot be everything to everyone, useful time and focus can be spent on improving programs and processes associated with determinate sentencing to give those with the most hope the best chance for success.

THREE DECADES LATER 147

Beyond these more study-specific policy implications, there is the usual list of suspects: pondering whether such blended schemes should continue in the future, or whether we should just send all the serious and violent juvenile offenders to an adult prison and be done with it, or whether the juvenile court should be abolished altogether. Another issue is that of the "success" of determinate sentencing. To a large degree, we avoided labeling determinate sentencing as successful or not successful. In our view, such labels are far too ambitious because of the many moving parts associated with determinate sentencing, from the initial charging decisions of the prosecutor to the determination hearing, plus all the decision points in between.[7]

Another run-of-the mill implied question is whether the get-tough atmosphere characteristic of juvenile justice over the last several decades should become more rehabilitative, or perhaps whether it is tough enough. Perhaps another implication is that more effort should be placed on prevention, with the hope that somehow serious and violent youthful offenders will then cease to exist. Still another policy implication stemming from this line of thinking could be to focus more on families and neighborhoods, drugs and gangs, religion and education, and so on. To be sure, more prevention programs, more intervention programs to curtail the influence of drugs and gangs, more education, more focus on family building, more discussion as to the nature of juvenile justice, and other such initiatives are generally beneficial. But at the end of the day, these things have been done and will continue to be part of future efforts to address youth violence, yet we will still have serious and violent juvenile offenders, and we will still be asking what to do about them. And if the goal is to find solutions other than simply locking them up for decades, then such questions need to be continually asked and evaluated.

We believe that at least in regard to Texas and determinate sentencing, the major policy focus should be on finding better ways of identifying the best risks and minimizing the damage (or potential damage) from the worst risks. Since determinate sentencing appears to be here to stay, we believe this is the ultimate policy implication. To some degree, this starts with a better understanding of the targets of blended sentencing. Future research could focus on the case study method or other more qualitative methodologies to more broadly understand decision making relevant to determinate sentencing at both the prosecutorial stage and the stage where release or transfer is decided. Researchers could also employ survey methodologies and focus on prosecutors to more accurately determine what factors go into the decision to pursue determinate sentencing rather than regular juvenile justice processing or adult court certification. As it stands, there is just very little information on the factors that matter in these decisions, and hence there is insufficient understanding of why two similarly situated youths may receive entirely different outcomes. Further, the judges and correctional officials who make the decisions regarding release or transfer could also be surveyed and studied to better understand the factors that drive their decision making on the back end of blended sentencing.

In a related vein, researchers and practitioners could pool resources and explore the application of existing risk assessment inventories, or the development of new ones, in the release or transfer decisions of sentenced offenders, and to gauge whether such instruments emerge as valid and reliable. Perhaps one of the greatest shortcomings of determinate sentencing is that it has left unresolved questions such as who becomes the target of determinate sentencing and why, and who gets released versus transferred. These are important considerations in understanding blended sentencing and assessing whether everything that can be done is being done to provide serious and violent juvenile offenders a chance at redemption while at the same time protecting the citizens of the great state of Texas.

CONCLUSION

This book began with a simple question: What happened when determinately sentenced offenders—a group responsible for some of the most serious and violent crimes in Texas—were temporarily spared adult justice and given one more chance at redemption? In the process of answering this question, we have provided a window into the lives of Texas's sentenced offenders as they navigated their way through the Texas juvenile justice system, specifically TYC, on their way to eventual release back to the community.

We have answered the initial question that spurred this book. But beyond all of the statistics presented, at the end of the day there must be recognition that society will continually be confronted with serious and violent juvenile offenders. They are not going away. This book, then, is only one effort to examine a unique attempt to deal with such offenders, and how that experience has turned out for one state and the 3,382 sentenced offenders studied within these pages. We have found that some sentenced offenders made their way back to the straight and narrow path—but that many others still held tight to the path of lost causes as they entered young adulthood. In these pages, we have tried to examine the factors behind those two different trajectories. Chapter 8 concludes our exploration with final thoughts and insights on this broad finding.

THE LAST WORD

ON MANY LEVELS, it is difficult to write a book with coauthors. Different writing styles, experiences, insights, and so on sometimes make "getting on the same page" hard to do. But these differences can also be benefits. The authors of this book have many combined years of experience in juvenile and criminal justice systems as juvenile correctional officers, juvenile probation officers, juvenile parole officers, and jailers. We also have years of experience as professors and researchers and students examining juvenile justice–related topics such as the determinants of youth delinquency, juvenile law, juvenile justice system decision making, institutional violence and misconduct, and juvenile offender recidivism.

Because of our diverse practical, academic, and research experiences, we believed a unique feature of this book would be the opportunity for each author to give his or her own thoughts, opinions, and perspectives as they relate to determinate sentencing in Texas, the sentenced offenders, and the findings of this book. These insights are presented next, with the goal that the reader can make up his or her own mind about them.

THE CONSEQUENCES OF HOPE: CHAD R. TRULSON

It was July 2013, just over twenty years to the day that Elizabeth Pena and Jennifer Ertman were savagely raped and murdered near T. C. Jester Park in northwest Houston. I was with my wife and daughter, driving back to north Texas from Galveston after a camping trip on the Gulf of Mexico beaches. Heading north on I-45 en route to US Highway 290 West (which incidentally leads directly to TYC's Giddings State School, where many of the sentenced offenders are sent and where the Capital

School building, Gatesville State School for Boys, ca. 1975. Courtesy of the Texas Department of Criminal Justice.

and Serious Violent Offender Program is based), I happened to look up and by chance notice the exit to T. C. Jester Boulevard, which runs right along White Oak Bayou and directly to T. C. Jester Park. When I saw the exit sign, I could not help but think about my wife and young daughter, and what I know I would do if they ever had to face the horror that Elizabeth and Jennifer endured that night in June 1993, who like us were just traveling home.

Emotionally, it is hard for me to reconcile that a large portion of the most serious and violent juvenile offenders in Texas faced just two to three years of incarceration for their acts before being released directly to the streets and neighborhoods of Texas's cities. Indeed, roughly 70 percent of all sentenced offenders from 1987–2011 who had a determination hearing were released from secure TYC facilities and avoided transfer to the Texas prison system. And this group of TYC direct releases included roughly four hundred aggravated sexual assault commitments (65 percent of all such offenders who had a determination hearing were released instead of transferred to the Texas prison system), nearly two hundred murder commitments (52 percent of all murder commitments who had a determination hearing were released), and almost one hundred capital murder commitments (45 percent of all capital murderers with a determination hearing were released), among other serious and violent offenders. As we now know, more than half of all those released reoffended, often for another felony offense, and therefore continued to be a drain on our society. These were the youths determined to be the best risks for TYC release instead of Texas prison transfer, and their success rate is no better than a coin flip. This is not good enough. The consequences are too high.

I also think about the victims of these offenders. No one really wants to talk about the victims. Sure, judges and prosecutors and journalists do, but outside of the courtroom we hear little about the victims, save for a newspaper article here and there. It is easy to forget the horrors they faced when their stories are moved to the back burner. Instead, the bulk of attention seems to always be on the youthful offender with a poor life history—bad parents, a poverty-stricken home, authority issues, substance abuse issues, poor school performance, and so on. We are reminded about their poor lot in life every time a decision must be made concerning their future. The hand-wringing has no end. This type of hyper-attention and hyper-sympathy for the offenders instead of the victims is hard for me to reconcile when it comes to such destructive offenders. These are the sob stories that make normal people feel somehow guilty for being outraged, that somehow elevate offenders over victims and afford offenders wide leniency never enjoyed by their victims. To me it is absurd.

I believe there are juvenile delinquents who are too dangerous and too far gone to risk giving them another chance. Despite our good natures and our efforts to try to save even the hardest cases, I cannot help but think that maybe more emphasis should be placed on saving future generations of victims who will more likely than not face these offenders on the streets of Texas. Some will argue that is what determinate sentencing is trying to do—save future generations by treating and rehabilitating these offenders before they become entrenched career criminals. I get the argument. But after looking at the facts in this book (and the mounting evidence of high failure rates for other similarly situated serious and violent juvenile offenders), I am not sure I buy it when the chances of change are no better than a coin flip. Some offenses are just too destructive to receive any benefit of the doubt, and certainly not after just two or three years. Sometimes sacrifices have to be made. Why do law-abiding individuals always have the burden of sacrifice?

Related to the last point and the notion of sacrifice, it should be noted that the 3,382 sentenced offenders studied in this book are really just a drop in the bucket compared to the thousands and thousands of other delinquents in Texas juvenile courts each year who are less risky and have much more potential to desist from further delinquency. While all of the 3,382 may or may not be lost causes (we know some released sentenced offenders were not officially rearrested during the recidivism follow-up period), on an emotional level, one must question whether they are even worth the effort and risk. I realize it is difficult to talk about sentenced offenders as if they were all equal in seriousness and depravity and so on. They are not. Equality in this sense is a fleeting concept. But in a broader context, the riskiest offenders are just a drop in the bucket. Why chance it?

Further, it is worth repeating that almost all of the sentenced offenders had been in contact with the juvenile justice system before the offenses that led to their determinate sentence. Looking back, we should have seen the results of this book coming. Almost all of the offenders had accumulated long and sordid juvenile justice histories before their determinate sentence commitment to TYC. For most, the determinate sentence was not a second chance, but a third or fourth chance. And despite the appearance that some made substantial progress while at TYC, it is a reality that there is a deep canyon between the institutional world and the real world. The results of this book generally back up that fact. If serious and violent offenders are to be released instead of transferred to the adult prison system, I just think more should be demanded of them first.

Beyond emotion, the second way I view determinate sentencing and the sentenced offenders is on a more rational level, as a professor and researcher and onetime practitioner. Well before I was a professor, I walked the halls and dorms of juvenile facilities and interacted with these types of offenders on a daily basis. I liked the kids. Even the most serious and violent of them had redeeming qualities. Later on as a juvenile parole officer, I witnessed firsthand the transition of these youthful offenders back into society. Even for the most problematic offenders from the worst backgrounds, in almost all cases I saw caring and concerned parents and grandparents and other custodians willing to do whatever it took to help the paroled delinquents. The reentry circumstances for most of the offenders were not as deplorable as many would paint the picture. Even so, few of the offenders I remember demonstrated a whole lot of motivation and investment toward change. Most still possessed a fatalistic "oh well" attitude about most things.

My overall sense when working with these offenders was that none of them really wanted to go back to confinement, but few were overly bothered by the prospect. As a professor and researcher, I have also had the opportunity to study juvenile offenders for more than a decade, particularly their institutional behavior patterns and their recidivism outcomes following state juvenile incarceration. I am no rube when it comes to juvenile offenders.

On a rational level, I am a broad proponent of determinate sentencing in Texas. I believe juveniles, even those who are serious and violent offenders, are generally more malleable than adults and have greater capacity to change—whether through personal industry, juvenile system intervention, or both. I have seen successes across the whole spectrum of youthful offenders, but mostly I have witnessed failures. I still broadly believe change can happen for youthful offenders. Yet just because change can happen does not mean it will. Change is hard to find in the pages of this book among the sentenced offenders. Oftentimes, the lost causes choose to be lost.

I also believe juvenile offenders, like the sentenced offenders studied in this book, are not fully rational actors and deserve some latitude because of their young age and less-than-perfect backgrounds. Research has generally established this lower level of rationality and maturity, and this is why juveniles are no longer subject to the punishment of death or mandatory life without parole sentences. While they may deserve some latitude, they do not deserve full latitude. That is why blended sentencing is attractive to me—because of the potential option for adult imprisonment if the front-end rehabilitative option at TYC fails. That said, one must be willing to use the punishment option and, more importantly, be adept at picking those who have the most promise from those who don't. I think we are falling behind on these aspects of determinate sentencing in Texas. Most sentenced offenders do not transfer to Texas prisons, most still skirt rules and are involved in violations while institutionalized, most reoffend once back out on the streets, and most of those reoffend for felonies. I do not believe this was the change that was envisioned. Again, more needs to be demanded of such offenders.

I also believe that determinate sentencing provides a better fit for certain juvenile offenders than does solely traditional juvenile court processing or the other end of the spectrum in adult court certification. The sentenced offenders of this study were simply not appropriate for traditional juvenile court. Traditional juvenile courts were not meant for killers and rapists; they were meant for truants and vandals, among other relatively nonserious delinquents. And if the hope is to fix or somehow rehabilitate a juvenile, a direct adult prison stint by way of adult court certification offers perhaps the least hope for that type of change. It is not that adult imprisonment cannot benefit a onetime juvenile offender or that the "bad" prison has nothing to offer but a life of crime. I am simply saying that the chance of change after adult prison time (compared to juvenile time) is lower for a variety of reasons. But again, if determinate sentencing is going to be used, we must improve upon our ability to identify the best and worst risks after the initial period of TYC confinement, because for some, exercising the adult prison option may be the best option we have to contain risk.

Also on a rational level, I believe that two to three years of juvenile incarceration is too short a time for such serious and violent offenders. I believe it is too short from a justice perspective, considering the crimes committed. Indeed, analyses in this book showed that very few sentenced offenders received the maximum allowable sentence for their crime. Even if they did, there are mechanisms in place to shorten that time (e.g., minimum lengths of stay). More importantly, I believe two to three years is too short from the perspective of expecting successful outcomes. On average, TYC-released sentenced offenders are around nineteen years old when they reenter society. This is an extremely high-risk age for such offenders. At release, they are still very young and still very far behind on the life chance ladder. They are immature and emotionally stupid. They lack empathy. They still largely cling to an institutional mentality that centers on selfishness and blame and, ironically, have adopted a fully formed victim attitude—in the old TYC they used to call these "thinking errors." In Texas, most of the emphasis on the sentenced offenders is during their incarceration, but less emphasis is placed on their transition back into mainstream society. It requires no wizardry or sophisticated statistical analyses to know that placing an offender back into the same circumstances (e.g., peer influences, lack of employment) from which he or she came is a recipe for more failures than successes, especially if nothing has really changed. Much more emphasis needs to be placed on this reentry transition if success is reasonably sought for sentenced offenders who spent only a few years under juvenile confinement for extremely serious and violent crimes. I go back to the old juvenile facility adage I learned long ago from people smarter than me: if nothing changes, nothing changes.

Lastly, when deciding whether determinate sentencing in Texas is "good" or "bad" or "useful" or "not useful," a variety of considerations must be taken into account. Certainly the institutional behavior and recidivism outcomes of the cohort of sentenced offenders examined in this book are noteworthy and should hold sway in such a determination. The fact that determinate sentencing provides a more flexible vehicle to deal with offenders who are not fit for traditional juvenile court but are somehow inappropriate (e.g., too young) for adult court also must be considered in the context of the utility of determinate sentencing from a system administration perspective.

Beyond those considerations, a final point must be made: under current laws, all determinately sentenced offenders in Texas will be released back into the free society. Some will be released directly from TYC, and they will be in their late teens, like the offenders studied in this book. Others will first be transferred to the Texas prison system, and most of these will get out in their twenties, early thirties, or, for a select few, their forties and fifties. But make no mistake, they are all going to get out.

For the TYC-released sentenced offenders, the results of this study suggest that a good portion of them will reoffend for further felony-level offenses. While we have no crystal ball, there is little in the way of evidence to suggest that most have changed their criminal ways into their twenties. Due to data limitations, we do not know what happened to the Texas prison transfers. But under current laws, all of them will get out too.

At the end of the day, one has to wonder whether two to three years in TYC and release to society for most of the sentenced offenders provides a better chance at change and/or less future victimizations compared to transfer to the Texas prison system, where rehabilitation opportunities are slimmer and the criminal attitude becomes stronger—but where release will occur during much less risky ages. Perhaps there is a middle ground between these options to fully maximize rehabilitation and further reduce risk. Either way, it is an honest question to consider, because again, they are all coming back.

In the foreword to this book, Professor Marquart began with a discussion that children are precious resources and that the job of parents, and sometimes of the state, is to support, invest, refine, and assist them. When our children misbehave, they need our help and efforts at correction. In most of these cases their deviations are minor and short-lived. But the question of what to do and what has been done about those few who engage in serious and continued aberrations constituted a main focus of our exploration into determinate sentencing in Texas.

The rehabilitative impulse among us is strong, especially when involving children. Even for the serious and violent delinquents that were the subjects of this book, we yearn for stories of redemption and seem wired to root for underdogs. As evidenced with determinate sentencing in Texas, second chances are stylish in our society, even for the most destructive offenders. Yet as much as we want to believe that all delinquents are redeemable, failing to appreciate that lost causes do exist seems a hell of a price for the innocent to pay to be stylish.

I end this section with an observation about humanity that is a bitter pill to swallow—a pill that just might be right no matter how much faith we put into the human tinkering trades. As the late James Q. Wilson noted years ago: "Wicked people exist. Nothing avails except to set them apart from innocent people . . . When we 'trifle with the wicked' we make sport of the innocent, and encourage the calculators. Justice suffers, and so do we all."[1]

We need to do a better job at identifying those who deserve second chances and those who do not when it comes to determinate sentencing. For the former group, our standards must be exceptional. For the latter group, all that is left for us to do is to wash our hands of them. The consequences of hope are simply too high to do anything less.

POSTSCRIPT

In 2009, fourteen-year-old Damien Ray Torres of Fort Worth received a thirty-year determinate sentence after shooting sixteen-year-old Zuly Ledesma to death during a gang-related drive-by. Roughly five years later, in August 2014, Torres was released from TYC on parole supervision just prior to turning nineteen years old. On February 22, 2015, Ernesto Rodriguez was shot multiple times outside a Fort Worth club. He died on March 2, 2015. The accused shooter was nineteen-year-old Damien Ray Torres.[2]

EQUALIZING THE JUVENILE PLAYING FIELD: DARIN R. HAERLE

My quest to understand the group of sentenced offenders examined in this book began in the fall of 2007. I was taking a criminal justice policy class during my master's program at the University of North

Texas, listening as Professor Trulson reviewed course material on recent rehabilitative efforts for juvenile offenders. There was one page of our textbook that mentioned the Capital Offender Program that is described in this book (and used as a predictor of recidivism in our analyses). Not even a full page was devoted to this program—it was really just a paragraph or two that touched on the program's existence. I remember holding up the class for a few minutes, raising my hand to get clarification on what exactly we had just read.

I was completely shocked that juvenile offenders who were just a few months or even a few weeks shy of turning seventeen (and thus being considered adults in Texas) could potentially be released thirty-plus years early for a capital crime. Granted, they were released after potentially participating in an intensive therapeutic treatment program and other TYC programming, but also after possibly serving only a few years of their determinate sentences within a juvenile correctional facility. Regardless of the context, this seemed like an extremely soft-on-crime approach, given the gravity of their crimes. It was that much more surprising to me that this long-standing determinate sentencing policy and treatment program existed in Texas, of all places—the state responsible for the largest number of executions in our country. This seemed a shocking setting for a clear and tangible swing of the punitive pendulum back toward the rehabilitative ideal on which the juvenile court was founded.

Like my coauthors, I pursued graduate education in criminology and criminal justice because of prior experience in the field. I worked as a group living counselor for female juvenile offenders in a residential treatment facility in Aurora, Colorado. This position required duties more similar to those of a juvenile correctional officer than to a "counselor," and this nonprofit facility housed offenders from all across the country. We provided long-term rehabilitative care for these youths and provided them with a high school education. Anecdotally—perhaps unlike the experiences of my coauthors—I remember witnessing more successes than failures. This practical experience provided insight into many broken state juvenile justice systems, revealed firsthand that rehabilitation can work, and was the catalyst for me to work toward figuring out what works to rehabilitate (and punish) these youthful offenders.

While we are all trained to be unbiased researchers, many of us entered academia because of such prior experience in the fields of juvenile and criminal justice. To suggest that we each left those biases and experiences behind would be dishonest and may even do a disservice to our work. The important thing, though, is that rather than drive our work with any emotional bias, we drive any advocacy with methodologically sound empirical research. The efficacy of policies like determinate sentencing must be evaluated from many perspectives—a necessity that is emphasized by our diverse viewpoints presented in this concluding chapter. I believe the findings of this book also need to be situated within the contexts of adolescent development, institutionalization, and jurisdictional considerations that allow for maximum exposure to rehabilitative efforts within juvenile correctional facilities.

Research consistently shows that a peak in delinquent and criminal behavior should be expected during mid-adolescence (typically around ages sixteen to seventeen). A huge gap exists between high levels of intellectual maturity and low levels of psychosocial maturity between the ages of sixteen and twenty. As a result, youths are more impulsive and engage in more risk-taking behaviors during this period of time. Adolescents are also poorer (arguably less rational) decision makers than adults, as evidenced by a large gap between high levels of arousal and low levels of self-control during that same period of mid-adolescence.

It is easy for criminologists to focus on the age-crime curve, but in reality the same peak during mid-adolescence exists for other outcomes such as drug use, automobile crashes, accidental drownings, and self-injurious behaviors. When all outcomes are appreciated, the data reveal the larger picture of an age-recklessness curve, of which the age-crime curve is merely one piece.[3] Furthermore, more than 90 percent of juveniles desist from crime by the time they reach their mid-twenties, as they approach the age of twenty-five and exit what has been recently referred to as emerging adulthood. The findings of this book need to appreciate both points in time: the age at which delinquency and criminal behavior peaks, and the age at which most juveniles desist.

While the challenges of adolescence abound, the silver lining is that youths are also more malleable than adults when it comes to treatment and rehabilitation. Even though most youths will age out of crime, the need exists to capitalize on their youthful malleability by exposing even the worst juvenile offenders to evidence-based treatment during their terms of incarceration. Nearly three-fourths of all sentenced offenders in our sample received at least one form of specialized treatment while committed to TYC. Given that most were committed to TYC just before their sixteenth birthdays, during the period of mid-adolescent development, this is the optimal time to capitalize on that youthful malleability. TYC has long-standing specialized treatment programs to target sex offenders, mentally ill offenders, chemically dependent offenders, and capital/violent offenders. Participation in the Capital Offender Program as examined in this book significantly reduced recidivism compared to nonparticipation, suggesting that such intensive therapeutic treatment duration has the potential to redirect the trajectory of even the most violent offenders.[4] Unfortunately, however, the supply of treatment programs is outweighed by the high demand for them among this violent cohort of juvenile offenders.

Determinate sentencing in Texas is appealing because, in theory, it provides a rehabilitative option before imposing the harshest part of the punishment. The key word in that sentence, though, is "option." For youths to capitalize on their potential to rehabilitate, they have to be given the option to participate in treatment programs during juvenile incarceration. Approximately half of the youths in this sample reoffended, but how many of those recidivists were eligible for intensive treatment and did not receive it during their term of commitment to TYC? This is a question that deserves consideration.

Yet even with some seemingly rehabilitated by specialized treatment programs or other help from TYC, roughly half of those youths released still recidivated—many by committing a new felony offense. These serious and violent offenders are released at an average of nineteen years of age, and after two to three years of incarceration. I believe this is an insufficient amount of time for a severely violent youth to be incarcerated—from a public safety/victim standpoint, a cost-benefit standpoint, and a rehabilitative standpoint. Given our five-year follow-up time, recidivism is measured on average from the age of nineteen to twenty-one up to around the age of twenty-four to twenty-six. The possibility remains that a large proportion of these offenders may desist beyond the age of twenty-five, a determination we are unable to make in this book. Chapter 6 does, however, provide support for this trend of aging out by revealing that the greatest risk of recidivism occurred within two years of release, with that same risk declining during the next three years. Rather than necessarily speaking to the failure of juvenile facilities, I think these findings provide further support for developmental research.

A report recently released by the Bureau of Justice Statistics revealed that across thirty states between 2005 and 2010, approximately three-fourths of incarcerated offenders released were rearrested within five years. While roughly 75 percent of the overall sample recidivated, 84 percent of those twenty-four and younger committed a new offense.[5] While a direct comparison cannot be made of our sample to that nationally representative sample, it is worth noting that the TYC recidivism rates are significantly lower. The coin flip of recidivism for the offenders in this book provides less than desirable odds, especially considering the gravity of their offenses. However, a combination of determinate sentencing and rehabilitative efforts within TYC facilities is making some headway in curbing recidivism rates compared to those for other offenders in the same age range released across the nation.

While recidivism is understandably in the forefront of everyone's mind as the most important outcome, the link between misconduct and recidivism needs to be more fully appreciated. Chapter 4 reveals numerous predictors of institutional misconduct, and misconduct is then revealed in chapter 6 to be a robust predictor of recidivism. A stronger empirical bridge needs to be built between these two outcomes, meaning that determinate sentencing needs to be evaluated from the perspective of institutionalization and prisonization, appreciating the impact that these processes have on released offenders.

Incarceration deprives inmates of certain liberties, and such deprivation has been shown to influence a greater degree of prisonization, as evidenced by the adoption of institutional culture.[6] The ideal model to use is a hybridized version that appreciates factors related to both deprivation and importation, or extra-prison factors such as inmate characteristics or external influences. Some of the assumptions related to deprivation theories have been challenged by providing evidence that importation factors such as time must be considered: the closer an inmate is to release, the better that inmate will behave because he or she is leaving the subcultural norms of the prison behind in favor of the anticipated socialization of returning to the community.[7] Determinate sentencing provides a different kind of knowledge for the youths under study in this book: knowledge of possible rather than inevitable transfer. If youths are unsure of what their "release" date really means, what does this mean for institutional theory? If youths with lengthy determinate sentences have concerns that they may be transferred to adult prison at age eighteen or nineteen rather than released to parole supervision, then this may trigger anticipatory *criminalization* rather than socialization.[8] Whether at nineteen from a juvenile facility or possibly over the age of thirty or forty from an adult prison, we must appreciate the fact that release is inevitable for these youths.

Rather than argue for premature release of such violent offenders after a term of two or three years of juvenile incarceration, I am arguing for an extension of juvenile correctional jurisdiction. Research consistently shows that adult court–waived youths are at a significantly higher risk of physical and sexual victimization within adult prisons than are youths who are incarcerated within exclusively juvenile correctional facilities.[9] Waived youths also display higher rates of recidivism than their juvenile court counterparts, no doubt in part due to a higher proportion of time served enduring victimization and criminalization on the adult side.

While providing due process to juveniles within the adult venue of criminal court, waiver often subjects them to adult incarceration that arguably violates other constitutional rights, such as the prohibition of cruel and unusual punishment. Forst, Fagan, and Vivona eloquently support this position by suggesting that "a rather cruel and ironic form of punishment is accorded to waived youth, where retribution for crimes against society occurs through victimization by staff and inmates" [in adult prisons].[10] Taking the extant research into account as well as other evidence I have found among incarcerated youths in California, I have to argue that—given the release of each offender is inevitable—it would be better to release them from juvenile facilities at twenty-five than to transfer them to prison at eighteen or nineteen and release them from there at twenty-five, after years of adult incarceration.

How, then, do we best transition from theoretical support into more practical evidence-based policy? I agree with Professor Trulson's previous statement that youths do not deserve full latitude—they should not escape all culpability for committing violent crimes. However, I agree with others that juvenile offenders do deserve a youth discount of some kind—even for the most violent "adult" crimes—as a way for the system to incorporate developmental immaturity as a mitigating factor in sentencing.[11] If not a discount to the sentence itself, then perhaps the justice system can provide them with a discount on the amount of time they have to spend incarcerated within adult prisons by extending the jurisdiction of juvenile correctional facilities.

The first two chapters of this book told the story of Jennifer Ertman and Elizabeth Pena, two young girls who were victims of the most heinous murders imaginable. Victims like Jennifer and Elizabeth, as well as their families, deserve the assurance that (1) the criminals responsible are adequately punished, and (2) society is safe from such criminals for an adequate amount of time. The concern for public safety becomes doubly important if the criminals are in the midst of adolescent development and overwhelmed by impulsivity, propensity for risk-taking, and poor decision-making abilities.

I think it may be best for such youthful offenders to age well beyond the peak of the age-crime curve while under juvenile correctional supervision. The longer they are incarcerated within TYC, the more likely it is that they will gain access to effective specialized treatment, and the less likely that they will be further criminalized and victimized within adult prisons. In California, similarly violent juvenile court youths are protected by juvenile jurisdiction until the age of twenty-five, while adult-court youths are transferred to adult prison at around age eighteen. Whether waived to adult court or determinately sentenced, all youths deserve an equalized playing field that provides the same chance for redemption to all, and that strikes the right balance between adequate punishment and opportunity for rehabilitation from mid-adolescence through emerging adulthood. I am not sure what the point of determinate sentencing is if we are unable to capitalize on the second chance it offers by providing adequate, long-term therapeutic rehabilitation while also ensuring public safety and protecting notions of justice. Given the challenges in achieving this and the evidence presented in this book, determinate sentencing in Texas may actually be better in theory than in practice.

TRADEOFFS: JONATHAN W. CAUDILL

Much like my coauthors, I have worked with hundreds if not thousands of juvenile offenders. As a probation officer, I investigated fresh charges, negotiated informal supervision plans, prepared pre-sentence investigation reports, supervised adjudicated offenders, and dealt with many failures. Additionally, I worked the dorms of a "camp" residential facility for TYC parole failures. In fact, some of the offenders under study in this book made their way through the camp's gates. Like Trulson, I am no rube when it comes to juvenile offenders.

The vast majority of juveniles at the camp reported gang membership and carried the tell-tale signs of "the life"—poorly inked teardrop and "set" tattoos, bullet and knife scars, "mean mugs," and relatively remorseless perspectives.[12] For many of them, "this time" meant a chance to step away from the heat or get off the lam. For others, "this time" meant a chance to shake the life and return to their community prepared to succeed. Of course, many returned to custody, and some returned rather quickly.

While it was easy to question the system in the wake of failures, it was obvious that factors well beyond the juvenile justice system were at play in the life course of these offenders. For some juveniles the rewards of the game—camaraderie, sex, and drugs—were too great. For others, the caustic environment to which they returned ate away their ambitions and left them callused. The long-term consequences of poor earlier decisions lingered with these offenders as well. Cumulatively, there is little doubt why some young adult offenders persist in criminal behaviors.

As a scholar, however, I have dedicated much of my time to understanding the more nuanced determinants of delinquent and criminal behavior and how public policy and practice react to these behaviors. I've had the fortune to conduct both quantitative and qualitative studies on adults in the criminal justice system and juveniles in the juvenile justice system.

This book was another of those opportunities. Just the notion that offenders who take the life of another person can be released some three years later smacks of a soft-on-crime stance. No doubt, some of these offenders were released prematurely given the recidivism findings. It is easy to dismiss the entire lot on the grounds that some are a menace to society. After all, many of these second-chance serious and violent offenders were rearrested, and rearrested for a felony offense, after release from TYC.

From a public policy perspective, it seems we could do a better job of estimating the likelihood of recidivism and allow these risk assessments to inform release decisions. While institutional behavior influenced release decisions for the sentenced offenders, other factors played a part as well, and some of those release decisions resulted in more crime. For example, Edward McCoy was released from TYC at his mid-sentence hearing because of the desires of the victim's family more so than the criminogenic factors of the case. To be fair, though, there is mounting evidence of an "evidence-based" culture developing in juvenile and criminal justice circles, where supervision levels and case plans are based on risk and needs assessments.

I am sure that previous generations of scholars, advocates, and administrators believed they too were on the verge of greatness with fresh crime panaceas. Indeed, the first juvenile court in 1899 was the product of the child-saving reformers who believed juvenile offenders to be inherently different from adult offenders and, therefore, requiring a softer touch due to their more malleable nature. A few short decades later,

Texas ratcheted down on juvenile offenders in an attempt to get tough on manipulative youthful offenders and reduce what appeared to be an out-of-control younger generation. Shortly thereafter the judicial system extended civil protections to marginalized groups, including juvenile offenders. This forced courts and correctional agencies to re-think how they dealt with juveniles. Texas's Determinate Sentencing Act (DSA), while presented as a determinate sentencing structure, seemingly walked the line between punishment and rehabilitation. It provided a second chance for serious and violent juvenile offenders motivated to change. At the same time, it provided Texans some level of security in knowing there was the potential for long-term incapacitation for dangerous or habitual offenders either unwilling or unable to conform to societal (and institutional) expectations. This blended sentencing legislation has the markings of an individualized focus, where offender-specific characteristics trump broad-based classification strategies. Of course, the evidence presented here suggests caution in the search for a cure-all to serious juvenile crime.

On a grander scale, however, determinate sentencing in Texas is an example of the delicate dance of crime control within the limitations of the law. In essence, the law both authorizes and restricts official intervention. Along this line of thought, the rehabilitative and punitive shifts in the juvenile justice system may be more akin to adjustments of formal social control in a shifting-sands legal environment than to major philosophical stances. In other words, innovations in juvenile crime policy may work to balance more exactly public safety and protection of individual rights. Inherent in this model, then, is the sacrifice of correctional efficacy for individual liberty.

While this may seem perfectly logical and aligned with major ideological preferences, these attempts to balance public safety and individual liberties may relate directly to the proliferation of serious and violent juvenile offenders. Specifically, the extension of civil rights to juvenile delinquents has restricted correctional options, thus requiring more sophisticated delinquent behaviors before official intervention. As presented in the early chapters in this book, evidence suggests that engagement of juveniles in the most serious offenses has escalated over time in the United States. It is quite possible that unfettered formal intervention in low-level juvenile delinquency during the early twentieth century precluded more serious and violent outcomes. If this is in fact a contributing factor to juvenile delinquency, then we have shot ourselves in the *parens patriae* foot.

Of course, this does not necessarily suggest that extension of civil rights protections to juveniles is a bad thing. What it does suggest, however, is that we should not anticipate or promote silver bullets for crime or delinquency. There are just too many opportunities for punishment avoidance resulting from legal protections against government intervention. The current culture of evidence-based correctional practices and programs has opened the door for partnerships in crime reduction between academics and practitioners, but these collaborations should be located within the reality of legal restrictions and based on realistic expectations.

Those factors considered, our study of serious and violent juvenile offenders in Texas provides some insight into their criminal trajectories. Although Texas reserved determinate sentencing for specific offenses, our findings suggest other factors than the committing offense contributed more to these offenders' successes or failures. Our most consistent determinants of persistent delinquency (institutional misconduct and recidivism) were associated with informal social control complications. Those youths originating from chaotic home environments and experiencing greater numbers of out-of-home placements—potentially the product of inadequate parental supervision—were consistently more likely to participate in institutional misconduct and recidivism once released from custody. Furthermore, those juvenile offenders responsible for institutional misconduct were more likely to recidivate after their incarceration. Ultimately, there was evidence suggesting that the home environment matters in a cohort of serious offenders, which frankly should not strike anyone as odd given what we know about childhood development of interpersonal relationships and emotional stability.

There's another side to these stories, however. For every serious offender, there is a victim. The negative consequences of violent victimization are, at least in part, a motivation for the justice system to deem an offender unfit to remain in mainstream society. Regardless of what one believes about the negative effects of incarceration, the judicial system has the responsibility to dispense justice to all involved parties. Victims deserve justice as well.

Serious crime does not always fit into the neat categories and limited sentencing structures afforded by the justice system. At the same time, however, the system has the responsibility to act in the best interests of the people. This idea of justice for all has molded the way in which the system recognizes the damages created by these offenders and how it strives to prevent further victimizations, while operating within legal standards. These competing objectives—retribution, rehabilitation, and individual liberty—make the process complex. In many cases, complexity leads to inefficiency, and inefficiency creates uncertainty. Uncertainty in the context of serious and violent crime means that someone will pay unduly. Excessive costs may apply to the offender sitting in a six-by-eight cell or to the unsuspecting next victim of a prematurely released habitual and serious offender. The question we must answer is which is worse.

A WINDOW INTO THE LIFE-COURSE-PERSISTENT OFFENDER: MATT DELISI

One of the most influential theories in criminal justice is Terrie Moffitt's developmental taxonomy. Moffitt suggests there are three basic types of people in regard to antisocial behavior and delinquency. The first group, abstainers, does not engage in antisocial behavior at all. Although it was believed that youths who were abstainers lacked social skills and opportunities for delinquency, the reality is that the behavior of abstainers is simply "better" than that of other children and adolescents. They do not dabble in misbehavior and mischief because it never occurs to them. Abstainers are healthier psychologically and are more likely to be high achievers in school. They are also rare, constituting perhaps 10 percent of the population.

The second group, adolescence-limited offenders, makes up about 80 percent of the population. As their label implies, adolescence-limited offenders engage in minor to moderate levels of antisocial behavior during their middle to late adolescence, and then quickly stop delinquency upon adulthood. These youths primarily engage in trivial mischief, such as truancy, vandalism, and minor assaults (e.g., fistfights at school) along with low-level drug experimentation with alcohol, tobacco, and marijuana. Their adolescent angst, so to speak, is produced from the difficulties of adolescence as they navigate the transition from child to adult. Once they realize the legal, social, and financial consequences of bad behavior, they stop. Most juvenile delinquency occurs within this group.

The third group, life-course-persistent offenders, accounts for the remaining 10 percent of the population. As their label indicates, these youths begin displaying pronounced problem behaviors very early in life, even before entering kindergarten. During elementary school, they are discrepant from their peers in terms of their aggressiveness, their deficits in self-control, their deficits in attending to school, and their cognitive problems. They also are more likely to have a poor home life characterized by high parental abuse, low parental involvement, low parental warmth, and poverty, among other deleterious circumstances. Their neuropsychological deficits create countless negative interactions with their parents, their siblings, their peers, their teachers, other adults, and ultimately with social work and juvenile justice officials. Unlike the relatively trivial delinquency of adolescence-limited youths, these children engage in more serious forms of problem behaviors and are more inclined to use interpersonal violence. They are children who will mature into full-fledged delinquents and often career criminals.

Although I doubt most people contemplate Moffitt's theory, they intuitively understand that some kids appear perfect, most kids are generally good with some minor mischief, and some kids are deeply troubled. As such, juvenile justice systems do a generally good job of weeding abstainers and adolescence-limited youths from formal juvenile justice processing—relying on diversion and other informal mechanisms to address their behavioral issues. Consequently, juvenile justice resources are disproportionately used to treat and supervise the most demanding cases.

None of the 3,382 youths studied in this book fit the abstainer or adolescence-limited labels. These are life-course-persistent antisocial individuals for whom TYC confinement is just the latest stage in what will be a recurrent pattern of offending and noncompliance, probation and institutionalization. That these children were already adjudicated for capital murder, murder, armed robbery, rape, and other serious felonies attests to the severity of their behavioral deficits. Many of these youths never had a chance to lead normal lives, for they were reared in homes of severe dysfunction, violence, and poverty. Many of them were exposed to criminal behavior as children. Instead of being raised by their parents, most were lowered by them.

In other words, youths who are found in deep-end placements in the juvenile justice system are very unlikely to make the transition from offender to functional member of society. Their deficits run too deep, and even before age twenty they have become habituated to criminal behavior. Blended sentencing makes sense, and I support it, but it makes the most sense when one considers the full spectrum of the juvenile offender population. Youths who are already committing the most serious felonies are not the ones to take a chance on, because the down-side is compromised public safety and enabling, or at least facilitating, the likely victimization of innocent people.

Delinquent youths themselves, including the 3,382 individuals studied in this book, generally give the same responses if asked about their future behavioral prospects. Delinquent youths are keen to point out the various social disadvantages that they have suffered and the various ways in which they did not get a fair shake in life. They are not incorrect. They often point to the difficulties they had in school, aca-demically and socially, and how it seemed that the system was out to get them based on the seemingly never-ending bad events they had to go through. This externalized locus of control is helpful for delinquent youths in thinking about why they are being suspended from school, or being expelled, or being placed in an alternative educational set-ting, or being placed in juvenile detention, or being sent to a commit-ment facility. And that, in the end, is the sad story of their life-course-persistent antisocial behavior. Moffitt was right.

CHAPTER 1: ORIGINS AND DISCOVERIES

1. D. Tanenhaus, *Juvenile Justice in the Making* (New York: Oxford University Press, 2004), 24.

2. D. Rothman, *Conscience and Convenience: The Asylum and Its Alternatives in Progressive America* (Boston: Little, Brown, 1980), 215.

3. Tanenhaus, *Juvenile Justice*, 24.

4. A. Platt, *The Child Savers: The Invention of Delinquency* (Chicago: University of Chicago Press, 1969).

5. P. Harris, W. Welsh, and F. Butler, "A Century of Juvenile Justice," in *The Nature of Crime: Continuity and Change*, ed. G. LaFree (Washington, DC: National Institute of Justice, 2000), 359–426. See also C. Brace, *The Dangerous Classes of New York* (New York: Wynkoop and Hallenbeck, 1880). For more recent discussions of the impact of immigration on crime or immigrant involvement in crime, see S. Bucerius and M. Tonry, eds., *The Oxford Handbook of Ethnicity, Crime and Immigration* (New York: Oxford University Press, 2013), which provides insight on the impact of immigrants on crime in the United States and abroad.

6. Harris, Welsh, and Butler, "A Century of Juvenile Justice," 361.

7. H. Snyder and M. Sickmund, *Juvenile Offenders and Victims: 2006 National Report* (Washington, DC: US Department of Justice, Office of Justice Programs, Office of Juvenile Justice and Delinquency Prevention, 2006).

8. To denote the wide discretion of juvenile courts over child-related matters of varying sorts, many states simply refer to juvenile courts as family courts.

9. See, for example, D. Wolcott, *Cops and Kids: Policing Juvenile Delinquency in Urban America, 1890–1940* (Columbus: Ohio State University Press, 2005) for a discussion of how police departments handled wayward youths in cities such as Detroit, Chicago, and Los Angeles before the formal development of juvenile courts.

10. B. Feld, *Bad Kids: Race and the Transformation of the Juvenile Court* (New York: Oxford University Press, 1999).

11. We use the term "wayward" broadly to denote both delinquent youths and those considered dependent (defined as having parents who want to take care of them but cannot) and neglected (the parents could take care of their child but do not). Early juvenile courts across the United States characteristically had wide jurisdiction over all child matters of concern regardless of whether the situation was one of delinquency, dependency, or neglect.

12. This section discusses the juvenile court and probation in a way that suggests all juvenile courts developed uniformly and followed the path of the Cook County juvenile court. This discussion is generic in nature as significant variations existed in the establishment and operation of juvenile courts across the United States. See Feld, *Bad Kids*.

13. J. Watkins, *The Juvenile Justice Century: A Sociolegal Commentary on American Juvenile Courts* (Durham, NC: Carolina Academic Press, 1998). It should

be noted that Illinois's juvenile court act revision of 1905 gave the court original and exclusive jurisdiction over all acts committed by males under seventeen years of age and acts committed by females under eighteen years of age. This included serious and violent juvenile offenders of the time. See, for example, D. Tanenhaus and S. Drizin, "Owing to the Extreme Youth of the Accused: The Changing Legal Response to Homicide," *Journal of Criminal Law and Criminology* 92 (2002): 641–706.

14. Feld, *Bad Kids*, 71.

15. D. Rothman, *The Discovery of the Asylum: Social Order and Disorder in the New Republic*, rev. ed. (Boston: Little, Brown, 1990), 225–226.

16. See Wolcott, *Cops and Kids*.

17. Feld, *Bad Kids*.

18. Rothman, *Discovery of the Asylum*.

19. For an excellent historical discussion of the houses of refuge that includes the routine and regimentation, see Feld, *Bad Kids* and Rothman, *Discovery of the Asylum*.

20. Rothman, *Discovery of the Asylum*, 210.

21. S. Schlossman, "Delinquent Children: The Juvenile Reform School," in *The Oxford History of the Prison: The Practice of Punishment in Western Society*, ed. N. Morris and D. Rothman (New York: Oxford University Press, 1995), 363–389.

22. Rothman, *Discovery of the Asylum*. The practice of placing wayward youths in the more tranquil setting of the countryside was not altogether unique. In this era it was not unusual for youths to be rounded up from urban city areas and placed with or bound out to foster homes, farms, and other placements in more rural areas such as the Midwest. Indeed, no one had ever seen a lazy or incorrigible farm kid, and so rural placement was thought to be just what was needed.

23. The change from houses of refuge to reformatories was largely symbolic. Such symbolism has been noted across the entire spectrum of changes to juvenile institutionalization. As noted by Hastings H. Hart, "Juvenile reformatories were known first as houses of refuge; when that term became opprobrious, they were called reform schools; when that term in turn became obnoxious, the name industrial school was used; when that name became offensive, they were called training schools." See H. Hart, *Preventive Treatment of Neglected Children* (New York: Russell Sage, 1910), 65.

24. Rothman, *Conscience and Convenience*.

25. This is not to say the newly named training and industrial schools did not feature some cell living. This is particularly true of those training schools that were simply renamed reform schools.

26. Rothman, *Conscience and Convenience*.

27. Ibid., 266.

28. For a description of the delinquent boys, see S. Glueck and E. Glueck, *Unraveling Juvenile Delinquency* (New York: Commonwealth Fund, 1950), 27–28. See also R. Sampson and J. Laub, *Crime in the Making: Pathways and Turning Points through Life* (Cambridge, MA: Harvard University Press, 1993).

29. Schlossman, "Delinquent Children."

30. Ibid., 373.

31. When discussing the "South," this generally refers to Alabama, Arkansas, Florida, Georgia, Mississippi, Louisiana, South Carolina, Tennessee, and Texas, but

can be expanded to include other states such as Kentucky, Virginia, and North Carolina. See V. Young, "Race and Gender in the Establishment of Juvenile Institutions: The Case of the South," *Prison Journal* 73 (1994): 244–265.

32. Ibid., 248.

33. Ibid., passim.

34. M. Colvin, *Penitentiaries, Reformatories, and Chain Gangs: Social Theory and the History of Punishment in Nineteenth-Century America* (New York: St. Martin's Press, 1997).

35. Due to abuses of prisoners supervised by private contractors under the lease, many southern states took control over transporting, supervising, and disciplining convicts at privately owned work sites. This system, called the contract system, was similar to the lease with the exception that state prison officials handled prisoner issues. The lease and contract systems functioned in the South into the 1900s but were all being dismantled by the 1920s.

36. C. Trulson and J. Marquart, *First Available Cell: Desegregation of the Texas Prison System* (Austin: University of Texas Press, 2009). See D. Walker, *Penology for Profit: A History of the Texas Prison System, 1867–1912* (College Station: Texas A&M University Press, 1988) and D. Oshinsky, *Worse than Slavery: Parchman Farm and the Ordeal of Jim Crow Justice* (New York: Free Press, 1996) for excellent descriptions of the convict lease in Texas and Mississippi. See also Colvin, *Penitentiaries, Reformatories, and Chain Gangs.*

37. Colvin, *Penitentiaries, Reformatories, and Chain Gangs.*

38. There simply was little effort to distinguish juveniles from adult criminals in the South in the years immediately after the Civil War. David M. Oshinsky even notes that in Mississippi, black children and adolescents constituted roughly 25 percent of all leased convicts. See Oshinsky, *Worse than Slavery.*

39. The number of juvenile offenders in the Texas prison system in the late 1800s to early 1900s would depend on how one defined "juveniles." See, for example, Walker, *Penology for Profit.*

40. See Walker, *Penology for Profit* for the numbers of Texas prisoners under fifteen, under sixteen, and from ages fifteen to nineteen in the years between 1880 and 1912.

41. In Texas the minimum age of adult criminal responsibility was not raised to age seventeen until 1918. Prior to 1918, the age of adult criminal responsibility was nine, meaning those nine and older could be sent to the prisoner lease camps or the state penitentiaries in Huntsville or Rusk. Before 1836, the age of adult responsibility was eight. Certainly, when discussing the evolution of the treatment of juveniles, in courts or within institutions, one must recognize the clash between the modern notion of a juvenile and the definitions of earlier years.

42. Young, "Race and Gender."

43. Colvin, *Penitentiaries, Reformatories, and Chain Gangs.*

44. W. Bush, *Who Gets a Childhood? Race and Juvenile Justice in Twentieth-Century Texas* (Athens: University of Georgia Press, 2010). See also W. Bush, *Protecting Texas' Most Precious Resource: A History of Juvenile Justice Policy in Texas (Part I and II)* (Austin: Texas Criminal Justice Coalition, 2008).

45. Bush, *Who Gets a Childhood?*

46. At about the same time Gatesville became operational, Texas pushed on with

the development of more institutions. To separate delinquent youths from those considered dependent or neglected, Texas opened the State Orphan Asylum in 1889 in Corsicana and also the Deaf, Dumb, and Blind Asylum for Colored Youth in Austin around the same time. On segregation, see, for example, Bush, *Who Gets a Childhood?*; and Trulson and Marquart, *First Available Cell.*

47. Bush, *Who Gets a Childhood?* 14.

48. Ibid.

49. It is interesting to note that in Texas, hard work in the prison farm cotton fields was more or less viewed as treatment. This same thinking was applied at Gatesville in the early years. In a letter to Texas prison officials in 1962, a former Gatesville ward, then incarcerated in the Texas prison system, wrote: "Sir, I have always been able to work and this is all that I have received. But my problem as I have stated is one very close to mental insanity. One that can neither be curbed or rechanneled by chopping cotton, or using my strength in the field that will serve to no avail to me when I am released from confinement." Trulson and Marquart, *First Available Cell*, 99.

50. See Bush, *Who Gets a Childhood?* 15–41, for an excellent discussion of the transformation of Gatesville due to these early changes, some symbolic and some real.

51. Ibid.

52. Bush, *Protecting Texas' Most Precious Resource*, 14.

53. For historical discussion of the development in Texas, see *Texas Youth Commission: An Inventory of Records at the Texas State Archives, 1886–1892, 1902, 1909–2003, undated (Bulk 1949–2000)*, accessed February 12, 2013, http://www.lib.utexas.edu/taro/tslac/20124/tsl-20124.html.

54. Bush, *Protecting Texas' Most Precious Resource*, 25.

55. Bush, *Who Gets a Childhood?*

56. Ibid.

57. Ibid. For further description of Mountain View, see also K. Wooden, *Weeping in the Playtime of Others: America's Incarcerated Children* (Columbus: Ohio State University Press, 2000).

58. See the William Wayne Justice Papers, Tarleton State University, accessed February 27, 2013, http://tarlton.law.utexas.edu/exhibits/ww_justice/morales_v_turman_page2.html.

59. *In re Gault*, 387 U.S. 1 (1967). This US Supreme Court case provided formal due process protections for juveniles during adjudication proceedings that might result in confinement in a secure facility.

60. See *Morales v. Turman*, 383 F. Supp. 53 (1974).

61. For details regarding the commitment of Johnny Brown and others, see Bush, *Who Gets a Childhood?* For another excellent treatment, see Wooden, *Weeping in the Playtime of Others.*

62. *Morales v. Turman*, 383 F. Supp. 53 (1974).

63. Ibid.

64. See the William Wayne Justice Papers and *Morales v. Turman*, 383 F. Supp. 53 (1974).

65. Many "office boys" allegedly graduated to the Texas prison system where they

became part of the notorious Building Tender system. Building tenders were inmate enforcers used by TDC administrators.

66. See the William Wayne Justice Papers.

67. The term "super-predator" refers to commentary from criminologists and others (John Dilulio, James Fox, James Q. Wilson, William Bennett, and John P. Walters, among others) in the 1990s warning of a coming onslaught of serious and violent juvenile criminals never before experienced in American society. Although predictions of massive crime increases into the new millennium never materialized, the notion of the juvenile super-predator sparked tremendous commentary and controversy surrounding juvenile offenders. See, for example, "Super-Predators," http://www.sparkaction.org/node/31984.

68. W. Bennett, J. Dilulio, and J. Walters, *Body Count* (New York: Simon and Schuster, 1996).

69. Beginning in 1996, juvenile offenders at least fourteen years of age could be certified to adult court for certain felonies, including capital murder, a first-degree felony, and an aggravated controlled substance felony. With these exceptions, certifications to adult court can occur for only those ages fifteen to seventeen. Moreover, following the Supreme Court decision in *Roper v. Simmons*, 543 U.S. 551 (2005), no juvenile offender can be sentenced to death. Further Supreme Court decisions have clarified that juveniles cannot be sanctioned to life in prison without the possibility of parole for a non-homicide (*Graham v. Florida*, 560 U.S.___[2010]) or a homicide offense (*Miller v. Alabama*, 567 U.S.___[2012]).

70. For the entire story, including updates on all of the offenders, see www.murdervictims.com/voices/jeneliz.html.

71. A. Turner, "Juvenile Killers Could Be Set Free by 2043," *Houston Chronicle*, March 4, 2005, available online at http://www.chron.com/news/houston-texas/article/Juvenile-killers-could-be-set-free-by-2043-1928601.php.

72. *Roper v. Simmons*, 543 U.S. 551 (2005).

73. This is by design, since 2008 state law prohibits misdemeanants from being sentenced to TYC. In the years immediately prior to 2008, roughly 20 percent of all TYC commitments were misdemeanants.

74. For the TYC commitment profile from 2006 to 2011, see http://www.tjjd.texas.gov/research/profile.aspx.

75. R. Smallheer, "Sentence Blending and the Promise of Rehabilitation: Bringing the Juvenile Justice System Full Circle," *Hofstra Law Review* 28 (1999): 262.

CHAPTER 2: THE DETERMINATE SENTENCING ACT IN TEXAS

1. *Violent or Habitual Offenders Act*, Texas Family Code Ann. section 53.045 (1987 and supp. 1995).

2. R. O. Dawson, "The Third Justice System: The New Juvenile-Criminal System of Determinate Sentencing for the Youthful Violent Offender in Texas," *St. Mary's Law Journal* 19 (1988): 943–1016; E. J. Fritsch and C. Hemmens, "An Assessment of Legislative Approaches to the Problem of Serious Juvenile Crime: A Case Study of Texas 1973–1995," *American Journal of Criminal Law* 23 (1996): 563–609.

3. Dawson, "The Third Justice System"; Fritsch and Hemmens, "An Assessment."

4. Dawson, "The Third Justice System."

5. Ibid.

6. D. P. Mears, "Evaluation Issues Confronting Juvenile Justice Sentencing Reforms: A Case Study of Texas," *Crime and Delinquency* 44 (1998): 443–463.

7. Dawson, "The Third Justice System"; Fritsch and Hemmens, "An Assessment"; Mears, "Juvenile Justice Sentencing Reforms."

8. R. O. Dawson, "Determinate Sentencing Proceedings for the Violent or Habitual Offender," in *Texas Juvenile Law*, 5th ed. (Austin: Texas Juvenile Probation Commission, 2000), 347–371; Mears, "Juvenile Justice Sentencing Reforms"; Texas Youth Commission, "Sentenced Offenders" (2007), accessed November 5, 2007, http://www.tyc.state.tx.us/about/sentenced_offenders.html; *Violent or Habitual Offenders Act.*

9. Deadly assault on a law enforcement officer was repealed as no longer eligible for determinate sentencing on September 1, 1994; see Dawson, "Determinate Sentencing Proceedings."

10. Ibid.; TYC, "Sentenced Offenders" (2007); *Violent or Habitual Offenders Act.*

11. Dawson, "Determinate Sentencing Proceedings."

12. This section relies heavily on Dawson's chapter in *Texas Juvenile Law.* For more details, see Dawson, Texas Family Code, section 53.045, table 2.1 (a list of offenses eligible for DSA prosecution) and figure 1 (a flowchart of DSA procedures).

13. For the entire story, including updates on all of the offenders, see www .murdervictims.com/voices/jeneliz.html.

14. Dawson, "Determinate Sentencing Proceedings." It is noted that any district court, criminal district court, family district court, or county court in Texas designated as a juvenile court can provide adjudication and disposition hearings in determinate sentencing cases.

15. This discussion focuses on what occurs following grand jury approval. Rejection (failure of nine members to approve the petition) triggers either normal delinquency proceedings to resume, petition to a different grand jury, or filing of a petition that requests discretionary waiver to adult court if the offender's age at the commission of the crime is eligible for such certification; Dawson, "Determinate Sentencing Proceedings."

16. A juvenile prosecuted under the DSA enjoys all rights available to adult criminal defendants, which include the right to a jury trial and the right to counsel. In Texas, all juveniles have the right to a jury, but this is not the case in other states.

17. Prior to 1999, the judge could provide a term of probation that lasted up to eighteen years of age. After DSA amendments in 1999, probation could be granted for any punishment of ten years or less. Even if a juvenile reaches the age of eighteen, the term of probation continues until the end of the ten-year term. If probation is revoked, a judge may order a new sentence, but it may not exceed the original ten-year punishment. Additionally, there is no minimum term of probation and a judge may discharge a juvenile from probation at any time. Probation is an option that effectively diverts less severe offenders from initial commitment to TYC, but this book examines only those who were not deemed eligible for probation and were instead sent to TYC; Dawson, "Determinate Sentencing Proceedings."

18. Minor modifications were made to these hearing proceedings for offenses committed after January 1, 1996. While it was still necessary for TYC to petition

the juvenile court for approval to release a juvenile before he or she completed the minimum length of stay, TYC was then granted authority to parole juveniles without court approval once they completed the minimum length of stay determined according to DSA modifications: a ten-year minimum stay for capital murder (and automatic transfer to adult prison at age twenty-one if still committed to TYC), three years for first-degree and aggravated controlled substance felonies, two years for second-degree felonies, and one year for third-degree felonies.

19. This option of release at age twenty-one, the maximum age of jurisdiction following the determination hearing, is also considered a form of being released without supervision as noted in chapter 5.

20. It should be noted that a sentenced offender released from TYC can be released to a nonsecure facility instead of immediately back home. Because these facilities are considered nonsecure, they are grouped as part of the "community" in this study.

21. A minimum length of stay (MLOS) can be much different than the sentence received from the juvenile court. A sentenced offender has the potential to be released after a MLOS, regardless of sentence length. Minimum lengths of stay are as follows: ten years for a capital felony; three years for an aggravated controlled substance felony or a first-degree felony; two years for a second-degree felony; and one year for a third-degree felony.

22. Mears, "Juvenile Justice Sentencing Reforms."

23. See www.murdervictims.com/voices/jeneliz.html.

24. Ibid.

25. D. Rothman, *Conscience and Convenience: The Asylum and Its Alternatives in Progressive America* (Boston: Little, Brown, 1980).

26. B. Feld, *Bad Kids: Race and the Transformation of the Juvenile Court* (New York: Oxford University Press, 1999).

27. E. J. Fritsch, C. Hemmens, and T. J. Caeti, "Violent Youth in Juvenile and Adult Court: An Assessment of Sentencing Strategies in Texas," *Law and Policy* 18 (1996): 115–136.

28. TYC, "Sentenced Offenders" (2007).

29. S. D. Levitt, "Understanding Why Crime Fell in the 1990s: Four Factors that Explain the Decline and Six that Do Not," *Journal of Economic Perspectives* 18 (2004): 163–190.

30. It is also relevant to note that determinate sentencing, related to the 1995 expansion of eligible offenses and also considering the inherent discretionary powers vested with the prosecutor, could have resulted in a situation where a determinate sentencing prosecution was used as leverage to entice plea bargains in the traditional juvenile court. For example, the youth could be presented with an opportunity to admit guilt in exchange for a traditional juvenile court adjudication hearing instead of a determinate sentencing prosecution and/or leniency in sentencing length and options. We have no evidence to suggest this is or is not the case, but it is worth considering this potential.

31. T. Wheeler-Cox, *Overview of the Texas Youth Commission's Specialized Treatment Programs* (Austin: Criminal Justice Policy Council, 1997).

32. Ibid.; TYC, "Sentenced Offenders" (2007).

33. P. Griffin, S. Addie, B. Adams, and K. Firestine, *Trying Juveniles as Adults: An Analysis of State Transfer Laws and Reporting* (Washington, DC: US Department of

Justice, Office of Justice Programs, Office of Juvenile Justice and Delinquency Prevention, 2011).

34. Mears, "Juvenile Justice Sentencing Reforms."

35. Dawson, "Determinate Sentencing Proceedings."

36. W. B. Connolly, "Nuts and Bolts of Juvenile Law: Same Difference—Determinate Sentencing," Texas Juvenile Probation Commission and Juvenile Law Section (2005), accessed February 8, 2007, http://www.juvenilelaw.org/Articles/2005/NB/Connolly.pdf.

37. D. M. Bishop, C. E. Frazier, and J. C. Henretta, "Prosecutorial Certification: Case Study of a Questionable Reform," *Crime and Delinquency* 35 (1989): 179–201; T. Fabelo, "Sentencing Reform in Texas: Can Criminal Justice Research Inform Public Policy?" *Crime and Delinquency* 40 (1994): 282–294; P. L. Griset, "Determinate Sentencing and Administrative Discretion over Time Served in Prison: A Case Study of Florida," *Crime and Delinquency* 42 (1996): 127–143.

38. Mears, "Juvenile Justice Sentencing Reforms."

39. P. Griffin, *Different from Adults: An Updated Analysis of Juvenile Transfer and Blended Sentencing Laws, with Recommendations for Reform* (Pittsburgh: National Center for Juvenile Justice, 2008).

CHAPTER 3: THE SHEEP THAT GOT LOST

1. For a classic discussion of the institutional intake ceremonies, see E. Goffman, *Asylums: Essays on the Social Situation of Mental Patients and Other Inmates* (New York: Anchor Books, 1961). Especially relevant is the first chapter, "On the Characteristics of Total Institutions."

2. Juveniles who have been adjudicated and sentenced under determinate sentencing in Texas are referred to informally as "sentenced offenders."

3. Marlin Orientation and Assessment was transferred to the operation of the Texas Department of Criminal Justice (TDCJ) on August 31, 2007, and repurposed as an adult correctional institution. This change and numerous other facility closings and reorganizations occurred as the result of many highly publicized instances of youthful offender abuse at several TYC facilities. When such changes are relevant to this current book, we will make note of them.

4. The age of initial jurisdiction in a determinate sentence case is ten to sixteen. It is possible for a youth to arrive at TYC as a sentenced offender after they have turned seventeen, for example, if they had previously been placed on determinate sentence probation and were revoked.

5. The data for this chapter and all subsequent ones was obtained from the Texas Youth Commission (TYC) under a research agreement signed on July 8, 2011. Data was retrieved at the end of calendar year 2011. This research was approved by the University of North Texas Institutional Review Board on July 18, 2011, Human Subjects Application No. 11321. All data received from the TYC was fully deidentified prior to being transmitted to the primary investigator. All names of determinately sentenced offenders found in this publication derive from published reports in newspapers and other public avenues, and not from the data provided by TYC. In no way was data derived from TYC able to be linked to an individual. In instances where a youth was identified by a public source, we have provided the specific citation. More specific

to the data in this study, TYC provided all information regarding offenders' social, familial, and institutional backgrounds, recidivism data, institutional behavior data, and information regarding the release of a sentenced offender from TYC to a community context or transfer to the Texas prison system.

6. This includes all youths who were remanded to TYC incarceration following adjudication under determinate sentencing. It should be noted that some offenders could have received determinate sentence probation during the time frame of this study, but are not included in the study unless they failed at the probated sentence and were incarcerated in TYC as a sentenced offender. Until 1999, the juvenile court judge or jury in a determinate sentencing case could have granted probation for a period up until the youth's eighteenth birthday. In 1999, Texas law changed regarding determinate sentence probation. After 1999, a juvenile in a determinate sentence case could receive a maximum probation sentence of ten years as long as the punishment time period assessed by judge or jury was ten years or less. This ten-year probated sentence could extend well beyond a juvenile's eighteenth birthday due to this new legislation. In those cases, the offender's probation could be extended into adulthood, being transferred to the criminal court upon the offender's eighteenth birthday. For more specific details, see R. Dawson, *Texas Juvenile Law*, 7th ed. (Austin: Texas Juvenile Probation Commission, 2008). Those youths who received determinate sentence probation are not included in this study. Only youths who received a sentence of incarceration in TYC are included. It is possible, for example, that an offender received determinate sentence probation, failed at that probation, and then entered TYC incarceration as a sentenced offender to serve the remainder of his or her sentence, including the potential transfer to prison. Those individuals are represented in this data.

7. Of the 3,382, four offenders died as indicated by TYC data relating to an offender's discharge from the agency. The circumstances of the deaths are unknown, but all appeared to have been released by TYC prior to the time of death. Those individuals who died are not considered in later chapters relative to recidivism calculations.

8. The numbers reference calendar year determinate sentences, not fiscal year determinate sentences.

9. The maximum length of a determinate sentence was changed from thirty to forty years in 1991.

10. There are perhaps numerous reasons for this drop in determinate sentences. The general decline in juvenile crime over the last several years is a contributing explanation. However, the youth abuse scandal of 2007 involving TYC facility administrators and staff reduced county-level confidence in TYC to treat and rehabilitate youthful offenders. As a result, local prosecutors and/or judges may have foregone determinate sentence proceedings to pursue adult court waiver proceedings, or, in other less serious determinate sentence–eligible cases, retained the youth in regular juvenile court. See, for example, J. Emily, "Judges Send Fewer Children to TYC," *Dallas Morning News*, April 9, 2007, 1A, 5A.

11. All references to individual juvenile names receiving a determinate sentence come only through publicly available documents (e.g., newspaper reports) that have identified the offender. The data used for this study is completely anonymous and deidentified.

12. P. Stone, "Youngest Davidson Felon to Be Released on Parole," *Palestine Herald Press*, May 9, 2007.

13. J. Smith, "McTear Admits Murder, Gets Maximum Sentence," *Austin Chronicle*, June 13, 2003, http://www.austinchronicle.com/news/2003–06–13/1636 65/, retrieved on April 11, 2013.

14. M. Buckley, "Life without Parole Is Sentence for Murder," *Brownsville Herald*, February 14, 2012, http://www.brownsvilleherald.com/news/valley/article _2f7e26b2-24e4-547d-8ofd-bd6efa391b77.html, retrieved on April 11, 2013.

15. P. Gately, "Teen Pleads Guilty in Local Man's Murder, Avoids Trial," KWTX-TV News, http://www.kwtx.com/home/headlines/90924959.html, retrieved on April 11, 2013.

16. For simplicity in presentation and analysis, subdivisions such as "attempted," "solicitation," and "conspiracy to commit" were not used in the tables and analyses. Among these subdivisions, there were thirteen commitments for attempted murder, ninety-four commitments for attempted capital murder, seven commitments for attempted sexual assault, ten commitments for attempted aggravated robbery, one commitment for attempted burglary, one commitment for conspiracy to commit capital murder, one commitment for conspiracy to commit aggravated robbery, and one commitment for solicitation to commit murder. Altogether, 128 or 3.78 percent of all 3,382 commitments fell in the attempted, conspiracy, or solicitation range.

17. It is interesting to note that a study comparing adult court certified and determinately sentenced juvenile offenders in Texas from 2005–2009 found that determinately sentenced offenders are no less serious than adult court certified youths in Texas, and in fact may be even more serious. Although there are numerous reasons for this, the author notes that adult court certification in Texas is not limited to only serious and violent offenses, as it usually is in determinate sentencing. For more details, see M. Deitch, *Juveniles in the Adult Criminal Justice System in Texas* (Austin: University of Texas at Austin, LBJ School of Public Affairs, 2011).

18. Dawson, *Texas Juvenile Law*, 524.

19. The data in this book on the histories of sentenced offenders reflects information about them at the time of their commitment to TYC.

20. The time period studied ends on December 31, 2011.

21. It is possible, once released to this community sentence, that an offender could violate the terms of his or her release and/or commit a new offense and be sent to the Texas prison system to continue the determinate sentence behind bars. Unfortunately, the data do not allow us to examine whether this occurred. While recidivism data in later chapters will examine if the offenders released to the community were rearrested, it does not allow us to examine any potential incarceration as a result of that arrest. While this is a common limitation in recidivism studies, it is a limitation nonetheless.

22. In cases where the sentenced offender resided in TYC until the maximum age of TYC authority (twenty-one before 2007, nineteen after 2007) or served their full sentence in TYC, a determination had typically been made not to send the offender to the Texas prison system. In short, when one of these types of options was received, it is likely that a determination hearing occurred in which the decision was made to retain the sentenced offender under the supervision of juvenile authorities.

23. For these forty-three offenders, the data did not include an indicator code of

their assignment following TYC release. Because there was no indicator of the destination of these offenders, they were grouped into the category of youths not receiving further community supervision.

24. For those transferred to the Texas prison system to continue the adult portion of their determinate sentence, this study does not have information on eventual release or other outcomes, such as institutional misconduct in TDC, for these offenders.

25. We include those who were indicated as "Died" in TYC's discharge reason for the time served calculations. Based on indicators in the data, these offenders appeared to have died following TYC release, and thus to have served their entire time in TYC. These offenders will be removed from the recidivism analyses, although they will be retained for institutional misconduct analyses in chapter 4 since they appeared to have served their entire time in TYC.

26. It should be noted that the determination of whether to release to the community or transfer to the Texas prison system almost always occurs between the youth's sixteenth and eighteenth birthdays. Although changes in the law detailed in chapter 2 have impacted this time frame, such a decision means that release to the community or transfer to the Texas prison system will be known for most youths by around age eighteen or nineteen.

27. The Capital and Serious Violent Offender Treatment Program, which functions exclusively at TYC's Giddings State School, has been highly touted as an effective approach for serious and violent juvenile offenders. This program initially started as the Capital Offender Program or Capital Offender Group but was later changed to admit other types of serious and violent offenders in addition to capital offenders or murderers. This program and some of its participants were thoroughly highlighted in J. Hubner, *Last Chance in Texas: The Redemption of Criminal Youth* (New York: Random House, 2005). Despite the promise of this program, as noted, only 17 percent of the youths in the current study received some dose of the residential program. Not shown in tabular form is that of the 17 percent (or 338) of youths who received this program, approximately 58 percent were homicide offenders. Other offenders who received this program ranged the gamut of offense types, but most included offenders committed for aggravated robbery and aggravated assault. The lack of assignment to this program relates to the program's small-group nature, and that it is only operated at Giddings State School.

28. For an excellent qualitative discussion of the extreme backgrounds and delinquency of the sentenced offenders, see Hubner, *Last Chance in Texas*.

CHAPTER 4: DOING TIME IN THE TEXAS YOUTH COMMISSION

1. S. Schlossman, "Delinquent Children: The Juvenile Reform School," in *The Oxford History of the Prison: The Practice of Punishment in Western Society*, ed. N. Morris and D. J. Rothman (New York: Oxford University Press, 1998), 325–349, quote on p. 327.

2. These estimates are consistent with other studies of confined juvenile offenders. A large-scale study of 2,520 serious and violent delinquent offenders found that the cohort engaged in more than 200,000 instances of minor misconduct and nearly 19,000 forms of major misconduct. This included more than 9,000 assaults against other wards, more than 1,400 assaults against staff, more than 1,400 instances

of gang-related activity, and over 200 incidents of sexual contact. See C. R. Trulson, M. DeLisi, J. W. Caudill, S. Belshaw, and J. W. Marquart, "Delinquent Careers behind Bars," *Criminal Justice Review* 35, no. 2 (2010): 200–219.

3. For examples of the deprivation model, see D. Clemmer, *The Prison Community* (New York: Holt, Rinehart, and Winston, 1958); R. A. Cloward, D. R. Cressey, G. H. Grosser, R. McCleery, L. E. Ohlin, G. M. Sykes, and S. L. Messinger, *Theoretical Studies in Social Organization of the Prison* (New York: Social Science Research Council, 1960); N. S. Hayner and F. Ash, "The Prison as a Community," *American Sociological Review* 5 (1940): 577–583; G. M. Sykes, *The Society of Captives* (Princeton, NJ: Princeton University Press, 1958). For examples of the importation model, see J. Irwin and D. R. Cressey, "Thieves, Convicts, and the Inmate Culture," *Social Problems* 10 (1962): 142–155; P. Gendreau, C. E. Goggin, and M. A. Law, "Predicting Prisons Misconducts," *Criminal Justice and Behavior* 24 (1997): 414–431; M. D. Cunningham and J. R. Sorensen, "Predictive Factors for Violent Misconduct in Close Custody," *Prison Journal* 87 (2007): 241–253; M. DeLisi, "Criminal Careers behind Bars," *Behavioral Sciences and the Law* 21 (2003): 653–669.

4. E. D. Poole and R. M. Regoli, "Violence in Juvenile Institutions," *Criminology* 21, no. 2 (1983): 213–232.

5. C. R. Trulson, "Determinants of Disruption: Institutional Misconduct among State-Committed Delinquents," *Youth Violence and Juvenile Justice* 5, no. 1 (2007): 7–34.

6. M. DeLisi, A. J. Drury, A. E. Kosloski, J. W. Caudill, P. J. Conis, C. A. Anderson, M. G. Vaughn, and K. M. Beaver, "The Cycle of Violence behind Bars: Traumatization and Institutional Misconduct among Juvenile Delinquents in Confinement," *Youth Violence and Juvenile Justice* 8, no. 2 (2010): 107–121.

7. J. MacDonald, "Violence and Drug Use in Juvenile Institutions," *Journal of Criminal Justice* 27 (1999): 33–44.

8. M. DeLisi, M. G. Vaughn, K. M. Beaver, J. P. Wright, A. Hochstetler, A. E. Kosloski, and A. J. Drury, "Juvenile Sex Offenders and Institutional Misconduct: The Role of Thought Psychopathology," *Criminal Behaviour and Mental Health* 18, no. 5 (2008): 292–305.

9. M. DeLisi, K. M. Beaver, M. G. Vaughn, C. R. Trulson, A. E. Kosloski, A. J. Drury, and J. P. Wright, "Personality, Gender, and Self-Control Theory Revisited: Results from a Sample of Institutionalized Juvenile Delinquents," *Applied Psychology in Criminal Justice* 6, no. 1 (2010): 31–46.

10. Readers who are interested in the full negative binomial regression model may request it from the authors.

11. Readers who are interested in the full logistic regression model may request it from the authors.

12. E. P. Mulvey and C. A. Schubert, "Youth in Prison and Beyond," in *The Oxford Handbook of Juvenile Crime and Juvenile Justice*, ed. B. C. Feld and D. M. Bishop (New York: Oxford University Press, 2012), 843–867, quote on p. 843.

CHAPTER 5: ANOTHER SECOND CHANCE

1. The amount of misconduct is surprising not because we presume being sentenced to TYC is a proxy for effective programming and treatment, but because so

many juvenile offenders with substantial Texas prison system time looming continue to engage in such high levels of misconduct, essentially providing evidence of the continuation of their delinquent career.

2. This determination hearing typically comes prior to a youth's eighteenth birthday, but sometimes sooner.

3. "Determination hearing" is a generic term indicating the decision point and process to release or transfer the offender.

4. In reality, release from TYC without supervision requirements could occur relatively soon after determination, or the youth could be sent back to TYC for any period of time just prior to his or her twenty-first birthday (before 2007) or nineteenth birthday (after 2007). In this instance, upon release to the community, supervision requirements include but are not limited to TYC parole, adult probation, or adult parole under the supervision of the Texas Department of Criminal Justice (TDCJ). A youth can also be released without a determination hearing. This could occur in cases where the youth completed his or her full determinate sentence length before reaching the need for a determination hearing. We examined this potential in the data, and with the exception of a handful of cases where age and sentence length/ minimum length of stay combined to less than age sixteen, most offenders were beyond seventeen when a decision was produced. For more specific details of determinate sentencing in Texas and nuances relative to release, consult R. Dawson, *Texas Juvenile Law*, 7th ed. (Austin: Texas Juvenile Probation Commission, 2008).

5. Once transferred to the Texas prison system, the remaining sentence length is subject to state parole and good-time laws.

6. B. Feld, *Bad Kids: Race and the Transformation of the Juvenile Court* (New York: Oxford University Press, 1999).

7. For a discussion of reasons for transfer and initiatives moving away from transfer, including blended sentencing, see J. Howell, *Preventing and Reducing Juvenile Delinquency* (Thousand Oaks, CA: Sage, 2003); and Feld, *Bad Kids*.

8. C. Trulson, J. Caudill, S. Belshaw, and M. DeLisi, "A Problem of Fit: Extreme Delinquents, Blended Sentencing, and the Determinants of Continued Adult Sanctions," *Criminal Justice Policy Review* 22 (2011): 263–284. See also E. J. Fritsch, C. Hemmens, and T. J. Caeti, "Violent Youth in Juvenile and Adult Court: An Assessment of Sentencing Strategies in Texas," *Law and Policy* 18 (1996): 115–136. For another excellent source on determinate sentencing in Texas, see R. O. Dawson, "The Third Justice System: The New Juvenile-Criminal System of Determinate Sentencing for the Youthful Violent Offender in Texas," *St. Mary's Law Journal* 19 (1988): 943–1016.

9. B. Applegate, R. Davis, and F. Cullen, "Reconsidering Child Saving: The Extent and Correlates of Public Support for Excluding Youth from the Juvenile Court," *Crime and Delinquency* 55 (2009): 51–77.

10. J. Brown and J. Sorensen, "Legal and Extra-Legal Factors Related to the Imposition of Blended Sentences," *Criminal Justice Policy Review* (2012), DOI: 10.1177/088740341246541.

11. See Howell, *Preventing and Reducing Juvenile Delinquency*.

12. It should be noted that blended sentencing schemes have also faced their share of criticism. Some have criticized the administration of blended sentencing schemes, especially those where adult judges instead of juvenile court judges make sentencing decisions. Others have criticized blended sentencing schemes as nothing

more than a "back door" to adult prison or a "punitive Trojan horse." Still others have criticized some blended sentencing schemes for unintended consequences such as that blended sentenced juveniles actually receive harsher punishment than juveniles waived to adult court or that some blended sentencing policies are implemented with little forethought or planning, leading to further unintended consequences such as focusing on the wrong types of juvenile offenders. For an excellent discussion of these criticisms, see Howell, *Preventing and Reducing Juvenile Delinquency*, 160–161.

13. L. Winner, L. Lanza-Kaduce, D. Bishop, and C. Frazier, "The Transfer of Juveniles to Criminal Court: Reexamining Recidivism over the Long Term," *Crime and Delinquency* 43 (1997): 548–563. See also D. Bishop, C. Frazier, L. Lanza-Kaduce, and L. Winner, "The Transfer of Juveniles to Criminal Court: Does It Make a Difference?" *Crime and Delinquency* 42 (1996): 171–191; Brown and Sorensen, "Legal and Extra-Legal Factors Related to the Imposition of Blended Sentences"; L. Lanza-Kaduce, J. Lane, D. Bishop, and C. Frazier, "Juvenile Offenders and Adult Felony Recidivism: The Impact of Transfer," *Journal of Crime and Justice* 28 (2005): 59–77; K. Johnson, L. Lanza-Kaduce, and J. Woolard, "Disregarding Graduated Treatment: Why Transfer Aggravates Recidivism," *Crime and Delinquency* 57 (2009): 756–777.

14. See C. Schubert, E. Mulvey, T. Loughran, J. Fagan, L. Chassin, A. Piquero, S. Losoya, L. Steinberg, and E. Cauffman, "Predicting Outcomes for Youth Transferred to Adult Court," *Law and Human Behavior* 34 (2010): 460–475; T. Loughran, E. Mulvey, C. Schubert, L. Chassin, L. Steinberg, A. Piquero, J. Fagan, S. Cota-Robles, E. Cauffman, and S. Losoya, "Differential Effects of Adult Court Transfer on Juvenile Offender Recidivism," *Law and Human Behavior* 34 (2010): 476–488.

15. This is a generalization. There are so many different types of waiver and types of blended sentencing that it is impossible to talk about these two sentencing divisions as if they were all the same. For an excellent resource providing information on the nuances of different waiver and blended sentencing provisions, see P. Griffin, *Transfer Provisions: State Juvenile Justice Profiles* (Pittsburgh: National Center for Juvenile Justice, 2010).

16. It is difficult to discuss waivers as if only one option existed. We are speaking of waiver in a broad and generic context.

17. Trulson et al., "A Problem of Fit."

18. Feld, *Bad Kids*.

19. Trulson et al., "A Problem of Fit."

20. K. Jordan and D. Myers, "The Decertification of Transferred Youth: Examining the Determinants of Reverse Waiver," *Youth Violence and Juvenile Justice* 5 (2007): 188–206.

21. See Trulson et al., "A Problem of Fit."

22. Jordan and Myers, "The Decertification of Transferred Youth." For perspectives on the impact of race on waiver, see also K. Jordan and T. Freiburger, "Examining the Impact of Race and Ethnicity on the Sentencing of Juveniles in Adult Court," *Criminal Justice Policy Review* 21 (2010): 185–201; and J. Lemmon, T. Austin, P. Verrecchia, and M. Fetzer, "The Effect of Legal and Extralegal Factors on Statutory Exclusion of Juvenile Offenders," *Youth Violence and Juvenile Justice* 3 (2005): 214–234.

23. As studies continue on waiver and new measures are considered on their im-

pact, it is likely that other factors determinative of waiver will be found. See, for example, J. Burrow, "Reverse Waiver and the Effects of Legal, Statutory, and Secondary Legal Factors on Sentencing Outcomes for Juvenile Offenders," *Crime and Delinquency* 54 (2008): 34–64 for evidence of judge experience as a determinant. See also C. Schubert et al., "Predicting Outcomes for Youth Transferred to Adult Court" and Loughran et al., "Differential Effects of Adult Court Transfer on Juvenile Offender Recidivism."

24. See also M. Podkopacz and B. Feld, "The Back-Door to Prison: Waiver Reform, Blended Sentencing, and the Law of Unintended Consequences," *Journal of Criminal Law and Criminology* 91 (2001): 997–1072.

25. Brown and Sorensen, "Legal and Extra-Legal Factors Related to the Imposition of Blended Sentences."

26. There is no predetermined time frame for this determination decision, with the exception that it must usually occur prior to an offender's eighteenth birthday. Depending on the age of TYC commitment, the time to this determination hearing varies for each individual offender, although the average time until decision was roughly three years.

27. It is possible that these offenders could have had their parole revoked and been remanded to the Texas prison system while on adult parole and upon new offending or continued violation of parole stipulations. Unfortunately, we do not have data to support whether this occurred for the sentenced offenders in this study.

28. Recall from previous chapters that maximum sentences can range from ten to forty years depending on the offense (or up to thirty years prior to 1995), but those are maximums, and previous data analysis showed that very few offenders received maximum sentences. In addition to maximums, sentenced offenders also have minimum lengths of stay: ten years for a capital felony, three years for a first-degree felony, two years for a second-degree felony, and one year for a third-degree felony. Provided the offender meets his or her minimum length of stay, and depending on the sentence length, it is possible for a youth to serve his or her full sentence without facing a determination hearing. Upon analysis of the data, there were a small number of cases (fewer than fifteen) in which an offender's age plus his or her sentence and/or minimum length of stay meant that the offender could have served his or her full sentence without having a determination hearing, which typically occurs around age seventeen. The determination for the other roughly 540 offenders was to allow them to serve the remainder of their sentences in TYC and be fully discharged without further supervision or Texas prison transfer.

29. In these instances, the youth was allowed to remain in TYC until reaching the age of correctional system majority/jurisdiction instead of being transferred on parole, sent to the Texas prison system, or released at an earlier age without supervision requirements. The offender had a determination hearing in which the decision was to recommit the offender to TYC until reaching the age of majority.

30. As noted in previous chapters, data suggests that these four offenders were released from TYC and died outside of TYC custody. We could not determine any further details from the data provided.

31. The specific test statistics were omitted for parsimony in presentation.

32. For coding purposes, commitment offense groupings are as follows: Homicide Commitment (capital murder, murder, and manslaughter); Sexual Commitment (ag-

gravated sexual assault, indecency with a child, and sexual assault); Robbery (aggravated robbery and robbery), Other Violent (aggravated assault, aggravated kidnapping, assault, and felony injury to a child or elderly individual); Drug (manufacture or delivery of a controlled substance and unlawful possession of a controlled substance); and Other (arson, burglary, deadly conduct, escape, intoxication manslaughter, and terroristic threat).

33. In the table, odds ratios were converted to percentages for ease of interpretation. Additionally, specific coefficients, including standard errors and significance levels, were omitted for parsimonious presentation. These values are available for interested readers upon request. It is also noted that all assumptions were evaluated, in particular for issues of multicollinearity. Upon an analysis for multicollinearity, the variable "previous referrals" was dropped from the analysis due to a high variance inflation factor. Inspections of correlations also revealed potential multicollinearity. Removal of "previous referrals" as a predictor remedied all issues of multicollinearity and all variance inflation factors were well within the acceptable range.

34. We realize that all of the offenders are violent offenders. But not all offenders receive the violent offender program due to its limited capacity. Moreover, this recognition suggests that while all offenders are violent, not all violent offenders are created equally, so to speak.

35. Unfortunately, for the specialized treatment measures, the data only indicated participation in these programs. There was not further information regarding time in treatment or whether or not a youthful offender fully completed the respective program, based on TYC criteria.

36. It is possible that longer time served in TYC was a function of youth progress. Thus it is not surprising that youths who served longer times in TYC were more likely to get released in some capacity.

37. In the MLR models, the percent of variance explained was slightly over 40 percent. This level of explained variance, which is relatively high, still suggests that more than 60 percent of the factors related to the determination outcome is unexplained by the variables in the model. Because such decisions are so highly specific to the offense/offender/victim/circumstances, it is not surprising that the majority of the variance was not explained.

38. See, for example, Burrow, "Reverse Waiver and the Effects of Legal, Statutory, and Secondary Legal Factors on Sentencing Outcomes for Juvenile Offenders." J. Burrow specifically looks at judge experience, at least involving reverse waiver decision, in "Examining the Influence of Matza's Principles of Justice and Their Impact on Reverse Waiver Decisions: Has Kadi-(In)justice Survived?" *Youth Violence and Juvenile Justice* 6 (2008): 59–82.

CHAPTER 6: THE BURDEN OF SECOND CHANCES

1. Death Row Information (2013), Offender Information: Danielle Simpson, *Texas Department of Criminal Justice*, Austin, accessed February 5, 2014, from https://www.tdcj.state.tx.us/death_row/dr_info/simpsondanielle.html.

2. D. Carson, "Danielle Simpson," *Texas Execution Information Center*, 2009, accessed June 17, 2013, from http://www.txexecutions.org/reports/445.asp.

3. P. Stone, "Teen Murder Convict to Be Freed," *Huntsville Item*, 2007, accessed June 17, 2013, from http://itemonline.com/archive/x518743527/.

4. Carson, "Danielle Simpson."

5. For Texas's most serious juvenile offenders, we included measures routinely found in other studies to affect recidivism outcomes. See R. Martinez Jr., "Predictors of Serious Violent Recidivism: Results from a Cohort Study," *Journal of Interpersonal Violence* 12, no. 2 (1997): 216–228; E. Mulder, E. Brand, R. Bullens, and H. van Marle, "Risk Factors for Overall Recidivism and Severity of Recidivism in Serious Juvenile Offenders," *International Journal of Offender Therapy and Comparative Criminology* 55, no. 1 (2011): 118–135; and E. S. Piper, "Violent Recidivism and Chronicity in the 1958 Philadelphia Cohort," *Journal of Quantitative Criminology* 1, no. 4 (1985): 319–344. To explore the notation of criminal persistence, see C. R. Trulson, J. W. Caudill, D. R. Haerle, and M. DeLisi, "Cliqued Up: The Post-incarceration Recidivism of Young Gang-Related Homicide Offenders," *Criminal Justice Review* 37, no. 2 (2012): 174–190, which focuses on the criminogenic effects of serious gang offending. C. R. Trulson, M. DeLisi, and J. W. Marquart, "Institutional Misconduct, Delinquent Background, and Rearrest Frequency among Serious and Violent Delinquent Offenders," *Crime and Delinquency* 57, no. 5 (2011): 709–731 provides a general perspective of factors associated with criminal persistence while incarcerated. For more research on identifying the next cohort of adult offenders, see C. R. Trulson, J. W. Marquart, J. L. Mullings, and T. J. Caeti, "In Between Adolescence and Adulthood: Recidivism Outcomes of a Cohort of State Delinquents," *Youth Violence and Juvenile Justice* 3, no. 4 (2005): 355–387, which explored recidivism for a group of paroled offenders.

6. J. W. Caudill, R. G. Morris, S. El Sayed, M. Yun, and M. DeLisi, "Pathways through the Juvenile Justice System: Predictors of Formal Disposition," *Youth Violence and Juvenile Justice* 11, no. 3 (2013): 183–195.

7. For a comprehensive analysis of recidivism-reducing treatment programs, see M. W. Lipsey and J. C. Howell, "Delinquency Prevention: A Broader View of Evidence-Based Programs Reveals More Options for State Juvenile Justice," *Criminology and Public Policy* 11, no. 3 (2011): 515–523.

8. J. C. Howell, ed., *Guide for Implementing the Comprehensive Strategy for Serious, Violent, and Chronic Juvenile Offenders* (Washington, DC: US Department of Justice, Office of Justice Programs, Office of Juvenile Justice and Delinquency Prevention, 1995).

9. Stone, "Teen Murder Convict to Be Freed."

10. Several previous studies may be of interest for those desiring a more specific understanding of how sociodemographic factors influence recidivism. See E. Mulder and E. Brand, "Risk Factors for Overall Recidivism and Severity of Recidivism in Serious Juvenile Offenders," *International Journal of Offender Therapy and Comparative Criminology* 55, no. 1 (2011): 118–135, for the influence of familial factors on criminality. On sociodemographic factors and recidivism, see Trulson et al., "Cliqued Up," which explored the interaction between gang affiliation and gang offending.

11. Persistent criminality has been the subject of many studies. Specific to serious and violent youthful offenders, see Martinez Jr., "Predictors of Serious Violent Recidivism"; Piper, "Violent Recidivism and Chronicity"; and Trulson et al., "In

Between Adolescence and Adulthood"; all of which provide a more comprehensive view.

12. Trulson et al., "Institutional Misconduct, Delinquent Background, and Re-arrest Frequency" provides more specificity on the association between recorded institutional behavior and post-release criminality.

13. Those interested in correctional treatment research should see M. W. Lipsey, "Can Intervention Rehabilitate Serious Delinquents?" *Annals of the American Academy of Political and Social Sciences* 564 (1999): 142–166.

14. Transition from an institutional environment to the community can be a struggle for some offenders. For example, J. Petersilia, *When Prisoners Come Home: Parole and Prisoner Reentry* (New York: Oxford University Press, 2003) suggested offenders released from California prisons carried with them a host of deleterious characteristics when released and that these factors may have complicated the re-entry process. Additionally, J. A. Bouffard and K. J. Bergseth, "The Impact of Reentry Services on Juvenile Offender Recidivism," *Youth Violence and Juvenile Justice* 6 (2008): 295–318 found support for incremental reductions in supervision for those released from incarceration.

15. Specifically, 19 percent of white offenders classified as recidivists compared to 25 percent nonrecidivists ($p < .01$) and 39 percent of Hispanic offenders classified as recidivists compared to 45 percent nonrecidivists ($p < .01$).

16. There were a total of 48 offenders classified as other race. Because of the low frequencies across the dependent variable, the authors collapsed other races with offenders classified as white for multivariate analyses.

17. Recall from chapter 3 that approximately 60 percent of offenders lived in poverty, approximately 71 percent came from chaotic home environments, one in five offenders reported emotional abuse, just less than one-fourth reported supervision neglect, and 77 percent reported a history of substance abuse.

18. S. Glueck and E. Glueck, *Unraveling Juvenile Delinquency* (New York: Commonwealth Fund, 1950).

19. J. H. Laub and R. J. Sampson, *Shared Beginnings, Divergent Lives: Delinquent Boys to Age 70* (Cambridge, MA: Harvard University Press, 2003).

20. J. H. Laub, D. S. Nagin, and R. J. Sampson, "Trajectories of Change in Criminal Offending: Good Marriages and the Desistance Process," *American Sociological Review* 63, no. 2 (1998): 225–238; R. J. Sampson, J. H. Laub, and C. Wimer, "Does Marriage Reduce Crime? A Counterfactual Approach to Within-Individual Causal Effects," *Criminology* 44, no. 3 (2006): 465–508.

21. Texas Youth Commission, *Texans Changing Lives: Annual Report Fiscal Year 2002* (Austin: Texas Youth Commission, 2002).

22. Other offenses include property crimes and institutional control crime (e.g., escape). Because there were so few offenders in these individual categories, the authors collapsed these low-frequency offenses into an "other" offense category to protect the anonymity of study subjects and for analysis requirements.

23. C. Trulson, J. Caudill, S. Belshaw, and M. DeLisi, "A Problem of Fit: Extreme Delinquents, Blended Sentencing, and the Determinants of Continued Adult Sanctions," *Criminal Justice Policy Review* 22 (2011): 263–284.

24. Trulson et al., "In Between Adolescence and Adulthood."

25. Although there was a statistically significant difference in recidivism group

classification based on treatment programming, one should use caution in drawing definitive conclusions of programming effectiveness. The reader interested in program effectiveness should turn to the more sophisticated event history analyses presented later in this chapter.

26. Analyses in chapter 5 provide a more comprehensive model, where several demographic, home environment, criminal history, and programming indicators predicted community supervision.

27. We use the broad term "event history analysis" to keep the focus on the recidivism outcomes of these serious offenders. Specifically, we used the Royston-Parmar event history analysis model, which estimates the correlation between individual characteristics and rearrest in the tradition of multivariate regression modeling. For the interested reader, we suggest reading J. M. Box-Steffensmeier and B. S. Jones, *Event History Modeling: A Guide for Social Scientists* (New York: Cambridge University Press, 2004); E. L. Kaplan and P. Meier, "Nonparametric Estimation from Incomplete Observations," *Journal of the American Statistical Association* 53, no. 282 (1958): 457–481; and O. O. Aalen, O. Borgan, and H. K. Gjessing, *Event History Analysis: A Process Point of View* (New York: Springer, 2006).

The Royston-Parmar event history analysis model provides scholars with more flexibility in estimating time-varying covariates and the baseline hazard function through regression splines and knots. Introduction of splines and knots—based on degrees of freedom—allowed us to first estimate the number and location of the knots given the covariation of independent variables over time. Additionally, the Royston-Parmar model permits a Bayesian approach to determine model scaling most closely associated with proportional risk of failure. We used the Akaike Information Criterion (AIC) goodness-of-fit statistic to optimize the number of knots and in selection of the most appropriate scale. The best AIC statistical values for four scales (hazard, odds, normal, Theta) and, within each scale, nine models with up to nine degrees of freedom was the hazard scale with three degrees of freedom. Based on this information, we used two equally distributed internal knots.

28. Crime statistics, for instance, are typically bound by some time frame (e.g., jurisdictional homicides per year reported by the Federal Bureau of Investigation's Uniform Crime Reports) to standardize them for comparison. This allows social scientists to develop crime rates across time. Additionally, this is a common practice in estimating individual-level risk of recidivism. Because traditional methods of estimating recidivism have relied on statistical procedures that hold elapsed time constant, time becomes a static measure within these models. This process classifies subjects into either nonrecidivist or recidivist groups without consideration for when within the period the recidivism event occurred. While this approach estimates recidivism within a predetermined period, the static influence of time is artificial.

29. D. R. Cox, "Regression Models and Life-Tables," *Journal of the Royal Statistics Society, Series B (Methodological)* 34, no. 2 (1972): 187–220.

30. Scholars have used event history analysis to explore and test a range of criminological phenomena and hypotheses related to case processing and offending; see, for example, M. A. Scott, L. Snowden, and A. M. Libby, "From Mental Health to Juvenile Justice: What Factors Predict this Transition?" *Journal of Child and Family Studies* 11, no. 3 (2002): 299–311, which invokes event history analysis in considering

the micro-level determinants of entry into Colorado's juvenile justice system for youths receiving Medicaid-funded mental health care. In another example, M. S. Zatz, "Los Cholos: Legal Processing of Chicano Gang Members," *Social Problems* 33, no. 1 (1985): 13–30 implements event history analysis to explore the official labeling effects of gang affiliation on case processing for Chicano youths in Phoenix, Arizona.

Scholars have also used event history analysis in the study of micro-level factors associated with offending. See J. W. Caudill, "Back on the Swagger: Institutional Release and Recidivism Timing among Gang Affiliates," *Youth Violence and Juvenile Justice* 8, no. 1 (2010): 58–70; C. DeJong, "Survival Analysis and Specific Deterrence: Integrating Theoretical and Empirical Models of Recidivism," *Criminology* 35, no. 4 (1997): 561–575; R. R. Gainey, B. K. Payne, and M. O'Toole, "The Relationship between Time in Jail, Time on Electronic Monitoring, and Recidivism: An Event History Analysis of a Jail-Based Program," *Justice Quarterly* 17, no. 4 (2000): 733–752.

31. Preliminary analyses of the at-risk period included estimating both a three- and a five-year model. The life table demonstrates higher recidivism risks at thirty-six months than at sixty months, suggesting less stability in the three-year model. The plateau effect of recidivism risk in the latter months, in concert with Caudill's use of a five-year at-risk period, supported this approach. This exposure restriction excluded any offender with an at-risk period shorter than sixty months based on the culmination of data collection efforts on January 1, 2012. In other words, offenders sentenced and then released to the community under Texas's blended sentencing law after January 1, 2007, were not included in event history analysis.

32. The recidivism level reported here differs slightly from the numbers of sentenced offenders rearrested and the percent of those rearrested reported earlier in this chapter because it is limited to a five-year time frame. Previous calculations of recidivism reported earlier in this chapter were not limited to a five-year time frame.

33. Gender and race were the most consistent predictors of recidivism for the full and offense-based models. In general, male and African American offenders were at significantly greater recidivism hazards than their counterparts. It should be noted that for race, specifically African American race, racial correlations were uncovered for all major outcomes in this text including misconduct participation, certain determination hearing decisions including prison transfer versus other determination hearing outcomes, and recidivism risk as examined in the current chapter. Although correlations with race (and gender) were associated with these outcomes, our goal with this book was not to examine the potential racial or gender effects of determinate sentencing. Moreover, even in the presence of effects related to race (e.g., that African American youths had a higher likelihood of prison transfer versus release with supervision compared to white or Hispanic offenders net the effects of other variables in the statistical models, or higher recidivism hazards compared with white or Hispanic offenders net the effects of other variables), we do not have access to data that could truly ferret out the reality behind any racial effects. The potential explanations for such effects are that the juvenile/determinate sentencing process is somehow discriminatory, or that being of a particular race/ethnicity is a proxy for some factor, legal and legitimate or otherwise, that leads to these outcomes, or that there is a combinational and cumulative effect of race or its proxy across the various stages of the process, producing the potential for more subtle discrimination or the appearance of discrimination. The reality among these options is that we do not

know, and we do not have the data to allow the kind of analyses that would provide such answers. Such an analysis and examination is undoubtedly important, but our lack of data means it cannot be given specific justice in this book. Any effort to do so would only be conjecture and speculation, which we believe would further muddle the issue.

34. "Full model" refers to the event history model that includes controls for offense group as opposed to event history models within offense groups. Also, we excluded one observation from the R-P modeling due to unexplained recidivism exposure exit.

35. The other offense control group included offenders sentenced for violent and other serious offenses—i.e., aggravated assault, aggravated kidnapping, arson, burglary, deadly conduct, escape, injury to a child or elderly individual, manufacture or delivery of a controlled substance, or unlawful possession of a controlled substance.

36. Texas's DSA was legally authorized for relatively few but was intended for serious and violent offenses.

37. Offenders sentenced for robbery, sexual, homicide, and other violent and drug-related crimes (the comparison group for the full event history analysis) made up approximately 95 percent of the sample. Small frequencies of other offense categories precluded a broader perspective.

38. Other independent variables were held constant at their respective means in the smoothed linear function of each observation (L. Breiman and J. H. Friedman, "Estimating Optimal Transformations for Multiple Regression and Correction [with Discussion]," *Journal of the American Statistical Association* 80 [1985]: 580–619.)

39. Five sexual offenders recidivated within the first month and one sexual offender experienced immediate rearrest after release from TYC. We suspect this immediate rearrest (rearrest = 1 and time to rearrest = 0) was the product of an administrative transfer between criminal justice agencies. With that said, we excluded this offender's case from further analysis given the lack of information.

40. Eighty-two percent (n = 196) of homicide commitments participated in the COP according to official records. Given the limitations of our measure of program participation, we encourage caution when interpreting these findings. Program enrollment is unspecific and does not consider treatment cooperation, case plan fidelity, and other important treatment program measures.

41. The relatively small sample size of the homicide offender group precluded use of race, gender, staff assaults, and the general treatment proxy in the graphic presentation, even though both were significant when correlated with recidivism hazard. Instead, we held constant these factors in similar fashion as the other covariates to maintain observations for the low-risk and high-risk groups.

42. Petersilia, *When Prisoners Come Home.*

CHAPTER 7: THREE DECADES LATER

1. Although more youths have been prosecuted and adjudicated under DSA, some were given determinate sentence probation in the original instance. We do not have information about those who received determinate sentence probation.

2. This claim is not just hyperbole, and we realize that some might argue that youths certified to adult court might be more serious offenders. It is interesting to

note that in a study comparing adult court certified and determinately sentenced juvenile offenders in Texas from 2005 to 2009, the author found that determinately sentenced offenders are no less serious than adult court certified youths in Texas, and in fact may be even more serious. Although there are numerous reasons for this, the author notes that adult court certification in Texas is not limited to serious and violent offenses, as is determinate sentencing for the most part. For more details, see M. Deitch, *Juveniles in the Adult Criminal Justice System in Texas* (Austin: University of Texas, LBJ School of Public Affairs, 2011).

3. D. P. Mears, "Evaluation Issues Confronting Juvenile Justice Sentencing Reforms: A Case Study of Texas," *Crime and Delinquency* 44 (1998): 443–463.

4. See, for example, M. Podkopacz and B. Feld, "The End of the Line: An Empirical Study of Judicial Waiver," *Journal of Criminal Law and Criminology* 86 (1996): 449–492; M. Podkopacz and B. Feld, "The Back-Door to Prison: Waiver Reform, Blended Sentencing, and the Law of Unintended Consequences," *Journal of Criminal Law and Criminology* 91 (2001): 997–1072; J. Burrow, "Examining the Influence of Matza's Principles of Justice and Their Impact on Reverse Waiver Decisions: Has Kadi-(In)justice Survived?" *Youth Violence and Juvenile Justice* 6 (2008): 59–82.

5. For an excellent discussion of determinate sentencing in Texas and these types of broader evaluative issues, see Mears, "Juvenile Justice Sentencing Reforms."

6. M. G. Vaughn, C. P. Salas-Wright, M. DeLisi, and B. R. Maynard, "Violence and Externalizing Behavior among Youth in the United States: Is There a Severe 5%?" *Youth Violence and Juvenile Justice* (in press); T. E. Moffitt, "Adolescence-Limited and Life-Course-Persistent Antisocial Behavior: A Developmental Taxonomy," *Psychological Review* 100, no. 4 (1993): 674–701.

7. Indeed, the notion of success concerning determinate sentencing is complicated and largely subjective. For example, determinate sentencing might be considered a success for prosecutors who have more charging options or leverage for plea bargains. Success may be found for judges who have more sentencing leeway beyond the regular juvenile court or that offered by adult court certification. It may be found for correctional staff and others who arguably have more leverage over youth behavior in institutions. It may be found for youths who avoided a certification to adult court. Success might not be found in terms of the victims of the sentenced offenders. The notion of success can be considered across a variety of contexts. We, however, do not go so far as to provide this subjective label to determinate sentencing.

CHAPTER 8: THE LAST WORD

1. James Q. Wilson, *Thinking about Crime* (New York: Random House, 1985), 206.

2. Deanna Boyd, "Fort Worth Teen Paroled in Murder Case Is Accused in Second Slaying," *Fort Worth Star-Telegram*, March 12, 2015, http://www.star-telegram.com /news/local/crime/article13880906.html, retrieved March 16, 2015.

3. L. Steinberg, "Punishment and the Adolescent Brain: The Role of Developmental Science in Recent U.S. Supreme Court Decisions about Juvenile Offenders," Center for Psychology and Law Brown Bag Series, lecture given at University of California–Irvine, March 2014.

4. Other research uses propensity score matching to reveal that such intensive therapeutic treatment for capital and serious violent offenders, when delivered in an adequate dose (ideally six months), significantly reduces the likelihood of recidivism compared to similar offenders who were eligible for but did not receive such treatment. See, for example, D. Haerle, "Dosage Matters: Impact of a Violent Offender Treatment Program on Juvenile Recidivism," *Youth Violence and Juvenile Justice* (forthcoming).

5. This study examines mostly adult offenders, but 17 percent of the sample is twenty-four years of age or younger; see A. D. Cooper, M. R. Durose, and H. N. Snyder, *Recidivism of Prisoners Released in 30 States in 2005: Patterns from 2005–2010* (Washington, DC: US Department of Justice, Office of Justice Programs, Bureau of Justice Statistics, 2014).

6. See D. Clemmer, *The Prison Community* (Boston: Christopher, 1940); E. Goffman, *Asylums: Essays on the Social Situation of Mental Patients and Other Inmates* (New York: Anchor Books, 1961).

7. S. Wheeler, "Socialization in Correctional Communities," *American Sociological Review* 26 (1961): 697–712.

8. I (Haerle) conducted interviews with a sample of incarcerated male juvenile offenders ages twelve to twenty-three in California. While similarly violent juvenile court youths are protected by juvenile jurisdiction until the age of twenty-five, the adult court youths are transferred to the adult side at age eighteen. Mixed methods research shows that knowledge of this transfer influences their behavior during this term of juvenile incarceration. More specifically, the more they articulate a strategy for survival on the adult side, the higher the rate of violent misconduct they engage in during juvenile incarceration.

9. See D. Bishop, "Juvenile Offenders in the Adult Criminal Justice System," *Crime and Justice* 27 (2000): 81–167; A. Kupchik, *Judging Juveniles: Prosecuting Adolescents in Adult and Juvenile Courts* (New York: New York University Press, 2006).

10. M. Forst, J. Fagan, and T. S. Vivona, "Youth in Prisons and Training Schools: Perceptions and Consequences of the Treatment-Custody Dichotomy," *Juvenile and Family Court Journal* 40 (1989): 1–14 (quotation on 9).

11. See B. Feld, "Abolish the Juvenile Court: Youthfulness, Criminal Responsibility, and Sentencing Policy," *Journal of Criminal Law and Criminology* 88, no. 1 (1997): 68–136; B. Feld, "Adolescent Criminal Responsibility, Proportionality, and Sentencing Policy: *Roper, Graham, Miller/Jackson*, and the Youth Discount," *Journal of Law and Inequality* 31 (2013): 263–330.

12. In my practitioner experience, I (Caudill) observed very little remorse for the damage created by the offender's behavior. Instead, most of these juvenile offenders expressed remorse in terms of "getting caught." TYC parole-violating gang members typically "chalked it up to the game" when they were "caught slippin'" and taken into custody. It was a game where the strong manipulated the weak and the remorseful typically were with the latter.

Page numbers in italics indicate photographs.

abuse (physical, emotional, and/or
sexual) in the home, ix, 59–61, 68, 72,
117–118, 144, 168, 188n17
abuse of juvenile offenders, 7, 9; in adult
prisons, 162; at Gatesville, 22; by TYC
officials, 26–27, 178n3, 179n10
adjudication history: of average released
sentenced offender, 61, 122; as a predictor of the determination hearing
outcome, 93, 97, 104; as a predictor
of institutional misconduct, 74; and
recidivism, 119–120, 124, 127. *See also*
delinquent history
administrative segregation. *See* solitary
confinement
adolescence, 162–163; peak in delinquent behavior during, 159; sexual
aggression during, 75; and Terrie
Moffitt's developmental taxonomy,
167–168, 169
adult correctional facilities, 17–20, 89–
90, 162, 163; chance of rehabilitation
after time spent in, 155. *See also*
Texas prison system
adult court certification/waiver, 2, 40,
47, 111, 176n15, 179n10; blended sentencing as an alternative to, 135,
143, 144, 148, 154–155, 192n7; criticism of, 90, 184n12; different types
of, 184nn15–16; factors influencing,
91–93, 96, 104; lowering the age for,
8–9, 35; processes, nationwide, 31,
48; and recidivism, 91; and seriousness of crimes, 191–192n2; in Texas,
7, 28, 46–47, 135, 180n17; youths
who receive, and increased risk of
physical and sexual victimization,
35–36, 162
adult offenders. *See* offenders, adult
African Americans: female, school for

delinquent, 5; and institutional misconduct, 82, 84–85, 137; and juvenile
justice in the South, 18–20; among
leased convicts in the South, 173n38;
and likelihood of being released at
determination hearings vs. going to
prison, 101–103, 106, 138; percentage
of, among juvenile sentenced offenders in Texas, 54; and recidivism,
115, 129–131, 133, 139, 190–191n33
age: of adult criminal responsibility,
raised, 5, 173n41; at commitment,
as a risk factor in institutional misconduct, 73, 75, 82, 84, 85, 137, 138; of
initial jurisdiction in a determinate
sentencing case, 178n4; of juvenile
sentenced offenders in Texas, 54,
173nn39–40; as a predictor of the
determination hearing outcome, 93,
104, 109, 139; at time of determination hearing, 181n26, 183n2, 185n26.
See also adolescence
aggravated assault, 31, 57, 138, 181n27,
185–186n32, 191n35
aggravated kidnapping, 9, 36, 185–
186n32, 185–186n32, 191n35
aggravated robbery, 31, 57, 181n27, 185–
186n32; attempted, 180n16
aggravated sexual assault, 9, 31, 36, 38,
41, 57, 65, 138, 151, 185–186n32
antisocial tendencies, 70, 74, 75, 84, 86
arson, 138, 185–186n32, 191n35
assault (as an offense), 138. *See also* aggravated assault; aggravated sexual
assault
assaults, institutional, by sentenced
offenders: averaged, 122; directed at
other wards, 74, 78, 87, 97, 120, 122,
127, 129, 130, 131, 132, 133, 137, 139, 140,
181–182n2; directed at staff, 74, 79,

87, 97, 127, 133, 181–182n2; as a factor
in determination hearing outcomes,
97, 105, 106, 108, 110; and recidivism,
120–121, 127, 129, 130, 131, 132, 133, 137,
139, 140
Augustus, John, 13

Bad Boys, 79
Bercu, Steven, 25–26
"Black Codes," 18
blacks. See African Americans
blended sentencing, 8, 31–32, 34, 45, 144,
145, 154, 165, 168; basis for, 90–91;
criticism of, 183–184n12; development of, in the 1980s, 90; different
types of, 184n15; efficacy of, 48–49;
future of, 147, 148; outcomes of, 93;
research on, 96, 148; spread of, 143.
See also determinate sentencing
boys. See males
Brady State School for Delinquent
and Dependent Colored Girls. See
Colored Girls Training School
Brown, Johnny W., 25
Brown, Martha, 25
Brown and Sorenson, 93
Brownwood State School, 51
building tenders, 27, 174–175n65
Bureau of Justice Statistics, 160
burglary, 31, 185–186n32, 191n35; attempted, 180n16

California, 162, 163, 188n14, 193n8; California Youth Authority (CYA), 74, 75
Campbell, Henry, 11, 29
Cantu, Peter, 30
Capital and Serious Violent Offender
Treatment Program (CSVOTP), 47, 68,
105, 150–151, 181n27, 186n34. See also
Capital Offender Program
capital murder, 9, 31, 36, 57, 80–81, 152,
175n69, 176–177n18; attempted, 36,
180n16; conspiracy to commit, 180n16
Capital Offender Program (COP), 38, 114,
121, 139, 140, 158, 160, 191n40; and
Edward McCoy, 112, 122; implementation of, 38; and recidivism, 131–132,

133; success of, 114, 181n27. See also
Capital and Serious Violent Offender Treatment Program
Catholics, 12
chain gangs, 18, 19, 20
Chavez, Arturo, 56
child abuse. See abuse (physical, emotional, and/or sexual) in the home;
abuse of juvenile offenders
child neglect. See neglected children
"child-savers," 11–12, 17, 31, 164
Christina Melton Crain Unit, 8
civil rights of juvenile offenders, 165–166
Civil War, 18, 20
Coke, Richard, 19
Colored Girls Training School, 6
Colquitt, Oscar B., 22
Connolly, Bill, 47–48
contraband, possession of, 79, 87
contract system, convict, 173n35
convict leases, 18–19, 173n35
corporal punishment, 7
correctional officers/staff, 2, 9, 27, 52,
141, 192n7. See also assaults, institutional, by sentenced offenders:
directed at staff; abuse of juvenile
offenders
Corsicana State Home, 5. See also Texas
State Orphan Asylum
Cox regression, 123
crime, juvenile. See juvenile crime
crime statistics, 189n28
criminal desistance, 118
Crockett State School, 8

Davidson, Clyde, 114
Davidson, Geraldine, 55, 111–113, 114
Davidson, Paul, 114
deadly assault on a law enforcement
officer, 9, 36, 176n9
Deaf, Dumb, and Blind Asylum for
Colored Youth, 5, 173–174n46
death penalty, x, 28, 30, 45, 89, 90, 154,
175n69. See also executions; Roper v.
Simmons
delinquency, juvenile. See juvenile
delinquency

delinquent history, 61–62, 68, 72–74, 119; and determination hearing outcome, 96, 100, 101, 103–104, 108; and institutional misconduct, 73, 74, 80, 82, 84–85, 137, 138; and recidivism, 118–120, 123, 133. *See also* adjudication history

demographics, 55, 83–85, 98, 102, 115–118, 126, 137. *See also* age; gender; race

dependent children, 8, 12, 13, 171n11, 173–174n46. *See also* home environment, problematic or disadvantaged; parenting

deprivation theories, 73, 161, 182n3

determinate sentencing: and commitment offenses, 37, 56–57; decision to pursue, 40–44, 143, 177n30; drop in, 179n10; and the Edward McCoy case, 111–113, 114, 122; and factors that influence the outcomes of determination hearings, 92–93, 94–108, 146; first long-term empirical study of, 136; future research on, 147–148; goals of, 152; improving, 146; and latitude in sentencing, 58; legal pathways of, 39; and number of determinate sentences in Texas, 54, 135; origins of, in Texas, ix–xi, 28–29, 35–38, 90, 144; process of, in Texas, 2–3, 31–32, 38–44; and recidivism outcomes, 110, 113–133, 136; and sentence length, 57–58, 59; success of, 147, 150–169, 192n7; theory of vs. practice of, 163. *See also* blended sentencing

Determinate Sentencing Act (DSA), 8–9, 28–29, 34, 36, 88, 111, 127, 135, 137, 165, 176n16, 191n1; efficacy of, in Texas, 45–49; first enacted, 36; milestones in, 38; modifications to, 37, 38, 176n17, 176–177n18

determination hearing(s), 41–45, 141–142, 180n22, 183n3; age at time of, 183n2; Edward McCoy's, 112, 114; outcomes of, and factors relating to, 62, 64, 88–89, 94–95, 100–110, 138–139,

151–152, 190–191n33; release of youth without, 183n4, 185n28; Venancio Medellin's, 44–45

double jeopardy, 47

drug-related offenses, 57, 118, 175n69, 185–186n32, 191nn35–37

drugs. *See* substance abuse; treatment programs, for juveniles: chemical dependency/substance abuse

DSA. *See* Determinate Sentencing Act (DSA)

due process, 26, 174n59

education: deficits in, as contributing to delinquency, 68, 87, 144, 152, 169; in juvenile reform schools, 15; lack of, in prison environments, 73; as a protective factor that buffers against misconduct, 84, 85, 137; and recidivism outcomes, 114; special needs, among youthful offenders, 61, 116

employment and criminal desistance, 118

environment. *See* home environment, problematic or disadvantaged

Ertman, Jennifer, 29–30, 41, 54, 109, 150, 151, 162

event history analysis, 123–133, 189n27, 189–190n30, 191n34

executions, 111, 113, 158. *See also* death penalty

Fagan, J., 162

family courts. *See* juvenile courts

Feld, Barry C., 13

felonies, 31, 154, 169; certification to adult court for, 175n69; maximum sentences for, 36, 37, 38, 57, 185n28; minimum lengths of stay for, 176–177n18, 177n21, 185n28. *See also* specific felonies

females, 26, 158; misconduct among, associated with psychiatric disorders, 75; offenses of, 25; schools/correctional facilities for delinquent, 5, 6, 51

Forst, M., 162

Gainesville State School for Girls, 5, 6, 26, 52

gangs, 52, 56, 157, 163; activity in, as a form of institutional misconduct, 79, 181–182n2; affiliation with, commonly seen in offenders' life histories, 59, 61; affiliation with, as a predictor of the determination hearing outcome, 92, 93, 104; affiliation with, and recidivism, 116, 121; affiliation with, as a risk factor in institutional misconduct, 73, 74–75, 79, 84, 137; as aggravating circumstance in sentencing, 92; prevention programs to curtail influence of, 147; renunciation programs for, 68; Venancio Medellin as member of, 30, 38, 41, 54

Gatesville House of Correction, 5, 21, 22

Gatesville State School for Boys, *xvi*, 1, 4, 6, 7, 34, 46, *51*, 63, 66, 67, 78, *100*, *112*, *151*; closing of, 2; hard work viewed as treatment at, 174n49; and the impact of *Morales v. Turman*, 25, 27–28; murders at, 24; opening of, 5, 173–174n46

Gatesville Unit for Women, 8

gender. *See* females; males

Giddings State School, 7, 8, 38, 52, 68, 122, 150, 181n27

girls. *See* females

Glueck, Sheldon and Eleanor, 17, 117, 118

Gonzalez, Rose Marie, 56

good-conduct time, 44

grand juries, 40, 41, 176n15

halfway houses, 52

Hart, Hastings H., 172n23

Hilltop Unit for Men (Gatesville), *xvi*, 6, 8, *12*, 63, 66

Hispanics: and institutional misconduct, 82, 84–85; and likelihood of being released at determination hearings vs. going to prison, 101, 106; percentage of, among juvenile sen-

tenced offenders in Texas, 54; and recidivism, 115, 188n15, 190–191n33

history of violence/delinquency. *See* delinquent history

Hoffman, William, Jr., 26

home environment, problematic or disadvantaged: in backgrounds of juvenile sentenced offenders in Texas, 58–62, 68, 117, 127, 144, 152, 166, 168, 188n17; belief that juvenile delinquency originates in, 17, 70; as a factor in institutional misconduct, 137; and recidivism, 116–118, 124, 127, 139

homicide, 108, 191n37; commission of, and determinate sentencing outcomes, 97, 104, 145, 185–186n32; as extreme institutional misconduct, 72; juvenile sentencing for, 175n69; offenders, treatment in the Capital Offender Program for, 114, 181n27, 191n40; rate in Texas, 8; and recidivism, 118, 128, 130–133, 134, 140, 191n41; statistics on, 189n28. *See also* capital murder; manslaughter; murder

houses of refuge, 14–15, 16–17, 20, 70, 89, 172nn19–23

Huntsville Unit (Texas State Penitentiary at Huntsville, also known as "Walls"), 19, 30, 113, 173n41

immigrants, 1, 12, 17, 171n5

indecency with a child, 57, 65, 185–186n32

individual liberties. *See* civil rights of juvenile offenders

Industrial School for Boys (Massachusetts), 17

industrial schools. *See* training and industrial schools

institutional misconduct, juvenile, 49, 64, 69, 72, 87–88, 120, 122, 156, 181–182n2, 182–183n1, 193n8; by commitment offense, 80–82; incidence and prevalence of, 73–82; as a predictor of the determination hearing out-

come, 93, 97, 100, 106, 108, 110, 139;
predictors of, 73, 82–85, 137–138, 161,
166; and recidivism, 120–122, 123, 127,
133, 139, 140, 166; in TDC, 181n24

Jester, Beauford H., 23
job training, 68, 105
journalists. *See* media coverage of juvenile cases
judges: adult vs. juvenile court, 183–
184n12; and blended sentencing,
92; and determinate sentencing in
Texas, 41, 44, 58, 109, 141, 145, 148,
176n17, 179n6, 192n7; early juvenile
court, 11, 13, 22; focus of, on victims,
152; and view of institutional misconduct, 88
juries, 41, 58, 176n16, 179n6. *See also*
grand juries
Justice, William Wayne, 7, 8, 26, 27
juvenile correctional facilities. *See*
Texas Youth Commission *and*
names of specific institutions
juvenile courts, 171n8; first in nation
(Chicago, IL), 11, 14, 15, 16, 21, 29, 31,
89, 164, 171n12, 171–172n13; development and expansion of, nationwide,
12–13, 171n9; in Texas, 21–22, 46, 164–
165, 176n14; traditional, 154–155
juvenile crime: drop in, nationwide, 46,
179n10; examples of, in Texas, 55–56;
increase in, in Texas, 8, 28, 31
juvenile delinquency, 2, 12; causes of,
70; "discovery" of, in the late 1800s,
89; as distinct from dependency and
neglect, 12, 13, 171n11; Glueck study
of, 17, 117–118; Moffitt's theory about,
167–168
Juvenile Delinquency Court Act (1907),
21
Juvenile Justice Code, 48
juvenile offenders. *See* offenders,
juvenile
juvenile reform schools. *See* reform
schools/reformatories

kidnapping. *See* aggravated kidnapping

lease system. *See* convict leases
Ledesma, Zuly, 157
life sentence without parole: disallowed
for juveniles, 175n69; mandatory, 154
Live Oak School (Gatesville), *12*, 66, 67
logistic regression, 82
Lowe, Doug, 114
Lyman School for Boys (Massachusetts),
1–2, 17

males: and institutional misconduct, 73,
75, 85; percentage of, among juvenile
sentenced offenders in Texas, 54,
122; and recidivism, 115–116, 128, 131,
133, 139, 190–191n33
Malone, Billy, 6
manslaughter, 57; intoxication, 185–
186n32
Marlin Orientation and Assessment,
51, 178n3
Marquart, James, 156
marriage and criminal desistance, 118
maturity. *See* offenders, juvenile: maturity of
McCoy, Edward "Pete," 55, 111–112, 113,
114, 122, 134, 164
McLennan County State Juvenile Correctional Facility, 51
McTear, Marcus, 55
Medellin, Jose, 30, 38
Medellin, Venancio ("Vinny"), 30–31, 32,
37–38, 40–41, 44–45, 54–55
media coverage of juvenile cases, 109,
146, 152
mental challenges, 61, 65
mental illness: as a risk factor in institutional misconduct, 137–138; among
youths in confinement, 61, 65, 74, 75,
116. *See also* treatment programs for
juveniles: mental health
minimum length of stay (MLOS), 42,
43, 53, 155, 176–177n18, 177n21, 183n4,
185n28
misconduct by institutionalized juveniles. *See* institutional misconduct,
juvenile
misdemeanors, juvenile, 10, 142, 175n73

Moffitt, Terrie, 167–168, 169
Morales, Alicia, 7, 25
Morales v. Turman, 8, 9, 25–28
Mosley, Ortralla, 55
Mountain View State School for Boys, 2, *21*, *24*, *29*, *71*, *88*, *136*; abuse at, 27; opening of, 7, 24, 31
multinomial logistic regression (MLR), 101, 105, 186n37
Mulvey, Edward P., 85
murder, 9, 36, 79, 80–81, 82, 151–152; attempted, 180n16; solicitation to commit, 180n16. *See also* capital murder; homicide; manslaughter

negative binomial model, 82
neglected children, ix, 8, 12, 13, 61, 171n11, 173–174n46. *See also* home environment, problematic or disadvantaged; parenting
New York House of Refuge, 14
Nuts and Bolts of Juvenile Law meeting, 48

O'Brien, Sean Derrick, 30
offenders, adult, 18, 28; belief that juveniles should be treated differently from, 14, 90; and the death penalty, x; focus on deterrence and punishment for, 33–34; juveniles treated as, in the early days, 19, 22, 173n38; as less malleable than children, 154, 159; stopping juveniles from becoming, 12, 31, 134; victimization of youthful offenders by, 35–36. *See also* adult court certification/waiver; adult correctional facilities
offenders, juvenile: commitment offenses of, 56–57; considered a danger to others, 61, 78, 120, 122, 137; considered a danger to selves, 62, 137; deaths of, 53, 64, 95, 179n7, 181n25, 185n30; defined, 178n2; demographics of, 54, 55, 83, 98, 102, 115–116, 126; institutional misconduct among, 73–82, 88; life-course persistent, 167–168; life histories of, 60–62;

maturity of, 90, 92, 109, 135, 144, 154, 155, 159, 162; outcomes for (release vs. prison time), 89, 94–108; petty, 17, 19, 20; picture of, as they transition from the lawful to the delinquent world, 53–62; and predictors of institutional misconduct, 82–85; profile of average, 122–123; progression of, through TYC, 62–64; and recidivism, 113–134, 139–140; and remorse, 193n12; sentences of, 58, 85, 104–106, 108, 109, 137, 139; serious and violent, 2–3, 9, 11, 16–17, 24–25, 28–29, 31, 32, 36, 46, 57, 58, 93, 113, 114, 122, 133, 135, 136, 138, 144, 146, 147, 151, 165, 175n67; time and activities of, while in TYC, 64–68; and transition from institutional environment to the community, 188n14; treated like adults, in the early days, 19, 22, 89–93, 173n38; victim attitude of, 155. *See also* adjudication history; delinquent history
"office boys," 27, 174–175n65
out-of-home residential placements, 93; average number of, among sentenced offenders cohort, 61, 119, 122; and institutional misconduct, 84, 137, 138, 166; and recidivism, 127, 129, 130, 139, 140, 166

parens patriae, ix, 33, 70, 165
parenting: absent, abusive, or criminal, 14, 17, 59, 144, 152, 166, 168, 171n11; caring and concerned, ix, 153
parole, 38, 42–43, 44, 52, 63, 69, 74, 94, 95, 138, 185n27; for Edward McCoy, 112; as a factor in reducing recidivism, 127, 128; failures, 163; for Venancio Medellin, 31, 44, 45. *See also* release to the community: with supervision
Pena, Elizabeth, 29–30, 41, 54, 109, 150, 151, 162
Perez, Efrain, 30
police: contacts with, as a predictor of institutional misconduct, 74, 75; departments, dealing with juveniles by, 171n9

poverty, 61, 72, 118, 144, 152, 168, 188n17

prison farms, 89

prisons. *See* adult correctional facilities; Texas prison system

probation, 13, 61, 63, 171n12, 179n6; failure of, 101, 103–104, 119, 176n17

Project Rio, 68

prosecutors, 88, 109, 141, 152; and discretion in determinate sentencing, 40, 41, 47, 48, 92, 143, 147–148, 177n30, 179n10, 192n7

public safety, 112, 114, 115, 122, 140, 160, 162–163, 165, 169

punishment: adult, 89, 90, 91, 136, 144; avoidance of, 166; cruel and unusual, 162; and determinate sentencing, 29, 136, 154, 160, 165; and first Texas juvenile courts, 21–29, 33–34; vs. rehabilitation, x, 33–34, 45, 48, 136, 147, 163, 165, 167; severity of, as matter for debate, 36

race: as a factor in determination hearing outcomes, 101–103; at Gatesville, 21; and juvenile justice in the South, 17–20; of juvenile sentenced offenders in Texas, 54; and recidivism, 124, 128, 129–130, 133, 188n15, 190–191n33; as a risk factor in institutional misconduct, 75; and segregation in juvenile correctional facilities, 7. *See also* African Americans; Hispanics; whites

Ramirez, Gilbert, 56

rape, 30, 56, 79, 82

recidivism, 3, 32, 49, 110, 113–133, 136, 139–140, 142, 145, 154, 156; and adult court–waived youth, 91, 162; and age at the time of commitment, 115; blame for, 146; Bureau of Justice Statistics on, 160–161; and the Capital and Serious Violent Offender Treatment Program, 131, 132–133, 158; and committing offense, 128–133, 134; and crime statistics, 189n28; and data on post-release incarceration, 142–143; and demo-graphic factors, 114, 115–118; as a determinant of persistent delinquency, 166; five-year life table of, 125; and gender, 115–116, 190–191n33; and homicide commitments, 118, 128, 130–133, 134, 140, 191n41; and institutional misconduct, 120–122, 123, 127, 133, 139, 140, 161, 166; and length of incarceration, 131, 132–133; and limitations of research on, 180n21; and post-release supervision, 127, 128, 134; and premature release, 164; and race, 115, 188n15, 190–191n33; and robbery commitments, 118, 128, 129, 131, 132, 133, 134, 139, 140; and sex offender commitments, 127, 128–130, 132, 133, 134, 140; timing of, and explanation for, 123–128, 139, 190nn31–32; and treatment, 114, 134, 160, 188–189n25, 193n4

Reconstruction, 18, 19, 20

redemption. *See* rehabilitation

reform schools/reformatories, 1, 15–16, 19, 20, 70, 172n23, 172n25

rehabilitation, 144, 152, 155, 156, 158; apparent, on the part of Edward McCoy, 114; and determinate sentencing, x, 2, 29, 36, 52, 90, 135–136, 160, 161, 163; and first Texas juvenile courts, 21–29, 33–34; impulse for, in society, 157; and institutional misconduct, 87–88; and malleability of youth, 159; progress toward, discussed at determination hearing, 42; vs. punishment, x, 33–34, 45, 48, 136, 147, 163, 165, 167; through treatment programs, 47, 68, 146. *See also* treatment programs for juveniles

release to the community, 64, 69, 106, 108, 110, 113; to a nonsecure facility, 177n20; without supervision, 43, 63, 89, 95, 96, 98–99, 100, 102–103, 105, 127, 133, 138, 140; with supervision, 42–43, 63, 89, 94, 96, 98–99, 100, 102–103, 104, 105, 106, 114, 123, 127, 128, 138, 140. *See also* parole; recidivism

retribution. *See* punishment

rioting, 7, 29, 79, 87

robbery, 104, 185–186n32, 191n35; and recidivism risk, 118, 128, 129, 131, 132, 133, 134, 139, 140; and sentence length, 108. *See also* aggravated robbery

Rodriguez, Ernesto, 157

Ron Jackson State Juvenile Correctional Complex, 51

Roper v. Simmons, 30, 175n69

Rothman, David J., 14, 16, 45

running away, 61, 103

Rusk State Penitentiary (Cherokee County, TX), 19, 173n41

Scared Straight, 79

Schlossman, Steven, 70

Schubert, Carol A., 85

self-harming behaviors, 79, 159. *See also* suicide/suicidal tendencies

sentenced offenders. *See* offenders, adult; offenders, juvenile

sentences: length of, 58, 59; long, as a predictor of the determination hearing outcome, 104–106, 108, 109, 139; long, as a risk factor in institutional misconduct, 85, 137; maximum, 3, 9, 30, 37, 38, 41, 53, 57–58, 155, 179n9, 185n28. *See also* minimum length of stay

sexual assault, 30, 38, 65, 185–186n32; attempted, 180n16. *See also* aggravated sexual assault; rape

sexual deviancy, 13, 62, 84, 121, 137

sexual misconduct/offending, 74, 75, 79, 104, 108, 113, 118, 181–182n2, 185–186n32, 191n35; and recidivism risk, 127, 128–130, 132, 133, 134, 140

Shelton, Pat, 44–45

Simpson, Danielle Nathaniel, 111–113

Simpson, Jennifer, 111

Simpson, Lionel, 111

slavery, 18, 20

Sleepers, 79

soft-on-crime approach, 158, 164

solitary confinement, 7, 28, 81

South, institutions for juvenile delinquents in the, 17–20, 172–173n31, 173n35

State Board of Control, 5, 6

State Home for Dependent and Neglected Children. *See* Waco State Home

State Institution for the Training of Delinquents. *See* Gatesville State School for Boys

State Juvenile Training Schools, 23

State Training School Code Commission, 6, 22–23

State Training School for Delinquent and Dependent Colored Girls, 6

State Youth Development Council, 6

statutory exclusion laws, 47

substance abuse, 59, 72, 147, 152, 164; in adolescence, 159, 167; and average released sentenced offender, 122; history of, at intake to state commitment, 61, 65, 72, 188n17; offenses related to, 118, 175n69, 185–186n32; and recidivism risk, 119–120, 124, 127, 129, 130, 133, 139, 140; as a risk factor in institutional misconduct, 73, 75, 85. *See also* drug-related offenses; treatment programs for juveniles: chemical dependency/substance abuse

suicide/suicidal tendencies, 62, 70, 72, 74, 79, 82

suicide watch, 51

"super-predators," 28, 31, 175n67

supervised release. *See* parole; release to the community: with supervision

TDC. *See* Texas Department of Corrections (TDC)

Texas Attorney General's Office, 9

Texas Blind, Deaf, and Orphan School, 5. *See also* Deaf, Dumb, and Blind Asylum for Colored Youth

Texas Board of Pardons and Paroles, 45

Texas Code of Criminal Procedure, 48

Texas Congress of Mothers, 22

Texas Constitution, 48

Texas Department of Corrections (TDC), 7, 8, 35, 52–53; and building tenders,

174–175n65; overcrowding in, 36. *See also* Texas prison system

Texas Department of Criminal Justice (TDCJ), 38, 111, 122, 178n3, 183n4; Parole Division of, 43, 63, 94, 122

Texas Department of Family and Protective Services (TDFPS), 8

Texas Department of Protective and Regulatory Services. *See* Texas Department of Family and Protective Services

Texas Federation of Women's Clubs, 22

Texas Juvenile Justice Department (TJJD), 10

Texas Juvenile Probation Commission (TJPC), 10, 48

Texas Legislature, 2, 5, 6, 8, 9; enacted the DSA, 36, 38; expanded the scope of the DSA, 37, 53; James Turman's influence on, 24; and juvenile justice, 20, 22–23, 35

Texas Office of the Inspector General, 9

Texas prison system: Building Tenders in, 27, 174–175n65; juvenile convicts in (1881), 19; overcrowding in, eased by moving out juvenile offenders, 19; transfer to, as possible outcome of determination hearing, x, 42, 43–44, 62, 63–64, 69, 89, 94–96, 97, 100, 104, 105–106, 136, 138, 142, 180n22, 181n24. *See also* Texas Department of Corrections (TDC)

Texas Rangers, 9

Texas Rules of Civil Procedure, 48

Texas Rules of Evidence, 48

Texas State Bar, Juvenile Law Section of, 48

Texas State Orphan Asylum, 5, 173–174n46

Texas State Training School for Girls. *See* Gainesville State School for Girls

Texas State Youth Development Council, 6, 23. *See also* Texas Youth Commission; Texas Youth Council

Texas Youth Commission (TYC), x, 2, 3, 38; abuse hotline, 9; high-security facilities of, 52; and the impact of *Morales v. Turman*, 25–28; increase in overall number of sentenced offenders committed to, 47; increase in serious and violent offenders among inmate population of, 25; institutional misconduct in, 73–86, 87–88, 137, 141; jurisdiction of, maximum age for, 43; length of incarceration in, and access to treatment, 163; length of incarceration in, and release to the community, 138–139, 186n36; length of incarceration in, and misconduct, 137; length of incarceration in, and recidivism, 131; Orientation and Assessment intake facility, 51–52; and parole failures, 163; percentage of offenders released from, 151; placed in conservatorship, 10; progression of sentenced offenders through, 62–64; and recidivism, 113–114, 121–122; sentenced offender histories before commitment to, 60–61, 72, 153; time and treatment in, 64–68; timeline of, 8–10; time served in, as predictive of the type of determination option, 104–105, 106, 110

Texas Youth Council, 6, 8, 23. *See also* Texas State Youth Development Council; Texas Youth Commission

therapy/therapeutic treatment. *See* treatment programs for juveniles

Torres, Damien Ray, 157

training and industrial schools, 15–16, 70, 172n23, 172n25

treatment programs for juveniles, 42, 47, 68, 121, 146, 158, 186n35; and average released sentenced offender, 122; capital offender, 64, 68; chemical dependency/substance abuse, 64–65, 105, 114, 121–122, 141, 160; evaluation for, during state orientation and assessment, 52; homicide offender, 114, 140, 181n27, 191n40; mental health, 64, 65, 105, 106, 108, 114, 121–122, 139, 160; participation in, as a predictor

of the determination hearing outcome, 105, 106, 108, 110, 139; and recidivism outcomes, 113, 132, 134, 188–189n25, 193n4; sex offender, 64, 65, 105, 114, 121, 160; violent offender, 105, 106, 108, 114, 160, 193n4; and youthful malleability, 159–160. *See also* Capital and Serious Violent Offender Treatment Program
truancy, 61, 85
Trulson, Chad, 158, 162
Turman, James, 6–7, 23–24, 26
Tuthill, Richard, 11, 29
TYC. *See* Texas Youth Commission

Unraveling Juvenile Delinquency (Glueck), 17
US citizenship, among sentenced offenders, 116
US Constitution, 48
US Department of Justice (Office of Juvenile Justice and Delinquency Prevention), 114
US Supreme Court, 25, 30, 174n59, 175n69

victims, crime, 141, 152, 166; interests of, 44, 152; participation of, in judicial process, 40, 109, 139; protection of, 92, 160, 167, 169

Villareal, Raul, 30
Violent or Habitual Offender Act. *See* Determinate Sentencing Act
Vivona, T. S., 162
vocational programs, 16, 68

Waco State Home (formerly the State Home for Dependent and Neglected Children), 5, 6
waiver. *See* adult court certification/waiver
weapons: possession of, 74, 79; use of, as aggravating circumstance in sentencing, 92
West Texas State School, 8, 9
whites: and institutional misconduct, 82, 84–85; and likelihood of being released at determination hearings vs. going to prison, 101–102, 106; percentage of, among juvenile sentenced offenders in Texas, 54; and recidivism, 115, 188n15
Williams, Khianna Laqua, 56
Wilson, James Q., 157
witnesses, character, 40
witnesses, crime, testimony of, 40
work camps, 89

Zuniga, Rudy, 55–56